European Family Therapy Association Series

Founding Editors

More information about this series at http://www.springer.com/series/13797

Maria Borcsa • Peter Stratton
Editors

Origins and Originality in Family Therapy and Systemic Practice

Springer

EFTA

Editors
Maria Borcsa
University of Applied Sciences
Nordhausen, Germany

Peter Stratton
University of Leeds
Leeds, UK

European Family Therapy Association Series
ISBN 978-3-319-39060-4 ISBN 978-3-319-39061-1 (eBook)
DOI 10.1007/978-3-319-39061-1

Library of Congress Control Number: 2016949371

Printed on acid-free paper

This Springer imprint is published by Springer Nature
The registered company is Springer International Publishing AG Switzerland

In memoriam Luigi Onnis

Preface

During the work on this book Luigi Onnis, Founding Member and Honorary President of EFTA, passed away. With him, we have lost not only an important figure for our association but also a truly admired person.

Having been active in the European Family Therapy Network that gave birth to EFTA, he followed enthusiastically his conviction that family therapy is due to gain an accurate place in the health policies of Europe - his commitment to these values is apparent in his chapter in this volume. His leading role in the field of family therapy was recognised all over Europe and his tireless activity, combined with his radiant personality, aroused the admiration and feelings of friendship in all who knew him.

He stays in our hearts and will always be a part of our conjoint memories.

We dedicate the first volume of the EFTA Book Series to Luigi Onnis with all our respect.

Nordhausen, Germany — Maria Borcsa
Leeds, UK — Peter Stratton

Contents

About the Authors

Maurizio Andolfi, M.D. Child psychiatrist and family therapist. Professor in Clinical Psychology, University la Sapienza Rome. Director of Accademia di Psicoterapia della Famiglia, Rome. Journal editor of *Terapia Familiare*. President of Silvano Andolfi Foundation. Co-founder European Family Therapy Association. AAMFT supervisor. Recipient of Award for Life Achievement from American Family Therapy Academy (2016). Among publications: (1994) Please, help me with this family, Routledge; (2013) Teen Voices, Wisdom Moon Publ.

Maria Borcsa, Ph.D. is Professor of Clinical Psychology at the University of Applied Sciences Nordhausen, Germany, accredited psychological psychotherapist, family and systemic therapist, supervisor and trainer. She is founding member of the Institute of Social Medicine, Rehabilitation Sciences and Healthcare Research at UAS Nordhausen, where she established the first Master's course in Systemic Counseling in Germany. Her research interests lie in qualitative research of couple and family therapy. She is journal editor (*Systeme*, 2001–2014; *Psychotherapie im Dialog*, since 2007) and founder of the EFTA Book Series. For many years she has served as a board member of the German Systemic Society (Systemische Gesellschaft) as well as of the European Family Therapy Association (EFTA), having been chair of the NFTO chamber 2010–2013. She served as President of EFTA 2013–2016.

Theo Compernolle, M.D., Ph.D. Independent international consultant, executive (team)coach, trainer and keynote speaker. Adjunct Professor at the CEDEP European Centre for Executive Development (France). Formerly Suez Chair in Leadership and Personal Development at the Solvay Business School, Adjunct Professor at the INSEAD, Visiting Professor at the Vlerick School for Management and TIAS and Professor at the Free University of Amsterdam. Founding member of EFTA.

Mony Elkaïm, M.D. is a psychiatrist. He is Honorary Professor at the Free University of Brussels and consultant at the Department of Psychiatry of the University Hospital Erasmus, Brussels. He is an approved supervisor under the

Founders Track of the American Association for Marriage and Family Therapy and Director of the "Institute for the Study of Family and Human Systems" (Brussels) as well as of "ELKAIM FORMATIONS" (Paris) and of the Journal *Cahiers Critiques de Thérapie Familiale et de Pratiques de Réseaux* (ed. De Boeck, Belgium). He is also President of the French speaking section of the "Belgian Group of Systemic Psychotherapists Trainers" and of the "Training Institutes Chamber" of EFTA.

Edith Goldbeter-Merinfeld, Ph.D. Em. Professor of Systemic Psychotherapy at Free University of Brussels (ULB), Doctor in Psychology, Director of Training at the Institut d'Etudes de la Famille et des Systèmes Humains in Brussels, trainer and family therapist, founding member of EFTA and of the Belgian Association of Family Therapists Trainers, and editor of the *Cahiers Critiques de Thérapie Familiale et de Pratiques de Réseaux*. She has directed systemic staffs in Psychosomatic and Psychiatric departments of University Hospitals in Brussels.

Julia Hille, B.A., M.A. systemic social worker, is a research associate and lecturer at the University of Applied Sciences Nordhausen and at the University of Applied Sciences Merseburg, Germany. She is writing her Ph.D. thesis on systemic couple therapy in the context of the international research project "Relational Mind in Events of Change in Multiactor Therapeutic Dialogues" at the Institute of Social Medicine, Rehabilitation Sciences and Healthcare Research at UAS Nordhausen.

Hugh Jenkins, Ph.D. moving from Cardiff, he worked at the Maudsley Hospital, 1981–1988; Senior Lecturer, Institute of Psychiatry 1988–2011 and Director of its Family Therapy Training Programme, 1988–1992; Chair, UK Association for Family Therapy, 1982–1985; Director, Institute of Family Therapy, 1987–1996. He received the Hungarian Family Therapy Association medal, 1996. He has worked regularly in Timişoara, Romania since 2002, establishing trainings widely recognised for their excellence. In full-time psychotherapy practice, London 1996–2012, he moved to East Anglia where he continues part-time. He has authored multiple articles, chapters, and was English Editor of *The Dictionary of Family Therapy*, 1995. He is a watercolour artist, exhibiting in East Anglia, with a solo exhibition in Romania, 2015.

Juan Luis Linares is psychiatrist and psychologist, Professor of Psychiatry at the Universitat Autònoma de Barcelona and Director of the Master in Family Therapy at the Universitat Ramón Llull. He is also Director of the Psychotherapy Unit and the Family Therapy School at the Hospital de la Santa Creu i Sant Pau in Barcelona. He has been founding member and President of the Societat Catalana de Teràpia Familiar (SCTF), the Federación Española de Asociaciones de Terapia Familiar (FEATF) and the European Family Therapy Association (EFTA), and he is Honorary President of the Red Europea y Latinoamericana de Escuelas Sistémicas (RELATES).

Luigi Onnis, Ph.D. (1944–2015) was Professor of Psychiatry and Clinical Psychology at the University of Rome "La Sapienza" and Director of Training for I.E.F.Co.S. (Istituto Europeo di Formazione e Consulenza Sistemica), Rome, Italy. He served as President of I.E.F.CO.S.T.RE, Cagliari. He was family therapy supervisor at the Family Therapy University School, Barcelona (Spain), approved supervisor of the American Association for Marriage and Family Therapy and honorary member of Association des Therapeutes Systemiques Françaises. Editor of the *Journal Rivista Psicobiettivo*. Member of the editorial board: *Journal of Systemic Therapies*, *Cahiers Critiques de Therapie Familiale*, *Reviste de Psicoterapia*. He was member of the European Family Therapy Network and founding member and Honorary President of EFTA.

Jorma Piha, M.D., Ph.D. is Emeritus Professor of Child Psychiatry at the University of Turku, Finland. He also served as the Head of the Child Psychiatry Clinic at Turku University Hospital. Additionally he is an Adjunct Professor of Family Psychotherapy. His research interests deal with child psychiatric epidemiology and follow-up and with risk factors in early parent-infant interaction. He is an accredited family psychotherapist, supervisor and trainer, and currently he is the Chair of the Finnish National Consortium of Universities for Psychotherapist Training.

Jacques Pluymaekers is a psychologist and family therapist. In 1970 he initiated a pilot project in one of the most underprivileged districts of Brussels which would develop the systemic approach and the family therapy in situations of crisis. This project also became the starting point of practices and many researches on the work of inter-institutional networks. He has developed, as of the 1980s, cycles of training in systemic approach and family therapy at the "Association Réseau Famille" in Montpellier (France), and at the "Institut Provincial de Formation Sociale" in Namur (Belgium). He was one of the founders of the Network "Alternative to Psychiatry" set up in 1975 in Brussels. He is Former Scientific Advisor at the School of Criminology of the Catholic University of Leuven, Belgium. He is Director and trainer at the Institute for Family and Human System Studies in Brussels and at the "Association Réseau et Famille" in Montpellier (France). Founding member of the European Family Therapy Association (EFTA), he was chairing CIM 2001–2013 and is today Honorary President of EFTA.

Kyriaki Polychroni, M.A., C.G.P., E.A.P. is a psychologist, systemic family and group psychotherapist and trainer at the Athenian Institute of Anthropos in Greece and a long-standing member of its Scientific Council. She is a certified EFT couple therapist, supervisor and trainer (ICEEFT), training and supervising professionals in couple and family therapy throughout Europe. Kyriaki is the Immediate Past President of the European Family Therapy Association (EFTA) and currently the Vice-Chair of its Chamber of Training Institutes (EFTA-TIC). She is a member of the American Family Therapy Academy (AFTA). Former Vice-President of the national branch of the European Association of Psychotherapists (E.A.P.). Founding member of the Hellenic Association of Systemic Therapy. Kyriaki Polychroni is joint editor of the journal *Human Systems*.

Florence Schmitt, Ph.D. is psychotherapist at the Department of Child Psychiatry of Turku University Hospital in Finland. She is an advanced level family therapist and trainer in family therapy, an individual psychoanalytically oriented psychotherapist for adults, and an early interaction psychotherapist. Her research and clinical work focused on supporting parenthood and parenting of both, mentally and somatically severely ill parents. Psychotherapy with dying parents and their children has been for the last 10 years a clinical priority.

Peter Stratton, B.Sc., Ph.D. Dip Psychotherapy. Fellow of the BPS and Emeritus Professor of Family Therapy at Leeds University, UK, he is a systemic family therapist and developmental psychologist with broad research interests and involvement in statutory processes that affect families. His research includes development of an outcome measure for families in therapy (the SCORE project); the effects of basing training on concepts of active learning and the dialogical construction of self; the relationships of humour and creativity during psychotherapy; and attributional analyses of family causal beliefs and blaming. He is founding editor of the journal *Human Systems*; Chair of European Family Therapy Association Research Committee and recently Academic and Research Development Officer for the Association for Family Therapy and Chair of the UKCP Research Faculty. Founding Director of Leeds Family Therapy and Research Centre and Managing Director of The Psychology Business Ltd.

Arlene Vetere, Ph.D., F.B.Ps.S., F.Ac.S.S. is Professor of Family Therapy and Systemic Practice at VID Specialized University, Oslo, Norway; Visiting Professor of Clinical Psychology at Universita degli Studi, Bergamo, Italy; and Affiliate Professor of Family Studies at Malta University. She lives in the UK where she is registered as a clinical psychologist, systemic psychotherapist and systemic supervisor. She joined the EFTA process in 1996 as chair of UK Association of Family Therapy, being a member of the working party that developed the three chamber structure of the new EFTA. Further she chaired the NFTO Board 2001–2004 and was President of EFTA for two terms, 2004–2010.

Chapter 1
From Origins and Originality: Family Therapy and the European Idea

Maria Borcsa and Peter Stratton

Synopsis EFTA is a unique organisation which brings together in its three chambers the leading national family therapy organisations of each of around 30 European countries (with more than 50,000 family therapists throughout Europe), 125 of the training institutes of around 30 countries and 1100 individual member practitioners of high standing (2016). It works politically to support the profession and practice of family therapy throughout Europe and has a collaborative relationship with a number of like-minded organisations all over the world.

This chapter describes the development of the European Family Therapy Association from its beginning as a network to this complex organisation. The aims of EFTA and the ways of achieving them are summarised, the publication of a Book Series seen as one significant contribution to realise the scientific goals of the association. The concept of the publication series and a short outline of the chapters of this first volume are given.

EFTA: From a Network to an Association

When EFTA was founded officially in 1990, it had already been blooming for years as a network of 231 colleagues from Austria (6 members), Belgium (36), Bulgaria (3), Canada (4), Czechoslovakia (3), Denmark (5), Finland (7), France (45), Germany (21), Greece (3), Hungary (2), Ireland (6), Israel (2), Italy (28), Netherlands (10), Norway (9), Poland (10), Portugal (2), Sweden (1), Spain (5), Switzerland (8), the UK (10), URSS (2) and Yugoslavia (3). Their goal was "to establish a Europe-wide association of family therapists, to promote cross cultural training, research and scholarship" (Borcsa et al. 2013, p. 345).

M. Borcsa (✉)
University of Applied Sciences Nordhausen, Nordhausen, Germany
e-mail: borcsa@fh-nordhausen.de

P. Stratton
University of Leeds, Leeds, United Kingdom

M. Borcsa, P. Stratton (eds.), *Origins and Originality in Family Therapy and Systemic Practice*, European Family Therapy Association Series,
DOI 10.1007/978-3-319-39061-1_1

One document from the 25th of June 1990 signed by Mony Elkaïm states the following:

> *"The next meeting of the network will take place in two parts in October in Paris. A preliminary meeting will be held on October 6 during the lunchbreak at the congress 'Ethics, Epistemologies, New Methods' (October 4, 5 & 6, 1990 in Paris). The creation of the European Family Therapy Association and the elections will be held on Sunday morning, October 7, 1990 from 9.00 a.m. to 12 p.m. at the following address:*
> *Salon Borghese*
> *Hôtel Lutétia*
> *47, bd. Raspail*
> *75279 Paris"*

The location was well chosen: A meaningful place for Europe's past century in terms of architecture, arts and especially for politics, reflecting all in one: occupation, resistance as well as humanitarian aid (Assouline 2005). Even one President of the French Republic spent his honeymoon here—how symbolic!

Only 2 years later, in 1992, we can find in the Moniteur Belge (1992, p. 1797, the official journal of the Kingdom of Belgium, listing non-profit associations according to the Belgian law), the following names as founding members of EFTA: Maimonid Elkaïm (Belgium), Alia Samara (Greece), Maurizio Andolfi (Italy), Hugh Jenkins (UK), Edith Goldbeter-Merinfeld (Belgium), Elida Romano (France), Paul Igodt (Belgium), Jorma Piha (Finland), Camillo Loriedo (Italy), Esther Wanschura (Austria), Luigi Onnis (Italy), Jacques Pluymaekers (Belgium), Theo Compernolle (Netherlands), Rick Pluut (Netherlands) and Gian Franco Cecchin (Italy). Being registered as a charity organisation was the first step of institutionalising an idea, which was bringing together family therapists from all over Europe.

It was in the same year that the Maastricht Treaty (formally, the Treaty on European Union) was signed by the 12 members of the European Community in Maastricht, Netherlands. This was the most important step in the European Integration since the founding of the European Community and is the basis of today's European Union, including a joint currency, with the focus on a common foreign and security policy and cooperation on justice and home affairs.

These parallel processes reflect a belief in a European idea of cooperative discourses and decisions. Today, 25 years later, we may look back onto these political developments in Europe with a more disillusioned but still hopeful view. The guiding principles of peace and collaboration seem more relevant than ever- in our respective countries, in Europe as a continent and in our global community.

The Development of EFTA

The association started its work with individual members from 23 countries, publishing its first membership directory in 1992. At that time, the countries most represented were France, Italy and Belgium, followed by Switzerland, Greece and Spain. Arlene Vetere, President of EFTA from 2004 to 2010 recalls: "In 1995, the

EFTA leadership made the visionary move to invite representatives from the national and regional associations of family therapy across Europe, to discuss the possibility of the associations joining the EFTA. The move was greeted with enthusiasm and a series of meetings ensued, to debate the mutual benefits of such a partnership. Quite quickly a systemic problem emerged—the originators of EFTA wanted the national and regional associations to join an association of individual members. The national and regional associations recognised that a new structure was needed to accommodate different levels of membership, interests and goals. A working party was set up to develop a structure that enabled full participation for individual members, national and regional associations and the training institutes—who were invited to participate in the new structure." (Borcsa et al. 2013, p. 345).

Already in July 1999, the statutes went through a reformation process to give a place to NFTO and training institutes membership, and during the EFTA conference in Budapest, 2001 these changes were voted and approved. So, since 2001, EFTA has established a new structure made up of three "chambers": CIM, NFTO and TIC, thereby allowing for national associations for family therapy and training institutes to represent their particular interests. "The new EFTA had a tripartite structure: a chamber for individual members (CIM); a chamber of national associations of family therapy (NFTO); and a chamber of training institutes (TIC). Countries that had regional associations were offered a period of 5 years to organise themselves into one federation or national association for representation at EFTA. Each chamber of EFTA elected its own board of seven members, with a chair person, secretary and treasurer. The three boards constituted the general board of EFTA. The overall president was elected from within the full board. A co-ordinating body, consisting of the president and two members from each chamber board, was appointed to oversee and monitor co-operation between the three boards in the general board. Thus, decision making and participation was equitable across the three chambers." (Borcsa et al. 2013, p. 345).

This structure is governed by new statutes, giving as a mission of EFTA to increase exchanges between family therapists as much as between training institutes and the national associations which bring family therapists together in their countries. In the current statutes (http://www.europeanfamilytherapy.eu/statutes-of-efta) you can find the aims of the association in more detail as follows:

1. To link and co-ordinate European national associations, institutes and individuals in the field of family therapy and systemic practice.
2. To promote the highest level of competence and quality in practice, research, supervision and teaching in family therapy and allied fields.
3. To facilitate European co-operation and the exchange of ideas and experience among associations, institutions and individuals concerning medical, legal, social, psychological, gender, cultural, economic, spiritual and other aspects of human experiences in relation to systemic thinking and practice.
4. To spread information about family therapy and the systemic approaches throughout Europe to individuals, institutions and organisations concerned with the health and development of families and human systems.

5. To promote research, conferences, publications, audio-visual tools and other scientific material in this field through meetings and all other appropriate communicational methods.
6. To enhance the training of systemic professionals and family therapists at regional, national and European levels by organising and facilitating exchanges between individuals, and professional centres.
7. To create links with other organisations having common or compatible aims in and outside of Europe.

The activities for achieving the aims of the association are:

- regular international meetings
- conferences and seminars
- international congresses
- the annual publication of a membership list
- the spreading of information by all appropriate means
- professional exchanges between family therapy centres and therapists in training and trainers from different European countries
- creating links with parallel organisations beyond Europe
- the establishment of appropriate different committees
- and all such other activities as will advance the aims of the association.

One of the main ways of achieving these aims is the organisation of triennial international congresses. Reviewing the list of topics of these congresses we realise that each one was relating to actual matters in the systemic field, but also to the socio-historical developments of the respective time. Not only bringing together the family therapy and systemic community but also having invited speakers from other disciplines to enrich with contemporary and innovative concepts and new ideas, has been again and again a challenge for the conference organisers.

The list of conferences up to now reads as well as a journey through some of the most interesting cities of Europe:

1. Sorrento (Italy) November 1992: "Feelings & Systems: a Challenge for Family Therapy?"
2. Athens (Greece) April 1994: "Ethics & Freedom. Changing Contexts and Family Therapy"
3. Barcelona (Spain) October 1997: "Families and Therapists in Different Social Realities"
4. Budapest (Hungary) June 2001: "Travelling through Time and Space"
5. Berlin (Germany) October 2004: "Creating Futures. Systemic Dialogues across Europe"
6. Glasgow (UK) October 2007: "Beyond Oppositions: Individuals, Families, Communities"
7. Paris (France) October 2010: "60 Years of Family Therapy, 20 Years of EFTA… and after? New Ways for Systemic Practice"
8. Istanbul (Turkey) October 2013: "Opportunities in a Time of Crisis: the Role of the Family"

9. Athens (Greece) September 2016: "Origins and Originality in Family Therapy and Systemic Practice"

Coming back to Athens in 2016 has a special significance. The congress 2016 was initially planned to take place in Amsterdam, Netherlands, trying to come to life in the venue of a former factory. As the expenses of the "production" got higher and higher the organisers would have needed to increase dramatically the fees for participants. This would have put attendance out of the reach for numerous EFTA members and especially for most students and trainees—the organisers had to face ethical issues of exclusion in their own association. Having built the programme on the Dutch colleagues' fondness for Aristotle's philosophy of Ethos, Logos, Techne and Polis, nothing seemed closer than considering to accompany Aristotle on his journey to his origins and to change place by moving to the origins of Europe, to Greece. The year 2016 is proclaimed the Aristotle Anniversary Year (2400 years) by UNESCO which was an excellent coincidence with the congress theme. Mina Polemi-Todoulou, President of the Greek national association ETHOS and her Greek team took up the challenge with enthusiasm and engagement and we wish to thank them at this place, too.

Let's finalise this paragraph with some remarks on the committees of EFTA: One major structural format of working on specific topics in EFTA has been the work of committees. In terms of the development of the association, the most important were the Committees on Training Standards, Research and on Ethics—giving the association and the members important fundaments. The more recently established committees are taking responsibility of the fact that the association reached now the age of being "over 25"; a review of the EFTA regulatories is taking place in the Committee on Statutes/Bylaws. Taking care of the next generation and considering how younger colleagues can be mobilised to be active in EFTA is one topic of the Developmental Committee. And, last but not least, the work of the External Relations Committee reflects that we live in a globalised world: the cooperation with family therapy associations all over the world becomes a duty in fostering the global development of systemic thinking.

Aiming at Research

EFTA has valued the roles that research can play in supporting its political agendas as well as in training and advancing systemic couple and family therapy (SCFT). Especially outcome-research has been crucial for many national associations either to become part or—after the economic crisis—to stay in the national health care systems. With the development of the outcome measurement SCORE (Stratton et al. 2010, 2014) and the decision to translate the measurement into different languages, an ongoing major project of the research committee and the research working task force in the chamber of NFTO started. At a board meeting in Lisbon, 2010 it was decided to establish the existing research committee more formally. A decision was made to give the chair of the committee a standing position on the board ex officio, and Peter Stratton was elected as chair of the Research Committee. Since this time membership of the EFTA Research Committee has been through active participation in one of its projects. In 2016, we have five projects:

Project 1. To investigate the possibilities of funding for Europe-wide research. Under the leadership of Mauro Mariotti (Italy) we have submitted two major proposals for EU funding with participation by twelve EFTA organisations, which received positive feedback but finally were not accepted. Currently we are engaging with a major project funded by Italian companies which has the objective of significantly improving health and ecological viability in medium sized towns. We are presenting the case that families should be at the heart of the planning and that implementation should be using proven systemic interventions.

Project 2. A survey of research relevant to family wellbeing and health promotion, while looking for connections to the official rhetoric about it in each country. Led by Angela Abela (Malta) we are working on defining a research project into how systemic therapy in conjunction with a systemic way of intervening at a contextual level is the best way to help underserved families to re-edit their stories around trauma and poverty. We plan a pilot study within EFTA's own resources to be a basis for an application for EU funding for a substantive investigation.

Project 3. Collating research published in the last 10 years that is currently only available in the language of the country in which it originated. This project falls naturally to the NFTOs and we will start by creating a repository of quality student dissertations. We need to do basic work to create a central repository or Esource, before proceeding further.

Project 4. Researching potential uses of the SCORE Index of Family Functioning. The SCORE-15 has been translated by EFTA members into 18 European languages (all available on the EFTA website http://www.europeanfamilytherapy.eu/score-15) with data being collected to test the usability and validity of the version for each country. Several papers have already been published or presented from this work: Borcsa and Schelenhaus (2011), Rivas and Pereira (2015), Józefik et al. (2015), Vilaça et al. (2015) and several from Alan Carr's team, e.g. Hamilton et al. (2015), O'Hanrahan et al. (2016). Increasingly, through discussions and the survey we have in process we can compare outcomes and also different ways of using SCORE to support systemic therapy in the different countries.

Project 5. To gather data on the needs of training courses as they enhance their use of research in training. This project is led by Monica Whyte (Ireland) with support of the TIC and NFTO Boards: a questionnaire has been constructed to determine the research training of the providers of family therapy training across our network, the skills that our trainees are developing in research activity and the support needs that may be identified by the training institutes for the future. It has been extensively piloted and at time of writing a multilingual version is being created that can be distributed through the network of training institutes.

EFTA is also collaborating with research activities of other bodies. Angela Abela is our official representative on the Child and Family Therapy Section of the Society for Psychotherapy Research, and we are playing a full role in the Heidelberg series of International Systemic Research Conferences (see www.systemisch-forschen.de).

The EFTA Book Series

With regard to the 25th Anniversary of EFTA, the time was ripe to contribute to the scientific purposes of the association with its own book series. There is a high level of publication among EFTA members but the organisation has reached a stage in its development at which having its own book series would be both of use to members and also a value to the field of family therapy worldwide. The aim is to benefit from the unique scope offered by EFTA membership to display the healthy, vibrant, and richly varied state of systemic couples and family therapy in Europe. By having senior authors and experienced editors bringing together and co-ordinating state-of-the-art contributions from across the Continent we wish to create composite understandings of the most crucial issues in the systemic field. So each book will not just be a collection but aims to contribute to the advance of thinking and understanding about issues of major concern to therapists, their clients, communities and governments. They will be compiled in such a way that they can be used by practitioners in each country to indicate the contribution that SCFT can make to the well-being of families and systems. The series, edited by Maria Borcsa and Peter Stratton, shall contribute to maintain therapists' expertise in each of the essential areas and to become also a source for training future therapists.

The topics will alternate between those that make research findings accessible and of immediate value to practitioners and those that cover clinical or training areas. These are being chosen as being important to therapists or trainers in many countries and in which the experiences have created significant advances in practice that can be used throughout Europe and worldwide.

About This Volume

This volume has been written by founding members of EFTA—two of them, Luigi Onnis and Jacques Pluymaekers became Honorary Presidents of the association—as well as each of its past presidents. It is a mosaic of the origins and originality of systemic thinking in Europe, reflected in contributions from Belgium, Finland, Germany, Greece, Italy, Netherlands, Spain and the UK. Of course it can give only a fleeting look into the beginnings and the development of topics discussed by these significant persons—and by choosing them, we inevitably excluded other colleagues who greatly contributed to the association as well as to the systemic model.

Notwithstanding we do hope that this selection gives an indication about the richness and diversity EFTA was rooted in from its foundation.

Hence, the purpose of the book is at least twofold: to accompany these influential colleagues on their personal and professional journey with regards to their engagement in systemic thinking as well as to their personal influences in the development of EFTA. Their contributions are committed to paradigms, models and concepts, as well as to applications of the approach. Through their focus, they give us insight into their philosophical and epistemological as well as clinical background and development. The paradigmatic reflections build the fundaments for concepts we are using in therapy as well as for a certain therapeutic stance. Therefore the book starts with four chapters of "Paradigms". We are fortunate to be able to start with a definitive statement by Luigi Onnis of his analysis of the development of systemic thinking. He reviews the very starting points of cybernetics and the thinking of Gregory Bateson which were made useful for family therapy. The development of second order cybernetics goes hand in hand with that of an ethical stance, having at its heart the acknowledgment of difference, diversity and plurality. At core he sees the perspective of complexity as essential both for therapy and for a just society. Jacques Pluymaekers describes how a phenomenological background led to the creation and implementation of centres which create a difference to traditional medical and juridical institutions. In Chap. 4 Hugh Jenkins takes up the issue of time especially in relation to ritual, and how understandings from philosophy and anthropology could enrich therapeutic practice. The fourth of our paradigms is provided by Juan Luis Linares' concept of ultramodern family therapy as a more functional alternative to postmodern dogmatism. His position allows for therapist knowledge that can be shared with the family to enhance its relational base and role as an intermediary between the individual and society.

The second group of chapters is headed "Models and Concepts" and starts with an account by Mony Elkaïm of his route from his heady early days at the forefront of family therapy and application of systemics to societal and international conflicts. He progresses to place his famous concept of resonance within interrelationships of "assemblages" and a model of human systems as relationships between world view systems rather than between individuals. For Chap. 7 Edith Goldbeter gives us an extended exploration of her concept of the "nodal third". A whole range of practical ways of using the absence of people from the session for different reasons, perhaps by death, being the third party in an affair etc. Next Theo Compernolle offers a model to integrate concepts from many areas under the heading of an "eco-psycho-somatic" approach to therapy to coordinate knowledge from different scientific domains such as medicine, neurology, biology, psychiatry, psychotherapy, management and family therapy and to pay special attention to what goes on at the interface between them. Finally in this section Arlene Vetere describes the development of "attachment narrative therapy" as a way of providing content within the reflexive framework of systemics. Her integration of attachment theory, narrative theory, and trauma theory with systemic theory and practice provides a powerful explanatory model.

The third section moves to concentrate on "Applications" with a collection of unique and powerful practices. Maurizio Andolfi uses his practice of inviting a child into a role as a co-therapist to argue that therapists should place greater emphasis on the "magic tools" of playfulness and creativity. So as the child joins the therapist in their work, the therapist joins the child in their special capacity to play with issues such as clashes between generations, thereby providing a relational link. In Chap. 11 Jorma Piha and Florence Schmitt bring a radical variation on a familiar application by proposing non-verbal sculpting. Their description in detail how to operate this challenging process has wider value of providing an example of how therapists can (should) combine rigour with creativity, meticulousness with flexibility and seriousness with imagination. Kyriaki Polychroni launches from her origins and those of the Athenian Institute of Anthropos, and the concepts that were developed to tackle the major changes in family and community life of that period. Out of the theoretical solutions to the needs of that context come ways of working that combine the systemic family approach with operating in group settings, and currently applications of attachment and Emotionally Focused Therapy.

The final section, of "Outlooks" starts with Chap. 13 in which Maria Borcsa and Julia Hille reflect on two global developments: the increasing number of transnational families and the expansion of information and communication technologies (ICTs). They propose the Genogram 4.0 Interview for therapy, training and research. This tool scrutinises unquestioned certainties like the concept of "home" and focuses on the use of digital technology in everyday communication processes. This first volume of the EFTA series concludes with a chapter by the Editors which reviews significant examples of originality from each chapter, placing them in relation to each other under a new set of headings, and then looks to future possibilities.

To close, we may say that the chapters reflect different traditions of European thinking. The diversity in personal-professional focus and style is appreciated, as this is supporting development and exchange which we trust will be enhanced by this book.

References

Assouline, P. (2005). *Lutetia*. Paris: Gallimard.

Borcsa, M., Hanks, H., & Vetere, A. (2013). The development of family therapy and systemic practice in Europe: Some reflections and concerns. *Contemporary Family Therapy, 35*(2), 342–348.

Borcsa, M., & Schelenhaus, S. (2011). Der Fragebogen zur Erfassung der Wirksamkeit von Systemischer Therapie SCORE 15. Ein Werkstattbericht. *Systeme, 25*(2), 137–140.

Hamilton, E., Carr, A., Cahill, P., Cassells, C., & Hartnett, D. (2015). Psychometric properties and responsiveness to change of 15- and 28-item versions of the SCORE: A family assessment questionnaire. *Family Process, 54*, 454–463. doi:10.1111/famp.12117.

Józefik, B., Matusiak, F., Wolska, M., & Ulasińska, R. (2015). Family therapy process—Works on the Polish version of SCORE-15 tool. *Psychiatria Polska,* 1–13. Retrieved August 28, 2015 from doi: http://dx.doi.org/10.12740/PP/OnlineFirst/42894. http://www.psychiatriapolska.pl/uploads/onlinefirst/ENGverJozefik_PsychiatrPolOnlineFirstNr24.pdf.

Moniteur Belge (1992). 3704, 1795–1797.
O'Hanrahan, K., White, M. D., Carr, A., Cahill, P., Keenleyside, M., Fitzhenry, M., et al. (2016). Validation of 28 and 15 item versions of the SCORE family assessment questionnaire with adult mental health service users. *Journal of Family Therapy.* FEB 1, 2016. doi:10.1111/1467-6427.12107.
Rivas G y Pereira, R. (2015). *Validación de una escala de evaluación familiar: Adaptación del SCORE-15 con normas en español.* Paper presented at III Iberical Congress of Family Therapy.
Stratton, P., Bland, J., Janes, E., & Lask, J. (2010). Developing a practicable outcome measure for systemic family therapy: The SCORE. *Journal of Family Therapy, 32*, 232–258.
Stratton, P., Lask, J., Bland, J., Nowotny, E., Evans, C., Singh, R., et al. (2014). Validation of the SCORE-15 index of family functioning and change in detecting therapeutic improvement early in therapy. *Journal of Family Therapy, 36*, 3–19.
Vilaça, M., de Sousa, B., Stratton, P., & Relvas, A. P. (2015). The 15-item systemic clinical outcome and routine evaluation (SCORE-15) scale: Portuguese validation studies. *Spanish Journal of Psychology, 18*, 1–10.

Part I
Paradigms

Chapter 2
From Pragmatics to Complexity: Developments and Perspectives of Systemic Psychotherapy

Luigi Onnis†

Synopsis The optics of complexity nowadays can be considered as one of the more mature and articulated developments of system thinking and has greatly contributed to renew and enrich the same epistemological basis. Coming from transversal elaborations in various fields of scientific knowledge, the "paradigms of complexity" (Morin 1977) exerted a major influence on theoretical and methodological elaboration of many disciplines of contemporary science, promoting the overcoming of reductionism residues of the mechanistic classical tradition.

In systemic psychotherapy, along with other influences, the perspective of complexity has activated in the past 30 years a process of review and conceptual enrichment which seems to invest the entire field of psychotherapy.

This healthy trend to renewal is, in general, not only linked to the large increase in demand for psychotherapy, with the extensive range of answers that it requires, but also to a fertile resumption of epistemological reflection in psychotherapy to be intended mainly as a "reflexive" operation that researches the links and correlations between therapeutic practices and theories that inspire them.

Specifically with regard to systemic therapy, there is no doubt that the encounter with the evolutionary and constructivist paradigms on one hand and, on the other hand with the perspective of complexity, has led to a healthy questioning of some conceptual assumptions.

The purpose of this chapter is precisely to try to define the essential outlines of this critical review of systems theories which are no longer definable in a univocal way and at the same time it tries to point out the inevitable influences that this renewal of theories exerted on therapeutic practices.

L. Onnis (Deceased)
Psychiatry and Clinical Psychology in "La Sapienza" Rome University, Rome, Italy

Istituto Europeo di Formazione e Consulenza Sistemica, Rome, Italy

M. Borcsa, P. Stratton (eds.), *Origins and Originality in Family Therapy and Systemic Practice*, European Family Therapy Association Series,
DOI 10.1007/978-3-319-39061-1_2

The First Systemic Formulations and the Influence of G. Bateson

The general systems theory stems from the crisis of the mechanistic model, derived from Descartes and Newton, which is characterized by a rigid pattern of cause effect that proceeds through analytical scans of objects examined, fragmenting them into constituent components observed in isolation and seeking, then, between these, relationships of linear causality. The inadequacy of this model is evident because, as Bertalanffy writes (1956) "in various scientific fields issues concerning the whole, the dynamic interaction, the organization have been emerging. Within the framework of Heisenberg and quantum mechanics it has become impossible to resolve the phenomena in local events: problems of order and organization appear whether it concerns the structure of atoms and of the architecture of the protein, whether it regards the phenomena interaction in thermodynamics, or if we try to address the problems of modern biology."

Even more so, the mechanistic model did not seem sufficient to address the study of human behaviour and mental processes to which instead the application of systemic concepts seemed to give more useful clarification.

It is to this enterprise that, in the early 1950s, Bateson and his initial group of researchers, attempt to address the sensitive area of psychopathology of schizophrenia proposing, with the help of new conceptual tools, a vision profoundly innovative (Bateson et al. 1956).

The systemic model that, in the wake of these studies, Bateson gradually develops in the decade 1950–1960, is essentially based on three assumptions:

(a) The first is that the individual is considered as an open system capable of self-regulation, in constant exchange with the environment, in such way that the unit of study (later defined by Bateson as the "the unit of survival") is no longer the isolated individual, but the individual "plus" environment;
(b) The second assumption is that the exchange that takes place between the individual and its context is not an exchange of energy, but of information, which implies the norm of "retro-action" and, therefore, of circularity; the study of human behaviour is assimilated to the one of communication and, reflecting this orientation, the hypothesis is formulated that the same symptomatic behaviours are communicative behaviours, which are appropriate and consistent with specific interactive modalities of the context in which they appear;
(c) The third assumption, that is definitely one of the most significant, is the *conception of mental processes* that Bateson gradually developed. For Bateson, the "mind", as opposed to what was claimed by the traditional Cartesian dichotomy, is not to be separated from the soma, but it is identified with the same dynamics of systemic self-organization, expressing even the organization of all functions and assuming the character of *meta-function*, which at higher levels of complexity, acquires the typical quality non-spatial and non temporal that we attribute to mind in the traditional sense. Not only that, but Bateson in this view of "mental" takes a further step: the mind is not fully identified with the indi-

> vidual, but it invests also streets and messages that connect the individual and the environment, given their inseparable correlation. In this systemic vision, which becomes truly ecological, the individual does not adapt to a given environment but the individual and the environment co-evolve.

What is essential to emphasize of this original systemic model, developed by Bateson, is how relevant *the attention is and the importance that is given to mental processes*. In fact the distance taken from psychoanalysis was certainly not linked to the fact that it was considered as a mental or intrapsychic theory, but rather because even the psychoanalytic model was referring to energy as energetic concepts, rather than information.

I would like to emphasize here, although the subject cannot be expanded in this context, how the insights Bateson had have been confirmed by recent neuroscience studies. In particular, the spectacular discovery of mirror neurons made by a group of researchers from Parma University (Gallese et al. 1996; Rizzolatti et al. 1996; Rizzolatti and Sinigaglia 2006), shows clearly how the mental functions are based on relations starting from the neurological level: the mind would not be able to develop and operate without the "nourishment" that is provided from corporal relations, from others, from the environment (for an in-depth discussion on these themes please see Onnis 2009, 2016).

Despite the great importance Bateson gave to the mental functions, the first applications of the systemic model to therapy, which occurred in the early 1960s, do wrong to this original inspiration of Bateson. In fact, assimilating reductively the systemic theory to the "cybernetics first manner", has led to the development of a model strongly centred on the concepts of "self-correction" and "homeostasis", rather than potential development; on the observable "pragmatic" interactions; rather than on the "semantics" of communications and consequently on complexity of meanings and of what more "mental" exists in individuals and human systems; on the possibility that the therapist provides on the treated system an "objective" description rather than on the inevitability of a co-participatory interaction between the therapist and the system itself.

This trend, which is expressed, for example, in "*Pragmatics of Human Communication*" (Watzlawick et al. 1967) and in the authors that refer to it, despite having allowed often excellent therapeutic results, proposes a systemic epistemology more reductive and still greatly affected, as we shall see later, by the mechanistic model.

Theoretical and Epistemological Developments of Systemic Psychotherapy

It is exactly this epistemology that, in recent years (approximately in the past 25 years) has undergone a major revision, as mentioned at the beginning, based on cues frequently provided by research carried out in fields unrelated to psychotherapy or behavioural sciences, from physics, to chemistry, and biology, thereby repeating on one hand, the existence of isomorphism between different systems (in the sense of Bertalanffy) and on the other by stimulating a fruitful integration between the various fields of scientific knowledge. This interdisciplinary integration does not allow relapses in reductionist homologation of systems and different phenomena, but rather is born, this time, in recognition of "complex" realities and therefore tends to be seen as science of "complexity".

The main aspects of this epistemological revision have been marked by three encounters:

(a) The meeting with the *evolutionary paradigm* has questioned the rigid conception of systemic homeostasis and has affected the temporal and historical dimension of the systems and on the relationship of the present with the past and future.
(b) The meeting with the *constructivist and self-referential orientations*, which posed the problem of the relationship between observer and observed, between therapist and system to be treated and has had therefore implications on the conception of the therapeutic relationship.
(c) The encounter with the *perspective of complexity* which has helped to overcome the residual dichotomies, shunt mechanistic, still present in the systemic area, suggesting the existence of a multiplicity of complex levels of reality that are not in opposition with each other, but in complementary relationship.

I will try now, briefly, to better clarify which transformations caused in the systemic approach these influences and intersections.

The Encounter with the Evolutionary Paradigms from "Homeostatic" Models to "Evolutionary" Models

The so-called "homeostatic" models were certainly influenced by the fact that the first family therapists who attempted to apply the systemic theory in human systems, in particular the "Pragmatics" group from Palo Alto, i.e. from Jackson (1957) to Watzlawick et al. (1967), found themselves working with severely dysfunctional families, which presented a series of pathological conditions affecting one or more members. These families appeared as systems with self-regulation with a prevailing tendency to neutralize, through negative feedback, any amendment of its homeostasis, to a point at which any behaviour of members of the system, beginning with the symptom of the identified patient, seemed to cooperate for this purpose.

This conception, which emphasizes the homeostatic aspects of the systems and consequently neglecting symptoms and the possibilities of their evolution, is mainly affected by the influence of the conceptual framework, which is still the "first cybernetic", i.e. cybernetics studying machines equipped exclusively of capacity for self-correction of any deviation from equilibrium, through mechanisms of negative feedback. But in the description of human systems as negative feedback loops, repetitive and immutable (a description which also contrasts with the same vision of man as a "system of active personality" which Bertalanffy (1956) had clearly suggested), you lose especially one basic aspect: the dimension of time. The system is always equal to itself, and therefore it is a system with *no history*.

It is not difficult to understand, from these considerations, how this model still has many points of contact with the mechanistic model: despite epistemological assumptions, which are undoubtedly different, link circularly the symptom to the behaviour of other members of the family, the symptom remains a stabilizing element of the systemic disorder so, essentially expression of pathology; the dynamics of the system is evaluated mainly as an interactive game of "inputs" and "outputs", so similar to the pattern stimulus–response, original of classical behaviourism, where you lose (or are placed in brackets in the so-called "black box") values and meanings and all those processing elements which, between input and output, are "internal" to the system; the therapist, finally, in its claimed separated and "neutral" position, continues to consider the system as an "object" of observation, risking however to reify it, given the only apparently observable interaction in the present, in which past and future seem to dissolve.

This homeostatic model has now been widely exceeded in the systemic therapy by a significant epistemological modification, caused by the reference of new paradigms, evolutionary paradigms that helped define *evolutionary models*.

Maruyama (1963) with his concepts of "morphostasis" and "morphogenesis", underlined the systemic tendency not only to maintain but also to "change" its shape. We can, however, say that studies that have heavily contributed to the elaboration of an evolutionary model, are those of Prigogine on the thermodynamics of non-equilibrium, coming, therefore, from a field very distant from psychotherapy.

According to Prigogine (Prigogine and Nicolis 1977; Prigogine and Stengers 1979), the balance of a system is never static, but permanently dynamic exposed to oscillations or "fluctuations" (that's why Prigogine's talks of "non-equilibrium systems"). If for the effect of perturbations, internal or external to the system, these fluctuations are sufficiently amplified, the system reaches a critical stage, called "bifurcation", beyond which it may start a change of state, in directions and outcomes that are not predictable beforehand. This evolutionary trend is supported by a continuous circular interaction of positive and negative feedback that ensures the continuous development of the system, therefore we can speak of "evolutionary feedback", clearly indicating that a system is *never equal to itself.*

A first important aspect of this view is that it reintroduces the dimension of time in the system: there is, as Prigogine says with a happy expression, an "arrow of time" that indicates the direction of development of the system and determines its "irreversibility". This also means that, it regains importance a history of a system that, between differences and redundancies interrelated, but not identical to themselves, marks its development over time.

The implications that these new epistemological premises have on the therapeutic process are particularly significant and eliminate any mechanistic residues that the homeostatic model still seemed to contain.

First, the symptom is no longer considered as an element that tends to reinforce the pathological homeostasis of the system, but as a moment of extreme instability of the system itself, the point of "bifurcation", to use the terminology of Prigogine, beyond which different directions are possible as well as the evolution towards more mature levels of development. Consider how important it is, especially in situations of acute discomfort, in the "crisis", that the therapist grasps this evolutionary potential, contained in suffering and obscurely expressed.

Secondly, the re-introduction into the system of the diachronic dimension of time, not only returns a sense of belonging to a story giving a historical meaning to suffering itself, but retrieves the value of the past, not by returning to a flat causal conception that proposes that the past "caused" the present, but in the sense that the past "is" in the present and continues to live in it. It continues to live there through myths, ghosts, cohesive whole of values and meanings that characterize the image (or the "representation") that the family system has of itself, and that, therefore, can and should be investigated and sought.

This complex process, therefore, is certainly an attempt to recover that attention on the mental processes, centre of the theory of Bateson; it is an attempt to question the reasons, intentions, meanings that individuals attribute to their behaviour; it is a return of individuals on the systemic scene; it is a shift from the observable *pragmatic* interactions, to the *semantics* of the behaviours.

Family therapists find themselves, therefore, in front of the "black box" that the first cybernetics had considered irrelevant or unfathomable: they find themselves faced with a deeper and hidden level than that of the observable interactions, an "inner world" in the family where individuals are intensely involved and that we could call the "mythical level" (Caillé 1994; Neuburger 1994; Onnis et al. 1994b, 2012; Onnis 1996); it is the "emotional cement" deepened in the family, made up of beliefs, values and shared feelings.

With regards to the therapeutic implications, the exploration of this mythic level, such as the path of its construction, which usually has a tri-generational dimension, has greatly enriched the clinical practice and has inspired the creativity of family therapists toward the development of models of intervention more useful to bring out this dimension of family myths, being essentially pre-verbal and pre-conscious, which does not have direct access to the word. We refer to the richness of the therapeutic use of analogical and metaphorical language, in different methods of intervention (to name just a few examples of the "Floating objects" of Caillé and Rey 1994, and the "Family Time Sculptures" of Onnis et al. 1990, 1994a, 2012; Onnis 2004).

The Encounter with Constructive and Autoreferential Paradigms: The "Auto-observant" Systems

It is the second epistemological step that invested the systemic field, being perhaps more problematic than the former because it touches closely the therapeutic relationship and invests the position of the therapist inside the therapeutic process.

It proceeds from the critique of the mechanistic view, which results from empiricism, and suggests the possibility of an outside observer, separate and neutral in regards to the observed object (which, therefore in function of this separation can be "objectively" described).

This concept, already unsustainable in the field of physical-chemical science, where it is clear that the observer affects the observing field, could even more so, be criticized in a situation that directly involves the interpersonal relationship as the therapeutic process.

Also in this regard G. Bateson is a pioneer and an inspiration; in one of his first works from the early 1950s (Ruesch and Bateson 1951) he refers to psychiatry as a "reflexive science". Successively the so-called "second-order cybernetics", to use the terminology of von Foester (1984, 1994), the biological studies of Maturana and Verela (1980) on the self-referential of the systems, the constructivist guidelines in psychotherapy, explicate in a direct way the "constructive circularity" between the observer and the observed system. It results, in regard to therapy, that in the therapeutic system, being the therapist inevitably part of his own observation, is, in effect, "self-looking" and "self-referential".

In truth, the therapist becomes part of the system in the exact moment he starts observing it; in fact and paradoxically, he could not know it without being a part of it. This is why the representation that the therapist provides of the system can never be completely objective, because the therapist, at the same time, helps to "build" the reality described.

The shift from an *epistemology of description to an epistemology of construction*, from an epistemology of observed systems to an epistemology of self-observant systems, provides at least two important results:

- The first relates to the cognitive sphere: once the myth of neutrality and separation has been abandoned (but yet very present in the models related to first cybernetics) the therapist withdraws the pretence of an objective knowledge of the therapeutic reality interpreted as an "absolute truth".
- The second consequence relates more directly to the therapeutic process: the therapist losing its distant and "external" position, must also give up the claim to control the therapeutic process and predict outcomes. Its function is mainly to introduce in the system elements of greater complexity, to increase the range of choices in the stereotyped and single view that the system has of its own reality, so that it can reconsider it and restart the process of evolution. But it will be for the system itself to "create" the forms and directions, completely unpredictable, of the change, becoming ultimately, the "architect of his own healing" (to use one more expression of Bateson 1979).

This concept, which comes from an epistemological, self-referential, and constructivist orientation, is undoubtedly full of fascinating and important implications for psychotherapeutic practices.

By recognizing the creativity and autonomy capacities of the system being treated, the therapeutic process becomes free from any manipulation or control purposes. This is the reason why attitudes and techniques of "instructive" or "prescriptive" type are replaced, today, with other dialogical types, in which a redefinition of the situation is proposed, that is, providing alternative views of reality rather than the rigid and univocal shared by the family system, reactivating the autonomous creative potential (Caillé 1994; Elkaïm 1989; Onnis 2004; Onnis et al. 2012).

At the same time, the recognition of the therapist as a "co-constructor" of the therapeutic reality invests him with a new responsibility, an "ethical function" (Keeney 1985; von Foester 1994). The therapist becomes, in fact, co-head of both the definition of the disease (which is also a "construction of reality") and of the evolution and outcome of discomfort. In this frame, for example, a sharp revision of the concept of "chronicity" takes place: it is no longer considered as a natural result of the disease as suggested by the medical tradition, but it is seen as "a function of the therapeutic relationship". Numerous studies, today, sustain this view (see among others Onnis 1985; Onnis et al. 1985, 2001).

At this point a question arises legitimately. What meanings do these epistemological steps that so heavily influenced the systemic orientation have? Placing the emphasis on the evolving time and the history of the system means that today systemic therapists have returned to the exploration of the past and withdrew from the study of the interactions in the present? Or enhancing the position of the observer means giving priority to the construction of reality of the observing subject rather than the "owned" reality of the object observed?

Encounter with the Complexity View

The answers to these questions are provided with the third encounter, the third intersection we have briefly mentioned: the one between systemic approach and the *view of complexity* (Morin 1977). The view of complexity allows to reformulate those questions and to replace the dichotomous and oppositional logic, of Cartesian derivation, that still inspires them, with *a logic of complementary and dialectic correlations* (Onnis 1989, 1993, 1994). This epistemological orientation has greatly influenced the systemic psychotherapy and has introduced both in the systemic vision as well as in therapeutic work, a more complex structure of levels: the behavioural level taking place in the "here and now" and the diachronic level of history and its meaning, the phenomenology of current interactions and family myths, the specificity of individuals and the characteristics of the systems to which they belong; the therapeutic system (with all the implications that it entails) and the in-treatment system, as co-participants, both the one and the other, which are implied in the construction of a new reality.

The interest and value of this epistemological approach also lies in the fact that it is proposed as a significant attempt to recover the multidimensionality of mental processes which, as we have seen, inspired the conception of Bateson. It's definitely the more mature and important development that characterizes systemic psychotherapy today.

Yet it is my impression that some of these issues discussed today in the systemic field are not a heritage of this area, but find harmonies and resonances in other areas of psychotherapy, including the psychoanalytical field.

I think that many psychotherapy fields tend today to emphasize the existence of contiguity and continuity, rather than delimitation, between subject and relational plot in which it is immersed, between the inner and outer world, proposing, therefore, that psyche and relatedness are far from being apart and opposing spaces, but rather on different levels, related, of the same human reality (among others see Stern 2004, 2006).

And this to me does not seem random. It does not seem random because it reflects a widespread tendency today that goes beyond the boundaries of school: to move towards a "perspective of complexity" and to get out from the confines of reductionism, through the recognition of a multiplicity of complex levels of reality that, in their autonomy, propose themselves as complementary and circularly related. It is not a coincidence that "complexus", as suggested by Morin (1977) means "what is joined together to form a single fabric"; and to remain in this metaphor, you could add that the threads, on one side, maintain their specificity, on the other side they define their appearance and function as parts of a plot.

Towards a Complexity Ethics

Placing yourself in a prospective of complexity does not come without consequences on the methodological level. First, because of the recursive correlation of the multiple levels involved in the game, these classic Cartesian relationships of dichotomous opposition branching, are replaced by relationships of complementarity; consequently a disjunctive logic type either/or (either intrapsychic or relational, either inside world or the outside world, either individual or family etc.) are replaced with a logic of dialogical conjunctions of type both/and (intra-psychic *and* relational, inner world *and* outer world; individual *and* family etc.). Secondly an epistemology of complexity also differs from every "holistic" model claiming to be "all-encompassing" and exhaustive and, having the presumption to explain everything, it becomes dogmatic, because it does not allow other views of reality; these are models of "totality" which then tend to uniqueness of "totalitarianism".

On the contrary if there is a keyword within the paradigm of complexity it is *plurality*. The need for a plurality of points of view arises from the realization that each reference model (including the systemic model) is necessarily limited and partial. There are different points of view to be considered from different angles of observation, which may allow a better approximation in the knowledge of observed reality, thanks to the comparison and integration among them.

It can then be concluded that if, on one hand the perspective of complexity offers to the therapist the frustration derived by a healthy immersion of humility, however, on the other hand it points out, the need for cooperation and convergence between different psychotherapeutic orientations, in respect of each other's diversity.

In this sense, the optic of complexity recovers the richness of Bateson's lesson where only the "difference is the matrix of information and knowledge" (Bateson 1972). But in the optics of complexity one final comment is appropriate: it has extremely important implications that go beyond the field of psychotherapy. If in psychotherapy it favours the fall of dogmas, in the broader social field it promotes a culture of respect and tolerance.

There is an extensive need of this culture nowadays and, it is clear, especially in face of phenomena of resurgence of racism, discrimination against minorities, violence against women and children, and rejection of "diversity", which dramatically characterize current society.

It is for this reason that we believe that a systemic thinking inspired by complexity may have a function that goes beyond the specific field of psychotherapy and really acquires an ethical function.

Acknowledgment I would like to thank Dr. Gloria Gabbard for the English translation.

References

Bateson, G. (1972). *Steps to an ecology of mind*. New York: Ballantine Books.
Bateson, G. (1979). *Mind and nature: A necessary unity*. New York: E. P. Dutton.
Bateson, G., Jackson, D. D., Haley, J., & Weakland, J. (1956). Towards a theory of schizophrenia. *Behavioral Sciences, 1*(4), 251–264.
von Bertalanffy, L. (1956). General system theory. *General Systems, 1*, 1–10.
Caillé, P., & Rey, Y. (1994). *Les objets flottants, méthodologie systémique de la relation d'aide*. Paris: Fabert.
Caillé, P. (1994). *Un et un font trois—Le couple d'aujourd'hui et sa thérapie*. Paris: Fabert.
Elkaïm, M. (1989). *Si tu m'aimes, ne m'aime pas, Approche systémique et psychothérapie*. Paris: Editions du Seuil.
von Foester, H. (1984). *Observing systems*. Seaside, CA: Intersystems Publications.
von Foester, H. (1994). Etica e cibernetica di second'ordine. *Psicobiettivo, 14*(3), 47–57.
Gallese, V., Fadiga, L., Fogassi, L., & Rizzolatti, G. (1996). Action recognition in the premotor cortex. *Brain, 119*, 593–609.
Jackson, D. D. (1957). The question of family homeostasis. *Psychiatric Quarterly Supplement, 31*, 79–80.
Keeney, D. (1985). *L'estetica del cambiamento*. Roma: Astrolabio.
Maruyama, M. (1963). The second cybernetics: Deviation-amplifying mutual causal processes. *American Scientist, 5*(2), 164–179.
Maturana, H., & Varela, F. (1980). *Autopoiesis and cognition: The realization of the living*. Boston: Reidel.
Morin, E. (1977). *La mèthode (tome I): La nature de la nature*. Paris: Le Seuil.
Neuburger, R. (1994). *Le mythe familial*. Paris: ESF.
Onnis, L. (1985). *Corpo e Contesto*. Roma: NIS.
Onnis, L. (1989). Therapie systemique et optique de la complexitè. *Cahiers critiques de therapie familiale et pratiques de reseaux, 11*, 107–110.
Onnis, L. (1993). Psychosomatic medicine: Toward a new epistemology. *Family Systems Medicine, 11*(2), 137–148.
Onnis, L. (1994). Verso un'ottica della complessità. *Psicobiettivo, 14*(3), 59–64.
Onnis, L. (1996). *Les langages du corps*. Paris: E.S.F.
Onnis, L. (2004). *Il tempo sospeso*. Milano: Franco Angeli.
Onnis, L. (2009). Lorsque la psyché est le reflet du corps. Une nouvelle alliance entre les neurosciences et la psychothérapie. *Cahiers critiques de thérapie familiale et de pratiques de réseaux, 2*(43), 65–91.

Onnis, L. (2016). Restoring mind-body unity. *Journal of Family Psychotherapy, 27*(1), 1–19.

Onnis, L., Bernardini, M., Leonelli, A., Mulè, A. M., Vietri, A., & Romano, C. (2012). Les sculptures du temps familial. Une méthode de "narration analogique"? *Cahiers critiques de thérapie familiale et de pratiques de réseaux, 48*(1), 31–57.

Onnis, L., Tortolani, D., DiGennaro, A., Marinozzi, P., Petralito, G., & Roggi, D. (1985). *Il bambino con disturbi psicosomatici: La famiglia, la domanda, il servizio*. Roma: Il Pensiero Scientifico.

Onnis, L., Di Gennaro, A., Cespa, G., Agostani, B., Chouhy, A., Dentale, R. C., et al. (1990). Le sculture del presente e del futuro: un modello di lavoro terapeutico nelle situazioni psicosomatiche. *Ecologia della Mente, 10*, 21–48.

Onnis, L., Di Gennaro, A., Cespa, G., Agostini, B., Chouhy, A., Dentale, R. C., et al. (1994a). Sculpting present and future: A systemic intervention model applied to psychosomatic families. *Family Process, 3*(3), 341–355.

Onnis, L., Di Gennaro, A., Cespa, G., Dentale, R. C., Bendetti, P., & Forato, F. (2001). Prevention of chronicity in psychosomatic illness: Research study on the treatment of childhood asthma. *Family Systems & Health, 19*(3), 237–250.

Onnis, L., Laurent, M., Benedetti, P., et al. (1994b). Il mito familiare: concetti teorici e implicazioni terapeutiche. *Ecologia della Mente, 2*, 95–112.

Prigogine, I., & Nicolis, S. (1977). *Self-organization in non-equilibrium systems*. New York: Wiley.

Prigogine, I., & Stengers, I. (1979). *La nouvelle alliance. Métamorphose de la science*. Paris: Collection Bibliothèque des Sciences humaines, Gallimard.

Rizzolatti, G., Fadiga, L., Gallese, V., & Fogassi, L. (1996). Premotor cortex and the recognition of motor actions. *Brain Research Cognitive Brain Research, 3*, 131–141.

Rizzolatti, G., & Sinigaglia, C. (2006). *So quel che fai, il cervello che agisce e i neuroni specchio*. Milano: Raffaello Cortina Editore.

Ruesch, J., & Bateson, G. (1951). *Communication: The social matrix of psychiatry*. New York: Norton.

Stern, D. (2004). *The present moment in psychotherapy and everyday life*. New York/London: Norton.

Stern, D. (2006). Il dialogo tra l'intrapsichico e l'interpersonale: una prospettiva basata sulla psicologia dello sviluppo. *Psicobiettivo, 26*, 77–88.

Watzlawick, P., Beavin, J. H., & Jackson, D. D. (1967). *Pragmatics of human communication*. New York: Norton.

Chapter 3
The Story of an Encounter: The Systemic Approach at the Heart of Innovative Clinical Practice

Jacques Pluymaekers

Synopsis This chapter shows how a clinical psychologist's training was enhanced by being centred essentially on an open psychoanalysis very influenced by phenomenology, and within a radical project of a psychosocial clinic accessible to the most disadvantaged.

Indeed, in the end of the 60s the reality of psychiatry, with regard to the protection of young people, was to relegate rather than to take care of the people. Major changes were imperative.

This was achieved by the installation of a crisis pilot centre in a disadvantaged district of Brussels whose orientation was the systemic approach, new in Belgium at that time.

Family therapies, networking practices, systemic readings of institutional and inter-institutional logics as well as the creation of specific tools like the landscape genogram were developed there.

What was developed yesterday remains crucial today where the return of excessive specialisation starts again to create forms of exclusion.

The Story of an Encounter

Throughout the following few pages, the story of an encounter that none of us could have imagined when we started is unfolded with all its richness and innovative development. This encounter is in fact a series of stories that overlap and intermingle. And like any skein of wool it is almost impossible to unravel all the threads.

Like a watermark, it is the story of the great debates at the end of the sixties regarding the place and the role of psychotherapy or psychiatry and psycho-social

J. Pluymaekers (✉)
Institut d'Etudes de la Famille et des Systèmes Humains,
Bruxelles, Belgium
E-mail: jacques.pluymaekers@gmail.com; iefsh@scarlet.be

M. Borcsa, P. Stratton (eds.), *Origins and Originality in Family Therapy and Systemic Practice*, European Family Therapy Association Series,
DOI 10.1007/978-3-319-39061-1_3

work within society in general, which will be used as an intellectual guideline for all that was to emerge from it.

This is the very real story of a pilot project which generated for us, as young clinical practitioners, the means of updating the intellectual stances we were going to take, our wish for a new therapeutic clinic, but it was also about out political and militant commitment. It is also the story of the author of these few pages who could not then know that he was to become particularly sensitive to what was happening at the heart of the complexity of families, institutions and as a more general rule at the heart of our society itself.

Our study of psychology had not given us much insight into the world of psychiatry, the protection of young people and of psychotherapy. The latter used psychoanalysis as a reference and our training had a tendency to orient more towards this epistemology. On the other hand, as young professionals, faced with the reality of psychiatry and/or the protection of young people, we could not help questioning the situation…! Were we to collaborate with what was taking place in these institutions? Was analytical clinical practice the right response when faced with dehumanising acts that we could not condone?

Collecting all that we had been able to glean from our studies, we realised that our questioning was largely influenced by the phenomenological point of view as developed by several of our professors. Whether this was Jacques Schotte, Alphonse de Waelhens, Georges Thinès, Christian Debuyst and their colleagues. They had all initiated us and trained us to think using a more global vision of relationships than the psychoanalytical approach allowed us to do. It was impossible for us not to take into account what goes on in human relationships and more particularly the therapeutic relationship.

So it was impossible for us not to react, for it was so obvious that the psychiatric institutions that employed us as well as those for protecting young people relegated people rather than taking care of them. In fact abuse was frequent and was even part of the whole structure, if one thinks of the use of electric shock treatment, insulin treatment, solitary confinement, all kinds of other forms of punishment …!

Confronted on a day to day basis with so little respect for the patients' or the young people's suffering, motivated us to actually question or rather to rebel against this! In addition to this daily situation, there was the painful confrontation with the justification put forward by those in charge of management for whom it was not possible to work in any other way. With these patients and young people what else could be done, and if there was violence as an outcome, that was understandable…

In contrast to this more global vision that we wished to promote, we were forced to deal with a world of care in institutions where the patients and young people were considered as objects … to be reformed! So what did it matter what means were implemented if they meant that there could be improvement, submission to social norms … at the cost, of course, of rejection and exclusion!

And so it was that, with several professional friends, we hitched ourselves up to a dream that we would be able to change things. We needed to "see things differently". All that had so astounded us during our studies could not be ignored. For my friends and myself, 1969 and 1970 became a real time for developing a laboratory for ideas in which the writings of Merleau-Ponty (1964), the gestalists,[1] the young Lacan (2001), Binswanger (1954), Maldiney[2] as well as the courses given by Alphonse de Waelhens in 1965 (see also De Waelhens, 1958), Jacques Schotte[3] (see also Schotte, 2008), Christian Debuyst[4](1985), Georges Thinès (1977; 1991) or the general semantics seminars given by Korsybski not only created upheaval in everything that I thought or that we thought, but also about the way that clinical and psychotherapeutic work could be envisaged.

What is more, one of these friends from my student years at Louvain, who had left to do his Ph.D. in Psychology in Quebec, also shared what he discovered there with us: there was the development of Family Therapy with Jacqueline Prudhomme, the birth of local community service centres (CLSC).

Along with another childhood friend who had become a lawyer, Michel Graindorge, the very frequent institutional abuse carried out in "children's homes" revolted us. Through his initiative and with media support from the Belgian weekly "Pourquoi Pas" in 1970, which took the form of a public enquiry commission at Brussels University, a highly virulent confrontation between victims of these institutions and right-thinking people whether it be those responsible for social action, justice or in politics. They all considered that there was nothing to denounce. And most of the testimonies to the procurers were dismissed altogether!

I also had help and support from Jean Vermeylen, founder, in 1960, of the first sectored mental health service in Brussels, which was created based on the model set up in the XIII arrondissement in Paris and founded by Philippe Paumelle with the agreement and help of Serge Lebovici and Réné Diatkine. Clearly it is impossible to define precisely today what exactly was the most dominant factor, out of all those interactions within myself, the phenomenological aspects, all that I experienced in the institutions, all that was coming out of Quebec or from France. Was it the fact that I changed my way of seeing and of thinking that led me to develop another type of practice? Was it the fact of being confronted by the necessity to do things differently that led me to utilise concretely that which had taken place for me in my way of thinking? It doesn't matter, it was also just at this time that revolutionary books were being published and that were going to have an effect on us... we were not the only ones to believe that we must change these practices and innovate, with no fear of "wetting our shirts" with crazy ideas or diversions. "Asylums (Asiles)" by Erving Goffman was published in French in 1968; "Psychiatry and Antipsychiatry" by David Cooper was translated into French in 1970; "The Hidden Dimension" by E. Hall in 1971. Jacques Hochmann, after spending several months working in Palo-Alto, published an article in 1967 "La psychothérapie familiale: une arme nouvelle pour la sociopsychiatrie". He was to further develop these ideas in a book published in 1971 "Pour une psychiatrie communautaire" which, in its appendix, gave us a

[1] This is what I learned from the professors G. de Montpellier et G. Thinès à l'UCL.

[2] From his conferences at Louvain in 1968–1969.

[3] The courses he gave at UCL in 1965 and 1966.

[4] The courses he gave at UCL in 1965 and 1966.

summary of Paul Watzlawick's book "Pragmatics of Human Communication" which appeared in the USA in 1967. This summary reproduced among other things the concepts developed by Gregory Bateson which I had been able to study in the collection "Merleau-Ponty à la Sorbonne" published in 1951 in volume V and re-edited in 1964. Two of these courses developed Bateson's concepts under the name of Margaret Mead. Maurice Merleau-Ponty's (1964) illustration showing that child psychology could only be related to the children's relationship with adults is based on Margaret Mead's research. It was she who described how these relationships can organise themselves: the symmetric, the complementary and the reciprocal relationship, she said; taking up what her fellow researcher and future husband, Gregory Bateson had modelled (Merleau-Ponty, 1964, pp. 120, 334). In another of his courses, "Méthode en psychologie de l'enfant" (Merleau-Ponty, 1964, p. 109), Merleau-Ponty returned to the different types of relationships that had been described by Bateson and he insisted on the fact that it is impossible to imagine that there is a child psychology which can describe a child's nature (as if he or she were an object). Then he would talk of this relationship as being a reciprocal enveloping where, as he said in his course "L'enfant vu par l'adulte" (Merleau-Ponty, 1964, p. 260) there is no pure observation, any observation is already a form of intervention. He concluded by stating that as a general rule about theory and practice "these relationships are not linear but circular". And further on he would add, "this circular relationship cannot be avoided even if it implies a risk of illusion" (Merleau-Ponty, 1964, pp. 119, 334). The language of the second cybernetic comes before the definition.

Whatever the case, in 1970, it was clear to me that it was important to develop other ways of practising in the therapeutic and psychosocial domains. This marked the beginning of a pilot project that was not only clinical but also political. It came into being with the creation of a crisis centre in the most disadvantaged areas of Brussels: "La Gerbe". I was to be the organiser and leader, sharing the enthusiasm for putting our skills forward in order to serve the inhabitants of this district with several professional friends.

It was a pilot scheme because it was based first and foremost on this "seeing things differently" that brought us a phenomenological and systemic reading highlighting the importance of not reducing the difficulties to the individual or to the intrapsychic but rather in re-contextualising them.

Again it was a pilot scheme because it favoured reinsertion into the community, into the area in such a way that care for those who needed it was truly available and that it was right within the community that solutions were worked on thus reducing the need for having recourse to various types of exclusion.

It was also a pilot scheme in that it took action to develop a global vision where humanity is essential, a vision that is the opposite of the logic of specialisation which leads one to believe that science has the answer to everything.

The first text (Pluymaekers, 1974a)[5] developing this pilot project put the main emphasis on this type of specialisation logic which looked at the problems and the

[5] This text that had been written in 1970 to present the pilot project to the authorities of the commune and the ministries was to be published in 1974.

participants as a series or as being linear, avoiding the more global vision and promoting a position where all would retreat when confronted by the patient or the deviant. So what was important for me was to be as close as possible to the experience of the inhabitants of the district when they found themselves confronted by difficulties with relatives, in school, at the hospital, with the police or with the social services. This meant creating a context where the inhabitants could take their own responsibility for themselves, share, make the best of our skills if necessary and thus avoid it being too easy to leave it up to a specialist.

The systemic approach and its ideas form the driving axis for such interventions. As the requests still come as individual ones, it's up to the team to see how to re-contextualise them. The network practices and the proposals to implicate the environment whether it be the families, the teenage gangs, the buildings' inhabitants, the people who frequent the local park, the nursery,.... are developed out of this which mean it is possible to respond to this objective.

With our colleagues, we met numerous families, developed a number of community projects... and there were many things that brought us together to share experiences, check the reliability of our new ways of working, improve the quality of the interviews with the families and the networks while recording them in video (Pluymaekers, 1974b; 1981; 1987).

"A Pragmatic of Human Communication" by Paul Watzlawick, translated into French in 1972 was to serve as a common reference for the team. "Couple and Family Therapy" by Virginia Satir (1971) had also just been translated into French.

Rapidly we asked Siegi Hirsch to act as our supervisor. He brought us the richness of his experience, his knowledge of Salvator Minuchin's work with poor families.

Jean Marc Guillerme had regularly continued to inform us of new developments on family therapy in Quebec. When he came back to France in 1973, he created a training centre for family therapy in Brittany "An Oriant" This meant that I was able to meet up with Jacqueline Prudhomme (Ausloos, 2015) among others, and she introduced me to the working methods that were very similar to those of Virginia Satir.

But the richest and most formative for me was that the experience of la Gerbe quickly became well-known in France and in Quebec and was endorsed through invitations. In France, it was the Education Surveillée (Supervised Education) research centre in Vaucresson who wished to learn more about our experience. This centre's team, led by Jacques Sélosse, was extremely dynamic. It was looking for new ways of working with young delinquents. I was to work a great deal with them just at the time when Siegi Hirsch (Fossion & Rejas, 2001) was invited to present his experience in Holland and the emotional didactic groups which were to train Pierre Segond and his colleagues to work using family therapy started in March 1973.

In Quebec, it was one of Christian Debuyst's friends, Raymond Jost, who invited me to share my experience and that of the Bureaux Consultation Jeunesse (Youth Advice Office) which they had just put in place through the centre in Boscoville. In Belgium too, "la Gerbe's" experience and clinical practice was closely monitored by the Ministry for Justice and for Culture as well as by the Health Ministry.

These invitations and the need to model our action for prevention and care in the community gave me a taste for spreading knowledge about this and so it was quite natural that I accepted the invitation to become a trainer for the systemic approach and for the work with families carried out by special needs educators and social workers, at the same time continuing with my clinical practice. I was to write my first synthesis of this experience in training in an article that appeared in the Thérapie Familiale review (Pluymaekers, 1986).

In it I described how, within the therapeutic process, action and reflection are hinged together, questioning each other in a circular logic. It is no longer a matter of searching for the cause in a linear fashion in order to treat someone nor of programming for such and such an effect …! It is a matter of living through an encounter that is totally unique and through which something quite new will arise, inventing something perceptible, creating a distance that is not distant, emerging from that difference… out of this flows the essential attitude of the therapist. He or she must not only understand the function of family or institutional malfunctions but they must also contribute to the possibility of creating contexts where change can appear, accepting to live with its uncertainty.

They should also develop the capacity to be at the very heart of the encounter, just as much a part of its physical body as using their skills. This is crucial as the immediacy with which we react—even before I have ever said it (verbally), I have said it (non-verbally),—makes the actions we give back, our reactions, real reflections. Automatically, we send back into our own selves all that we have transmitted-received. It is in this way of becoming involved that it is possible to create that which de Waelhens called a non-distant distance where difference emerges. Within this hic et nunc in therapy, in training or in the encounters conducted in the socio-political project at la Gerbe, all of a sudden something moves, without us really being able to be certain where the "ressorts praxiques" were.

Following these first years, the work with families and the community in the area went ahead well. La Gerbe is at the same time a community leadership team that is recognised as such by the Minister for Culture, the first experience in Belgium of help in an open environment for young people and their families which had the support of the Youth Protection programme (Pluymaekers, 1974a, b) and within its status as a dispensary for mental hygiene for children and adults subsidised by the Ministry for Health, the third psychiatric sector in Belgium after that of Jean Vermeylen in Anderlecht and the one in Ixelles.

As a member of the Gerbe team, I was very much involved in negotiations with the Ministry for Health working on a law that explicitly developed the creation of psychiatric sectors much in the same way as had been done in France in 1960. The debate concentrated on the question of knowing whether these new institutions should be handled, as in France, by the heads of the psychiatric hospitals and hence depending on them. The Ministry for Health and in particular Monsieur Colémont and professionals with practical experience recommended that the organising bodies for these new Centres for Mental Health, as they were called, should be private or public organisations with no link to the hospitals. In fact it was feared that, working under the direction of the psychiatric hospitals, these new services would become the subordinates of the hospitals and would not respond at all to the problem of over hospitalisation... and to the needs of the sectors' inhabitants! There was also the fear that the local or neighbourhood work with the families and the community as developed at La Gerbe would not be possible when coming from the psychiatric hospitals which are very little integrated into the neighbourhood and are even badly perceived by most of the families. The decree setting out the Mental Health services was voted in March 1975 and barred them from being offshoots of the psychiatric hospitals.

When Mony Elkaïm finished his specialisation in psychiatry in September 1974 he came back from the USA. He did not know about la Gerbe and its integration into one of the run down areas of Brussels but, without realising it, we had a mutual friend: Michel Graindorge, the lawyer with whom I had worked in 1970 on that astonishing public enquiry commission into abuse within institutions. It was through him that we met and that was the start of a long friendship, as much on the tangible level of projects that we developed together as on the level of discussing those subjects that had stirred us, both from an intellectual and from an emotional point of view. As with any friendship, apart from those moments (which were numerous) of enthusiasm for what we held most dear, we have also experienced differences of opinion, yet our friendship is still there ... despite the passing years!

Mony was to come and enrich the Gerbe team that I led. His experience in the southern Bronx and all his direct experience in the USA with the founders of the family therapy approach were passed on to us with the richness and clarity that is typical of Mony. This meant that the team could increase its work with families and its networking practice (see also Chap. 6 in this volume).

For the team and for myself this was also a prolific moment when meetings with clinical workers who, like ourselves, were developing work with families whether this was as family therapy or in my more specific field of prescribed help as it was to be called later on.

In psychiatry as in the protection of young people, having global vision means including both the families and also the social and legal environment. Care was dispensed "under the orders" of judges or of the social services.

In the first instance, my thoughts led me to develop a systemic reading of what was happening in these relationships between the social, the therapeutic and the legal aspects. This meant that it was possible to set up what, independently from the official agendas, would be the roles and functions of each one, a relationship game that is very specifically between those making the mandatory injunctions (the judge or the social authority), the mandataries (the psychosocial team) and the family in difficulty. In this game, the implicit rules dictated to each one of them how they should be entering into the relationship which amplified the "institutional paradox" where the professional is "qualified" by the mandatory injunction made by the judge and implicitly disqualified by the same judge as far as the young people and the families were concerned by the very fact that the family is forced to want this help! (Pluymaekers, 1989). The family and the young person are therefore reduced to being the "object of the court order" which puts them into a very subtle double bind which hides behind its paradoxical dimension. In following this connecting thread,

Guy Hardy (2001; 2012), was to develop, working from his clinical work on compulsory help, a very elaborate description of the challenges and the means of dealing with them when working within this context. He said that, implicitly, the social workers' combined injunction was to be: "I want you to want to change and so that you do that, I want you to want help!". Is the family or the young person now in a double bind situation? As they are not being able not to react, they have to develop strategies. These will be either to refuse or to comply, either they adhere or even better they adhere in "a strategic way" in which they pretend to want this help. He added that very often this meant helping a young person to get themselves out of a problematic situation that he or she is said to have and that he or she doesn't accept that they have!

At the same time, my involvement as a clinical worker within sheltered care in institutions both in the area of psychiatry and the protection of young people had made me aware of what was going on between the various protagonists in the institutions (care workers, specialist educators, residents and the family) on a day-to-day basis. By then I had set up a method based on recording a video of this day-to-day life (meals, meetings, getting up in the morning, bedtime, recreational activities,...). When re-viewing these videos, what happened was that it was possible to discover that in the background of these moments that are considered to be routine, implicit rules on the level of relationships were going on. These were managing the gaps and even the contradictions that exist between the official and the real agendas. It was possible to observe how the educators as well as residents were affected by these rules and how they used them in their own turn in such a way as to regulate the very specific way the system was functioning and.... malfunctioning, which could cause a great deal of suffering! These implicit rules in the daily life of the institutions never ceased to turn in circles and to establish consensuses that were sometimes very rigid and in which all the members of the system participated. Our work consisted in softening the situation whereas often people working in these situations will attempt to change the official agenda in a linear manner, thinking that things would get better, but forgetting the strength of these implicit rules.

This research showed its real importance for the educators as well as for all the professional workers responsible for "daily life" there. Unravelling the implicit rules obviously means making it possible to develop non-conventional strategies that would favour the creation of contexts where change could take place.

Having a systemic reading of what was happening, asking questions about the function of the events, making a hypothesis and opening up other possibilities mean that the educational actions become creative and to find pleasure in getting problems to evolve when they only seemed to keep repeating themselves (Pluymaekers, 1989).

When faced with clinical situations of families with "multiple problems" and the recurring feeling of helplessness of the workers, I thought hard again about the games and the challenges within relationships between the social, the therapeutic and the legal aspects, and I was convinced that in these large systems there are also implicit rules that are being activated which, when decoded, could make it clear how much our conventional type of work, rooted in linear thinking which hopes to repair the situation, only reinforces the positions of the various people involved so that finally they turn out to be counterproductive. They contribute to maintaining symptomatic behaviour and can even make this absolutely "necessary".

There is the story of this young 17-year-old, placed in an institution by order of the judge. He was in love with a young girl, also placed in care by a judge, and they decided to have a child, certain that the judges would allow them to set up home as a couple ... and no longer be treated as "the judges' children". That is what happened, but, the young man developed the idea that getting teenagers pregnant would allow him to escape from the institution's claws ... One by one, over several years, he was to father nine children all born from a relationship with teenagers placed in an institution. Each time, he would live for the first year with each mother. He had a good job, a house and he was warmhearted ... with each separation, a judge would intervene as far as the babies were concerned as the mothers didn't seem capable of raising them. They would all be put into care ... but as each time the files were created in the mothers' names, neither the judges nor the social services examined what was going on in this situation, whereas, on the one hand, the father convinced that he was "doing his duty", was saving these teenagers from the claws of justice and on the other hand, the social and legal services who were also "doing their duty to protect" without realising how they were being manipulated and were reacting to the problem, while contributing to the repetition of these situations!

When re-reading the track record for patients in psychiatric wards, prisoners, young adults in difficulty, it is inevitable that one wonders about the succession of measures taken to help and the restrictions that are put into place, sometimes ever since these people were toddlers, which have only helped the problems to continue as if the workers were transmitting a reading of the situation which could be considered as saying "keep doing more of the same thing". Predictably, what follows is that when a new worker comes into a situation, they very quickly see that this family is being monitored by a dozen, or sometimes even more, social, therapeutic and legal services.

There again, implicit rules are emerging which will impose themselves on the psycho-social workers and on the judges in the name of consensus. Often, during conciliation meetings, the consensuses which are being created will become conspiracies against one or other of the actors and this means that it is impossible to take the families' skills or that of the workers into account. In developing this model of a systemic reading and its methodology, I named it "a systemic reading of the inter-institutional" (Pluymaekers, 1996, 1999).

In the area of health policies, the work of reflecting with the workers in the field and the representatives of the ministries carried on. On Mony Elkaïm's initiative, the team at la Gerbe were to organise a major event within the district itself and this was the symposium that took place in January 1975 whose subject was "Alternative à la psychiatrie" (an alternative to psychiatry). As Mony wrote in the preface to the book 10/18 recounting those days and the establishment of the international Network-Alternative à la Psychiatrie: "the success of this encounter was to go well beyond the hopes of the organisers... (they would all) insist on the necessity to refuse to adhere to a criticism of the psychiatric system ...(but) lead the fight against the process of marginalising the work within the family, the school, the workplace, etc..." (Elkaïm, 1977, pp. 7–8).

There is no doubt that the richness of the debates at this time strengthened the public health policy leaders' idea that there was a need to recognise the demands that really being in close proximity establishes between the inhabitants of the sector and the mental health professionals. For us, as militants, it was essential that the royal decree indicating that mental health teams be created should take up a clear position on the need for these teams to be independent of the psychiatric hospitals. This was the case, and was approved in the vote that took place in March 1975. The team at La Gerbe, who were already working on a defined territory was therefore to become "a mental health centre" with no structural link with the hospital.

At the same time as the opportunities which the growth of Réseau-Alternative à la Psychiatrie were to give us, the friendships and exchanges that we were then to develop were, for the team at La Gerbe as much as for me, a real source of excitement which made our clinic innovative, committed and critical. We were to share our approach on meeting families, discovering the richness of the various clinics, those of Luigi Cancrini, of Luigi Onnis, of Maurizio Andolfi's team, of Sylvana Montagano. We were also very aware of the network practices that Giavonni Jervis and Yvonne Bonner hosted in Reggio Emilia and of the political positions taken up by Franco Basaglia, and Robert Castel. I mustn't forget the critical but stimulating contributions that were conveyed by Félix Guattari and David Cooper.

What's more, for me, the reflection on the practice of district networking and the social work for the protection of young people continued. We had very heartening encounters with the team for the infant-juvenile sector in Villeurbanne (Lyon) led by Jacques Hochman and Francis Maqueda who were experimenting with community psychiatry. There were the discussions on practice for prevention in the underprivileged district of "south central" Montreal. The research centre for "supervised education" in Vaucresson who invited me to give them training sessions remains for me a place where we could exchange and work on our way of carrying on with our clinical practice. These were to be enhanced by Guy Ausloos' first articles published in the Vaucresson annals. He and I had met in Lausanne at the beginning of the 70s, both of us sharing the belief in the importance of the work with families … which at the time was not obvious!

For me, the history of La Gerbe, those meetings, those friendships, have been the pinnacle of a systemic clinical practice which could be thought through, modelled, and transmitted. So, since 1981 I was to be an initiator of the training course in the Systemic Approach and Family Therapy within the higher social education syllabus in Namur and founder of the association, Réseau et Famille in Montpellier which, ever since, has been organising 3 and now 4 year long term training courses every year.

That was to take place through the Institut d'Etudes de la Famille et des Systèmes Humains that Mony Elkaim created in 1979 and which was to be the basis for the review, "Les cahiers critiques de thérapie familiale et de pratiques de réseaux": but most importantly there were the congresses that we organised in the 80s in Brussels. These congresses were to be extraordinary places where we could carry out debates, discussions on the systemic approach and family therapy. So it was quite natural that we wanted the work of reflection and discussion to continue, punctuated by congresses. This was to lead to the creation of an international network of family therapists that Mony coordinated and of which I was to be the kingpin. EFTA was in its period of gestation and it was in 1990 that this network achieved its full structure as a non-profit, international association.

It was within this context of passionate encounters, discussions about our way of working, sharing and friendship that each of us at their own rhythm and according to their clinical background developed innovative concepts, effective methodologies, the inventive ways of practising that EFTA and its congresses displayed to their best advantage.

For me, I was so pleased to see the development of research on prescribed help especially that of Guy Hardy (2012) within social work and of Thierry Darnaud (2007) in support work for the elderly. In a different dimension, the landscaped genogram that I created with Chantal Hanquet for work on family history has proved its fruitfulness in the work on emotions in therapy, in intervention and in training (Pluymaekers and Hanquet 2000, and translation 2003a, b; 2007a; 2008a, and translation 2007b; 2008b).

It would seem that today we find ourselves more and more confronted by these new forms of specialisation logic. As before they seem rather to give answers to financial and management interests than to the needs of the people in difficulty whether it be on a psychosocial level or in mental health. So it is crucial that our systemic practice and family therapy should assert themselves so as to ensure the balance between the human being and the simplistic logic of specialisation.

Acknowledgment I like to thank Yvette Lilot for the English translation.

References

Ausloos, G. (2015). In memoriam Jacqueline Prud'Homme. *Thérapie familiale, 36*(1), 1–2.
Binswanger, L. (1954). *Le rêve et l'existence*. Paris: Desclée de Brouwer (Original work published 1930).
Cooper, D. (1970). *Psychiatry and anti-Psychiatry*. Paris: Le Seuil.
Darnaud, T. (1999, 2007). *L'entrée en maison de retraite* (2è ed.). Paris: ESF.
De Waelhens, A. (1958). *Existence et signification*. Louvain: Nauwelaerts.
Debuyst, C. (1985). *Modèle éthologique et criminologique*. Liège: Mardaga.
Elkaïm, M. (1977). *Réseau-alternative à la psychiatrie*. Paris: Union Générale des Editeurs. Collection 10/18 N 1175 7-8.
Fossion, P., & Rejas, M. C. (2001). *Siegi Hirsh: Au coeur des thérapies*. Ramonville: Eres.
Goffman, E. (1968). *Asiles*. Paris: Ed. Minuit.
Hall, E. (1971). *La dimension cachée*. Paris: Le Seuil.
Hardy, G. (2001). *S'il te plait, ne m'aide pas* (2èth ed.). Ramonville: Eres.
Hardy, G. (2012). *S'il te plait, ne m'aide pas* (2èth ed.). Ramonville: Eres.
Hochmann, J. (1967). La psychothérapie familiale. Une arme nouvelle pour la sociopsychiatrie. *L'information psychiatrique, 7*, 1157–1172.
Hochmann, J. (1971). *Pour une psychiatrie communautaire*. Paris: Le Seuil.
Lacan, J. (2001). Les complexes familiaux dans la formation de l'individu. In J. Lacan (Ed.), *Autres Écrits* (pp. 23–84). Paris: Seuil (Original work published 1938)

Merleau-Ponty, M. (1964). Résumé de ses cours établi par des étudiants et appouvé par lui-même. *Bulletin de Psychologie, 18*, 236.

Pluymaekers, J. (1974a). *Insertion et secteur*. Bruxelles: LBHM. Mosaïque, 17.

Pluymaekers, J. (1974b). L'éducation dans la rue. In Centre d'étude de la délinquance juvénile (Ed.), *Voies nouvelles de prévention* (pp. 111–119). ULB: Bruxelles.

Pluymaekers, J. (1981). Aussi gros que les montagnes de la gerbe. *Connexions, 32*, 97–131.

Pluymaekers, J. (1986). Agir et réfléchir…à l'infini.: la formation à l'approche systémique. *Thérapie familiale, 7*(2), 167–180.

Pluymaekers, J. (1987). *Réseaux et pratiques de quartier in Les pratiques de réseau*. Paris: ESF.

Pluymaekers, J. (1989). *Familles, institutions et approche systémique*. Paris: ESF.

Pluymaekers, J. (1996). *Traiter la maltraitance: une remise en question. Cahiers critiques de thérapie familiale et de pratiques de réseau*. Bruxelles: De Boeck.

Pluymaekers, J. (1997). Actuar y pensar…hasta el infinito: la formacion en el abordaje sistemico. *Systemica, 3*, 99–112 (Spanish translation).

Pluymaekers, J. (1999). La justice, le social et le thérapeutique face à la maltraitance. In AFIREM (Ed.), *La prise en charge de la maltraitance. Jeux et enjeux* (pp. 301–322). Paris: Khartala.

Pluymaekers, J., & Hanquet, C. (2000). Richesse du génogramme paysager: histoire familiale et actualisation psychodramatique. *Cahiers critiques de thérapie familiale et de pratiques de réseaux, 2*, 85–108.

Pluymaekers, J., & Hanquet, C. (2003a). Genograma y terapia familiar: riqueza del genograma paisajistico, historia famiiar y actualiazacion psicodramatica. *Systemica, 11–12*, 95–117 (Spanish translation).

Pluymaekers, J., & Hanquet, C. (2003b). O πλουτος του τοπιακου γενεογραμματος: Οικογειακη ιστορια και ψυχοεkδραματιση. *Τετραδια ψγχιατρικης, 84*, 62–77 (Greek translation).

Pluymaekers, J., & Hanquet, C. (2007a). Ricchezza del gnegramma in forma di paesaggio: un opportunita per i gruppi di supervisione. *Psicobiettivo, XXVII*(1), 89–108 (Italian translation).

Pluymaekers, J., & Hanquet, C. (2007b). Η εkπαιδευση των οικογενειακων θεραπευτων και το γενεογραμμα τονιου: ενα εργαλειο για την προσωπικη αναπτυξη και την εποπτεια. *Μεταλογος, 12*, 103–112 (Greek translation).

Pluymaekers, J., & Hanquet, C. (2008a). La formation des thérapeutes familiaux et le génogramme paysager: un outil de développement personnel et de supervision. *Cahiers critiques de thérapie familiale et de pratiques de réseaux, 41*, 97–106.

Pluymaekers, J., & Hanquet, C. (2008b). Training of family therapists and the Landscape Genogram: The meaning of therapist personal and private development and supervision. *Human Systems, 19*(3), 212–221.

Satir, V. (1971). *Thérapie de couple et de famille*. Paris: EPI.

Schotte, J. (2008). *Vers l'anthropopsychiatrie, un parcours*. Peronnais: Ed. Hermann.

Thinès, G. (1977). *Phénoménologie et science du comportement*. Liège: Mardaga.

Thinès, G. (1980). *Phenomenology and the sciences of behaviour*, essai, Londres, Allen and Unwin.

Thinès, G. (1991). *Existence et subjectivité*. Bruxelles: Ed. Université de Bruxelles.

Watzlawick, P. (1972). *Une logique de la communication*. Paris: Le Seuil.

Chapter 4
Time: An A-Theoretical Framework for Therapy and Healing

Hugh Jenkins

Synopsis Time is the insistent nattering monkey on my shoulder; one that is preoccupied with the nature of endless time when we say "time stands still", and those episodic temporal events that seem here one moment and gone the next. With this in mind I bookend the chapter with two images: Norwegian midnight sun and the Northern Lights, to touch on our temporary temporal occupation of this planet. In the body of this chapter an image of dwarfed human habitation suggest another context.

Preoccupation with time predates Parmenides but only infrequently becomes the focus for therapy. Ideas about "time-limited" therapy can obscure the importance of the quality of time experienced: we see as if with "eyes wide shut". Both statements are true; "We know what time is" and "We don't know what time is".

This chapter explores the importance of a temporal perspective in therapy, paying attention to ritual and time; ritual in therapy; therapy as ritual, as well as the spaces in between in moments of change. The often ignored "liminal" as a-temporal space for change opens alternatives that are non-specific to any particular model of therapy.

After reflecting briefly on psychodynamic and systemic models, and life cycle and transgenerational frameworks, the value to clinicians of exploring temporal

---

Hugh specialised in becoming a generalist as a psychotherapist, both in drawing on a range of therapeutic models as a way to avoid "orthodoxy" and in working with a whole range of presenting problems. His therapy is based primarily on the quality of the relationship between therapist and patient from which to begin. In his early practice this was in the community with families facing multiple disadvantages. He has lead or been extensively involved in training programmes in Hungary, Romania, and Singapore.

H. Jenkins, Ph.D. (✉)
Rowans, 4 Old Forge Close, Long Green, Wortham IP22 1PU, UK
e-mail: ventris@dircon.co.uk

M. Borcsa, P. Stratton (eds.), *Origins and Originality in Family Therapy and Systemic Practice*, European Family Therapy Association Series,
DOI 10.1007/978-3-319-39061-1_4

perspectives from philosophy and anthropology is discussed. This creates a unique perspective on time in therapeutic healing, considering what is common to good practice and unique for each individual.

Timeless Time

Here with the Midnight Sun there is a sense of timelessness. The sun never sets; light is constant, forever; night and day are un-boundaried. Inevitably the sun will wane, winter will come with its short dark days when the sun is no longer seen, but at this moment that seems incomprehensible. We are suspended almost in a liminal space (Stoller 2009), as is often the experience of patients in therapy sessions (Plate 4.1).

That Reminds Me of a Story …

There is a story of a man who rode his bicycle through customs at the American Mexican border, carrying a rucksack and two panniers full of sand. Every time he did this, customs officers emptied all the sand out to find what he was smuggling; nothing, every time. This went on for some considerable time. One day, as the man was returning, he stopped to have a beer just before the customs post, and some customs officers sitting there said: "We know you are smuggling something but can't find it. Please tell us, and we promise not to stop you. What is it?" "Bicycles" said the man.

Plate 4.1 Over Lofoten Islands: Norwegian Midnight Sun. Hugh Jenkins 2014

The Meeting of Three Ways: A Tripartite Structure

A simple tripartite image (Fig. 4.1) maps three perspectives for approaching time; philosophy, anthropology, and psychotherapy (Jenkins 2013). How might understandings of time from the first two disciplines enrich therapeutic practice?

This image recalls the meeting of three roads in the region of Phokis from Delphi, Daulis, and Thebes (Sophocles 1984) where Oedipus killed his father. Depending on where one stands, it is (Vickers 2007, p. 29–30) "a place of divergence or convergence. So it's a matter of which way you happen to be travelling, a widening of choice, or a narrowing … all roads will be travelled in the end. It's only a matter of time".

A three-way meeting point can be a place of unusual connections and choice. Choice means re-ordering ideas, perhaps how to respond when the sequential is experienced simultaneously or the fleeting present hovers tantalisingly beyond our peripheral reach. Such a convergence may feel like almost a "non-place" (Augé 1995) in its liminality. Therapy is a "liminal" space, inhabited by patient and therapist, located at the margins (Jenkins 2007). It is an ambiguous transitional territory of potential for psychological and emotional transformation, choice and uncertainty.

A short chapter can only touch on some general themes. If the reader's curiosity is aroused to explore further it may become a fascinating personal and professional journey and open ways of seeing that always present were not previously evident.

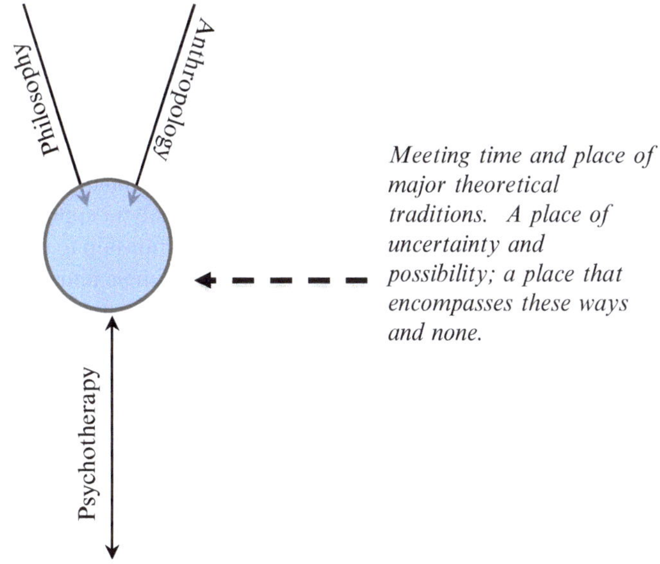

Fig. 4.1 Meeting of the three ways

"Time" is always present, though like the customs officials in the story, we may see it with "eyes wide shut" without recognition.

My professional practice is shaped in many ways by temporal perspectives. As a personal story, it is influenced by a childhood of multiple family house moves, multiple schools, including two boarding, a precarious balance between change and stability; an early apprenticeship for living in the marginal or "liminal".[1] It helps me understand why exploring my family tree with my godmother was important; how to thread security or continuity into discontinuity. I had not heard of genograms, "family scripts", "invisible loyalties", or "intergenerational transmission". I realise now that what I learnt from this is how to help people find *their* ways through ostensibly chaotic stories, to create hope from hopelessness; like the bicycle smuggler, to "see" what is there all the time but is so easily missed. The Romanian sculptor Brâncuşi captures the essence of this process: (Georgescu-Gorjan 2012, p. 359) "It is not birds I sculpt, it is flight". It is tempting to become preoccupied with the bird; its structure, weight, shape, colours, beak, talons—and to miss the essential; to miss flight.

I have in effect attempted to capture this sense of "flight" (Jenkins 2006), often through gendered stories over generations, women to women; women to men, and similarly for men, their flight journeys, exploring how these scripts (Byng-Hall 1988, 1995) often (re-) play through current relationships. David Malan describes how his "triangles", intrapersonal and interpersonal, "represented by a *triangle of time*" (Malan 1979, p. 80) inter-loop at different levels of description. These are temporal approaches, echoing Freud's thinking about time, those early experiences that replay again and again in later life through a "compulsion to repeat" (Freud 1926: Vol. XX). Time and temporality underpin Freud's work, how "today" becomes an attempt to deal with the past.

> Thus a man who has spent his childhood in an excessive and to-day forgotten attachment to his mother, may spend his whole life looking for a wife on whom he can make himself dependent and by whom he can arrange to be nourished and supported. (Freud 1939. Vol. XXIII, p. 75–76).

It is not necessary to embrace Freud's theories of repression or the Unconscious to accept such a view; but we need to see the familiar analytic approach with new eyes. In many ways future, present, and past and our relationship to these temporal dimensions is Freud's framework (Fig. 4.2). It is such a simple template abstracted from scholarship in many disciplines about time. Brâncuşi captures this process: "*Simplicity is complexity resolved*" (Georgescu-Gorjan 2012, p. 94). This in essence is the nature of psychotherapy and my underlying approach.

---

[1]Liminal comes from the Latin, *limen* meaning threshold. It is that place which is in neither space, betwixt and between. The Roman double-headed god, Janus, who looks in both directions, is the god of doorways. Hence subliminal; below the threshold. *Liminal* is an important concept for this chapter.

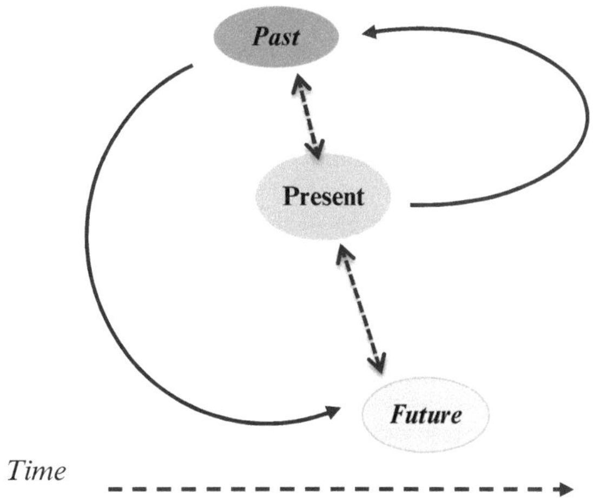

Fig. 4.2 Future, present, and past: a simple template for dealing with complexity (Jenkins 2006)

Background: Setting the Scene

We all have ideas about time, time as subjective experience, and how our experience of time changes according to our state of emotional arousal. Like the bicycle story, it is there but we do not necessarily "see" what we see. We know that "time" has different connotations in different cultures, whether we "use" time or "take" time, or are "in" time, even what it is to be late or early (Levine 2006). Yet like the fish in water that has no concept of water or wetness, we pay little conscious attention to time or the so-called "passage of time" from moment to moment.

Some dispute time's existence (Barbour 2000, 2008), or suggest time is not fixed but relative (Canales 2015; Einstein 1961). St Augustine famously wrote: "What, then, is time? I know well enough what it is, provided that nobody asks me; but if I am asked what it is and try to explain, I am baffled" (Augustine 1961, p. 264). When I look back on my career, I see how time in so many ways has been "the silent guest at the therapeutic table" (Jenkins 2013).

Recent History: Stepping Back

In the 1960s and 1970s in the UK many of us were strongly influenced by the work of R.D. Laing (1961, 1965, 1969; Laing and Esterson 1970). Psychiatric illness was no longer located discretely in the individual but in the social matrix in which the individual found her/himself. Current patterns and patterns of communication over time became the focus for intervention. Laing was influenced in his thinking by the work of anthropologist Gregory Bateson (1955, 1936/1958, 1960, 1964, 1969, 1970) in understanding behaviour through pattern, feedback, and communication in the individual's familial and social context. Other anthropologists were contemporaneously describing communication patterns (Leach 1976) as a way to understand other cultures. *Family Life* (Loach 1972), a powerful film of the era, reflects Laing and Bateson's thinking about "madness and the family". Laing and his followers challenged traditional psychiatry in the UK, as did Thomas Szasz (1972) in the USA. Julian Leff and collaborators took these ideas further in studies on Expressed Emotion (EE) (Leff 1979; Leff and Vaughn 1981, 1985).

Time is implicit in all therapy. However, little attention is given to qualitative changes in the patient's experience of time, nor time as a primary consideration. Descriptions of time are often given without explicit reference to the contribution of other disciplines. A notable exception in the systemic field is the work of Boscolo and Bertrando (1993). Texts on brief therapy rarely if ever give attention to the quality of time in healing; rather it is to the characteristics of therapy practised briefly.

In life cycle models (Carter and McGoldrick 1980, 1989; Jenkins 1981) time is to the fore in terms of stages; stages that have duration, as in adolescence (Jenkins 1981; Jenkins and Cowley 1985), or chronically disrupted families (Jenkins 1983); older people (Herr and Weakland 1979); or that are highly stressed for different reasons, such as when a parent is chronically ill or dies and a young person takes on "parental" roles beyond their years (Combrinck-Graham 1985). Transgenerational models emphasise a linear time where patterns of repetition are described over extended periods—inter- and trans-generationally (Boszormenyi-Nagy and Spark 1973; Bowen 1978; Lieberman 1978, 1979a, b), and the important work of John Byng-Hall bringing together attachment theory (Byng-Hall 1991) and systems thinking through family scripts (Byng-Hall 1973, 1980, 1986, 1988, 1995). These and many more form much of my foundational thinking.

Time to the Fore?

What happens when we put time to the fore, not as a novel model for psychotherapy, but to add an important dimension for all psychotherapeutic models? I have explored this elsewhere (Jenkins 2007, 2008, 2012, 2013, 2015a, b) putting time in the forefront and asking how the disciplines of philosophy and anthropology may enhance our practice as healers.

The ways we pay attention to time, depending on our model(s) of change, are mainly past or future. The future, we may say, has to pass through the present to become the past, as in McTaggart's "*A*" series (McTaggart 1927); from a nearer and nearer future to an increasingly distant past. This is a time that is fluid, changing, unlike his "*B*" series of "before" and "after", temporal moments that remain in fixed relationship.

In my practice I hold in mind a perspective of present, past and future (Fig. 4.2) irrespective of the therapeutic model. Too often the past remains painfully present for relationships in trouble and the future becomes impossible to envisage, especially in the intensity of individual (Jenkins and Asen 1992) or couples therapy (Jenkins 2006). This is often so in couple therapy (Jenkins 2006) with the complexity of "le tiers pesant" (Goldbeter-Merinfeld 1999, see Chap. 7 of this volume).

"Le tiers pesant" describes those multiple triangulations that the therapist must find ways to confront. They may be enacted in the room, or the "mind" of the individual patient, the couple or family, or the therapist may embody this third nodal point. In our work, the most difficult "time" to capture and describe is "the present moment".

> The present moment is the felt experience of what happens during a short stretch of consciousness. … It is the experience as originally lived. It provides the raw material for a possible later verbal recounting (Stern 2004, p. 32–33).

This sounds simple and self-evident. It is "slippery" and forever fleeting.

> What we usually overlook is that when we jump out of one present moment we simply jump into another (the next) present moment – in this case, the new present experience of wondering about the last present experience. But we act as if the second experience is from an objective perspective compared to the first. Actually it is still a first-person experience about trying to take a third-person stance relative to something that just happened (ibid).

Such is the complexity that so often has to be resolved. Only in the moment do we fully experience, yet when we try to describe or make sense of that experience (another present moment), we are no longer in it; present constantly becomes past (McTaggart 1927). Or more precisely we are immersed in a constantly fleeting quicksilver-like phenomenon that we can only *begin* to describe when no longer *in* the experience.

In order to begin linking this to practice, I describe two clinical examples, before returning to my development in the family and systemic field and the importance of holding models of "mind" that in Western thinking come from Freud and psychoanalysis *and* "mind" as Bateson (1970) describes, those transforms of difference in the whole recursive cycle of relationship: "The elementary cybernetic system with its messages in circuit is, in fact, the simplest unit of mind; and the transform of a difference travelling in a circuit is the elementary idea" (Bateson 1970, p. 433).

Clinical Vignettes

> *Dan*. I saw Dan and his wife in couple therapy. In the previous session Dan described how well a weekend camping in the New Forest with his adult son from his first marriage had gone. Now, he seemed despondent about himself as son, husband, and father, and he became increasingly enraged. Instead of articulating it symbolically in words, he began to roar, punching the table beside him until it partly collapsed. Still shouting, he picked up a pot-plant, struck it on the half-destroyed table, shook it at me, and made to leave. I quietly said: "Please sit down, Dan". After a pause he sat down, angry, now crying. Then came the story of all the men who had let him down; absent father, sexually abusing male teacher, his male therapist, me, among others; all those he wanted to annihilate. At that moment the invisible boundary between the symbolic therapeutic relationship, where he could talk out his despair, and the urge to act out his rage had blurred.

Here, in T. S. Eliot's words "Time present and time past/Are both perhaps present in time future/And time future contained in time past" (Eliot 2001, p. 3), he railed like a child. He lashed out at adults who again denied his elemental needs for comfort and affirmation while *simultaneously* fragilely conscious of the present.

Unlike patients who lose all sense of spatial or temporal location, his adult self was still accessible though momentarily overwhelmed by his primitive "narcissistic" hurt. This moment is not, as I will discuss, simply Parmenides' instant out of time (Plato 1997). It is more complex. It embodies thickness and depth (Husserl 1991) where past obliterates and becomes present, where the present disappears and temporal boundaries dissolve.

June. The second example is June. I had known Chris and June for a long time and seen them together, and then Chris on his own. Later June asked if we could meet. As she described situations that frustrated and irritated her endlessly, leaving her feeling unappreciated, evoking childhood memories of emotional neglect, I tried to make sense of this story. Cognitively, she knew that Chris loved and admired her. I said:

"You and Chris live in different timeframes. For Chris, events happen, things are said, mistakes are made, regrets even are expressed. For Chris that is the end of it. He gets on with the next thing. You are different. You remember, you connect events, history is important and you take a long-term view, you work very hard to make sense, and you reflect. It is that in important ways you live in different time or temporal worlds. Chris lives in *episodic time* while your time is *narrative* or diachronic. In this way you bypass each other, as if you spoke different languages."

From then on, with this in mind, June could begin to make sense of their struggles; that Chris was not repeating her painful story of, nor "personifying", a neglectful father whom she could never please.

Lurking in the background is another context; our psychology is our neurology. Simon Baron-Cohen (2003) describes how male and female brains differ. Antonio Damasio (2000a, b) describes our cerebral neurology, and therefore our mind. He links cognition and emotion and how we experience our worlds, while Solms and Turnbull (2002) address this from a neuro-psychoanalytic view. We experience time through our neuro-biology, and have scientific understandings of experiences of time, as for Chris and June. When we are deeply engrossed in a subject, or listening to music or watching a beautiful sunset, we lose track of time; an hour becomes an instant. Our brain waves change in these moments, changes that can be mapped with fMRI. None of this detracts from the visceral experience. Equally, when we are bored or having difficulty coping, a few minutes become an eternity. Our neurology, by virtue of our "wiring" linked in evolutionary terms to gender and states of emotional arousal, influence our experiences of time. It is not uncommon for a patient to reply when I say that we need to be finishing: "Really! I have only been here a few minutes." Experiences of time change; the time of therapy and the time of the clock are not the same. As in therapy and ritual, the *mundane* or everyday experience of time become part of the *sacred* or *sublime,* which as we will discover is another kind of temporal space.

Resources: Philosophy

Plato describes the *instant* in *Parmenides*. This strange phenomenon may hold the key to what often seems mysterious about when and how change occurs in therapy; why it cannot readily be planned or easily grasped.

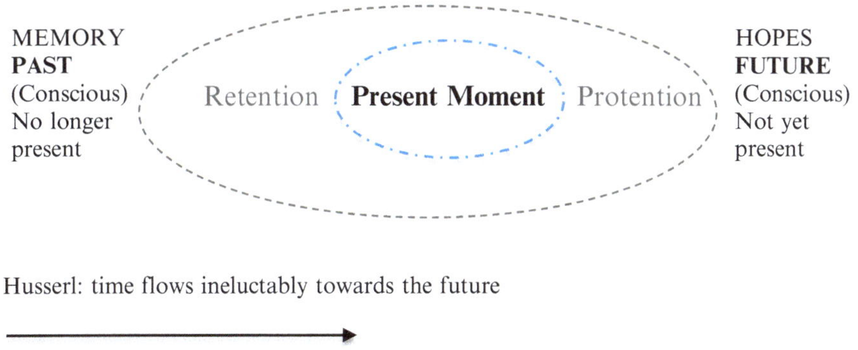

Fig. 4.3 Retentive and protentive aspects are constitutive elements of the present moment. They create a "thick" present

> The instant seems to signify something such that changing occurs from it to each of two states. For a thing doesn't change from rest while rest continues, or from motion while motion continues. Rather, this queer creature, the instant, lurks between motion and rest – being in no time at all – and to it and from it the moving thing changes to resting and the resting thing changes to moving. … But in changing, it changes at an instant, and when it changes, it would be in no time at all, and just then it would be neither in motion nor at rest. (Plato 1997, p. 388).

In the healing encounter, the moment/instant of "will be", "is", or "was" can scarcely be grasped, yet it seems likely "change" occurs in this liminal space we call the *instant*. This betwixt and between lies outside the logic of (*chronos*) time, in an intangible temporal experiential field (*kairos*). Jane will describe her experience of such an instant when we consider ritual.

Edmund Husserl describes a "thick present". This proposes time has "thickness". All therapy takes place in the present, but not all presents are the same. The present for Husserl includes elements of past and future. The past is *Retention*; the future is *Protention* (Fig. 4.3). The three temporal perspectives all exist in the present, but the Present Moment is paramount. *Retention, present moment*, and *protention*, constitute every moment. "Retention" differs from active memory, requiring conscious recall; the not-yet-present of "protention", unlike expectation, is also not held consciously. This tripartite present incorporates "no longer", and "not yet". This is reminiscent of Augustine, that there is only the present; the present of past, present, and future things.

Husserl's "thick present" can contain an active present, past (and future). He cites the example of a musical note lingering "continuously held in consciousness" that "remains present". Present in the past, "(t)he moment shades off and changes continuously, and according to the degree of change, [it] is more or less present" (Husserl 1991, p. 18). Present and past moments are a simultaneous "present moment of experience", but the "past" is forever receding, "shading off" into a further and further past. This prefigures McTaggart's (1927) *A* Series; a nearer and nearer future through to a further and further past without overlap.

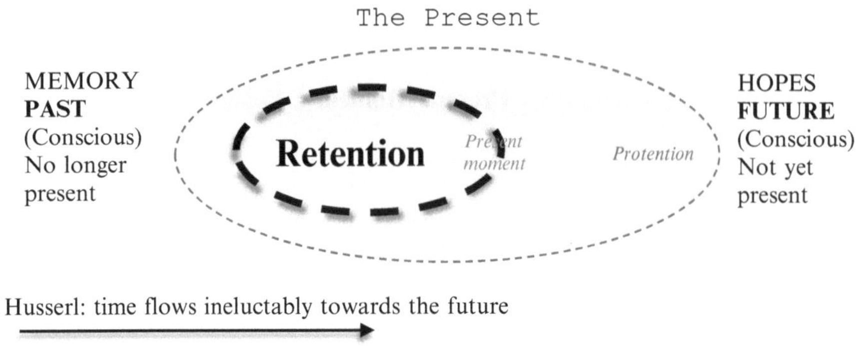

Fig. 4.4 The "thick" present; here "retention" dominates

In therapy the story is often different. Many patients experience a *past-remaining-present*; no "shading off". Their present-of-the-past remains intrusive and constant, a time that does not heal and forever stands still (Hall 1989); time with a qualitative difference. A past event that endures "is present now and present constantly, and present together with the new moment 'past'—past and present at once" (Husserl 1991, p. 19); a simultaneity of different times. Time emerging from relationship, since we are in time and not spectators, is not a succession of nows (une succession de maintenant), but in the thick instant "layers of time … thicken" (la couche du temps … s'épaissit; Merleau-Ponty 2011, p. 478).

When Dan became enraged and "saw red" his past hurts, abandonments, and abuse flooded and as in Fig. 4.4 "retention" overwhelms any sense of present and obliterates any possible future; a timeless past-present. If we reconsider this visually, present and protention recede; "retention" engulfs, defining all experience past and present (and feared future). Jane's account below brings some of these ideas to life.

Clinical Vignette

I saw Jane in therapy for over eight years. She had been regularly sexually and physically abused for forty-five years, suffering extremes of torture, imprisonment, broken bones, and three pregnancies during her adolescence by her father; aborted by her mother. Abuse by both parents continued during therapy. At the age of 68 they both received 30-year prison sentences for a lifetime of abuse.

At her suggestion, Jane took part in three research interviews about her experiences of therapy some two years after successfully ending therapy. At the beginning of the first interview I began:

> **HJ.** "What were some of your experiences of being in the therapy room, especially with regard to your experiences of time? You remember that I sometimes said that bringing you back into the present, when you seemed to disappear, was a bit like pulling you back in at the end of a rope."

Jane. "There were times when I wasn't in the room. It was a bit like watching T.V. and it goes from one camera to another, it was seamless, it would slide. I was never aware of the transition, this was before we did BMW,[2] and I would suddenly become aware of what was going on, and suddenly I was in a different place; the sights and smells from a different place and time. There was never any thought, 'how can this be possible'. I couldn't think this isn't possible because I was with Hugh, or that I was now a lot larger than then. … It was like being in a dream but still awake, it was terrifying because of the scary things that were happening. It was a re-enactment of what used to happen. Somehow it seemed to be worse than it had been in the first place; it seemed more frightening than it had been at the time. I would end up where I had been before, a moment that was leading up to a bad bit that I knew was going to happen, when before, in the real time, I didn't know beforehand exactly what was going to happen."

"It was like reading a book that you have read before and only part remember. At that moment, I could see the future and that made it seem worse than it had been. I was not aware of you in the scenario while experiencing the terror. I was completely oblivious of that."

In these moments all sense of time and place is lost and the distorted world of Alice in Wonderland is normal. It is essential for the therapist to have a way of understanding, experiencing even, these temporal confusions, and to be acutely aware of the moment-by-moment changes in the session so as to follow and help the patient recover from this world of timeless time and trauma. St Augustine's description of the present helps.

Augustine (1961) speaks of there being only the present: the *present of past things* (memory); the *present of present things* (direct perception); the *present of future things* (expectation). Time of Jane's present-of-past events freezes in the present. It is too present, and the present of present time in the session freezes, overwhelmed by the present-past and no present-future; Husserl's retention engulfs, in an accumulating retention of retention (Merleau-Ponty 2011). Past, present, and future, are an undifferentiated "one". All is "retention".

We can call on Kant for a different simultaneity of different times; time as points on a line; "… we reason from the properties of this line to all the properties of time, with this one exception, that while the parts of the line are simultaneous the parts of time are always successive" (Kant 2003, p. 77). Imagine "crumpling" this line into a "ball" where otherwise distinct sequential temporal points become an undifferentiated knot. Therapy with Jane resembles un-crumpling the Kantian ball and re-extending the line to help her gain control over her constantly re-lived past and present trauma, no longer dominated or defined by her history. Through therapy, sequential temporal points become less and less experienced as simultaneous and undifferentiated in her healing.

In trauma and dissociation, as with Jane, we see a temporal breaking apart and compartmentalising of the intrapsychic structure to protect the individual's integrity, at considerable personal cost. It is not a static but discontinuous state with splitting of mental imagery and affect, of flashback disconnected from the temporal context:

[2] BMW is a simple three-part ritual I created for her to help deal with moments of panic and dissociation that involves breathing (B), a personal mantra (M), and writing down (W).

"The memory of one's life has holes in it – a full narrative history cannot be told by the person whose life has been interrupted by trauma" (Kalsched 1996, p. 13).

The discontinuous effect of trauma on memory when events are experienced episodically fractures time; it seems to freeze the moment. The individual experiences a sense of powerlessness; their temporal world changes utterly. Jane's description of being in the therapy room,—her recurrent nightmares, intrusive recollections, and many other symptoms, including her dissociative states,—met the criteria for Posttraumatic Stress Disorder (DSM-IV DSMIV 2000 [309.81]: 463–468). However, an important element in understanding her trauma phenomenologically is the impact of time distortion, "the memory of one's life (*that*) has holes in it"; "a full narrative history cannot be told"; all is incomplete.

Resources: Anthropology

That the nature, place, and experience of time is different in different cultures is well documented and not the subject here (Levine 2006). Rather, I will touch on Plato's instant from the perspective of the liminal and then show how practices from one cultural context, the Balinese, can inform therapy. I will also draw on some of the anthropological literature on ritual and time for clinical practice.

Victor Turner suggests that the liminal occurs in unstructured space. If relationships are based on a structure of socio-politico-religious positions *inter alia*, "we must regard the period of margin or 'liminality' as an interstructural situation" (Turner 1967, p. 93). Change between states becomes possible in the "interstructural" moment. In the shift from one way of being, of quality of relationship or organisation, to another,

> … there has to be … an interval, however brief, of *margin* or *limen*, when the past is momentarily negated, suspended, or abrogated, and the future has not yet begun, an instant of pure potentiality, when everything, as it were, trembles in the balance. (Turner 1982b, p. 44).

Transition and transformation are often confused in systemic writing. Colin Turnbull suggests that through performance of ritual, "a transformation takes place, not a mere transition, and this has everything to do with our understanding of liminality" (Turnbull 1990, p. 73). The liminal is not an inert space even though unstructured in terms of "before" and "after". Liminality is "the process of transformation at work. The technique of consciously achieving transformation is the process of entering the liminal state" (Ibid, p. 79) in the in-between, in the "instant" out of time, between two structured periods.

This captures equally the dynamic of therapy when the rational is subverted in an experiential shift, after which present and future are changed utterly, and one's relationship with the past alters. In this subjective in-between description we enter a more complex world, between the "phenomenological experience of time and chronological time" (Perelberg 2007, p. xv). St. Paul's (liminal) experience, struck from his horse on the road to Damascus between two geographical places, between persecutor and convert, arguably changed the course of world history. His transformation phenomenologically was beyond rational explanation.

Leopold Howe describes how the Balinese calendar appears to return to "the same logical point" (Howe 1981) at different, regular moments, in a cyclical temporal sequence. It is a framework that I have found helpful working with couples. While "cyclicity does not entail non-durational time" in the Balinese calendar, there is a timeless quality of being unable to escape repetition. Eliade emphasises how in ritual time is annulled, only to begin again and again.

> ... every sacrifice *repeats* the original sacrifice and co-occurs with it. Every sacrifice is accomplished at the same mythical moment; through the paradox of ritual, mundane time and duration are suspended. ... to the degree that an act (or an object) acquires a certain *reality* through the repetition of paradigmatic movements, and not only those, but mundane time, duration, "history" even, are abolished ... (Eliade 1969, p. 49–50). [3]

Howe suggests: "The accumulation of these cycles is however usually of far less interest than the co-ordination of events within the cycle" (Howe 1981, p. 227). How patients "co-ordinate" events and relationships has therapeutic value. The "co-ordination of events within the cycle", social relationships, and harmony, are more salient for the Balinese than Western preoccupations with measurable *chronos*. In the spirit-filled world "people and gods are part of the same massive cycle" (ibid, p. 229); they exist *in* time.

Cycles of experience *do* accumulate in people's lives, often like silt imperceptibly changing a riverbed. Over time (duration) events are co-ordinated (without conscious or intentional process) so that repeated linear events acquire circular and patterned connections with some predictability (Keeney 1983). When the therapist is able to introduce a different temporal cycle of diachronic connection that challenges the patient's episodic compartmentalization, a powerful shift in relationships can occur. June was helped to see Chris' episodic world in contrast to her more relational diachronic realities, *and* she began to contextualise Chris' episodic behaviour as belonging to him, and not attribute it to her early history of emotional neglect whereby she would then confuse those temporal realities of her-past-of-present-things-present.

Figure 4.5 presents these two kinds of time: durational (cyclical) of repetition and time of the "logical point". The same number on the revolving circle and the straight-line represent the "same point" from cyclical and linear views. The intervals *between* two or more "points" represent "duration", (a *lawas* in Balinese or particular length of time). The rotating circle represents "cyclical time". A complete cycle is six "*lawas*" from 1 through 2, 3, 4, 5, 6, and "back" to 1. Points marking duration echo Plato's discussion of number in *Parmenides*.

---

[3] ...tout sacrifice *répète* le sacrifice initial et coïncide avec lui. Tous les sacrifices sont accomplis au même instant mythique du commencement; par le paradoxe du rite, le temps profane et la durée sont suspendus. ... dans la mesure où un acte (ou un objet) acquiert une certaine *réalité* par la répétition de gestes paradigmatiques et pas cela seulement, il y a abolition implicite du temps profane, de la durée, de l' "histoire"... (Eliade 1969, p. 49–50).

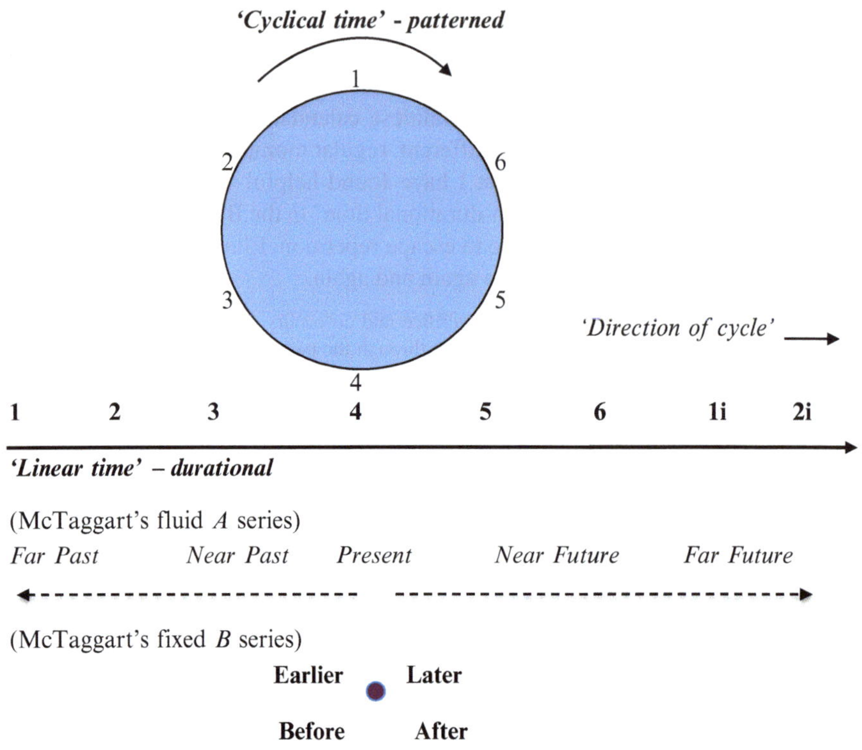

Fig. 4.5 Cyclicity/linearity: complementary perspectives

> So of all the things that have number the one has come to be first. … But that which has come to be first, I take it, has come to be earlier, and the others later; and things that have come to be later are younger than what has come to be earlier. … (Plato 1997, p. 385).

Plato's *chronos* number does not hold up in trauma as we saw; that which came first too often becomes present in the "number of now", as the Kantian length of string with knots in simultaneous sequence that when scrunched into ball really are experienced in undifferentiated simultaneity. We see some of this in Fig. 4.5, when number 1 repeated is not the same number 1.

The "*new* 1" at the start of the subsequent sequence is not the "*same* 1" marking the "beginning" of the cycle. It is at the same *logical* point but is at another *chronological* number point "along the linear time line" of number. This *different* 1 we can call 1i, then 2i, 3i, 4i, and so on. A further cycle becomes 1ii, 2ii, 3ii, and so on incrementally at each *logical point* and subsequent *durational* point of repetition; "when a cycle ends it does not return to the same *temporal* point; it returns, and this is a very different thing, to the same *logical* point" (Howe 1981, p. 231). In Balinese culture the cyclical aspect of duration predominates over linear'. Our Western cultures often emphasise duration and how to "*use*" time, while the Balinese tend to be *in* time. The difference between *using* time and *being in* time is important for thinking about time in psychotherapy. The patient in the session who loses all sense of duration is *in* time and in that moment more susceptible to change, in a "sublime" or "sacred" moment.

In couple therapy I find many examples of couples returning to "the same logical point", either in their current relationship in their history of relationships, and/or in family and cultural histories that affect attempts at intimacy, autonomy, power, nurturing, and so on. From a different model, this would be Freud's "compulsion to repeat". Therapy becomes a process to uncover these temporal patterns to help the couple block their preferred but failing ways of resolving their difficulty, and develop alternative ways to *be* and to relate.

Ritual

Ritual and ceremony are often confused: "Ceremony *indicates*, ritual *transforms*, and transformation occurs most radically in the ritual 'pupation' of liminal seclusion – at least in life-crisis rituals" (Turner 1982b, p. 80–81). Therapy and ritual are performative, intentional activities, concerned with continuity, transformation, and change (Jenkins 2013).[4] Both are structured and socially embedded in their culture. Ritual involves "more or less invariant sequences of formal acts and utterances not entirely encoded by the performers" (Rappaport 1999: 24). Rites of passage intend transformative, irreversible change, such as circumcision, the Jewish bar mitzvah, marriage, or funeral rites.

In ritual generally, and rites of passage particularly (Gennep 1960; Turner 1969), an important element is the initiate's experience of time suspended, of being beyond everyday time (Stoller and Olkes 1989). A general description suggests:

> Ritual ... functions on a psychological level. It provides a coherent framework for the disorienting aspects of human life, such as illness, danger, and life changes. It gives people a sense of control over disturbing and threatening events; an exorcism may not actually drive out any spirits, but it can drive out the sense of helplessness and despair associated with an illness. (Barfield 1997, p. 411).

Ritual brings cohesion to situations that otherwise risk disorder and chaos. Paradoxically, the task is often to ensure stability in the external world by channelling instability for socially sanctioned change, similar in many ways to therapy. The patient enters a symbolic reality and "feels a widening of the space in which he lives ... so that the past appears more coherent and the future more inviting" (Lifton and Olson 2004, p. 38).

Therapeutic ritual must encode avenues for change, for "the stability promoted by ritual is not an inertial inheritance but a continually renewed endeavour" (Torrance 1994, p. 70). Excessive system change creates systemic runaway and entropy, while excess stability risks system negentropy (Bateson 1973; Beer 1974). In ritual, anthropologists speak of time as "sublime" or "sacred". The sublime time

---

[4] A complex ritual interweaving past, present, and future to stop nightmares that had plagued the patient for over 40 years is described in Jenkins (2013: 262–265).

of ritual refers to events occurring outside the ordinary or "mundane", often in a location set aside. Although part of socially sanctioned transformation, these activities take place at the margins (Stoller 2009) in an in-between "liminal" spatial and temporal space.

Clinical Vignette: Jenny, a Ritual of Obliteration and Renewal

Jenny's story incorporates the main elements of all ritual. It is a single powerful act that requires the performative and an element of ordeal. It helps her "fix" time and re-establish a clear "before" and "after" in her life.

> Jenny's partner had betrayed her. After having a child by her he began an affair with a married woman with whom he subsequently had two children. In her late forties, Jenny saw little hope of more children. Her hurt was palpable. There came a point in therapy when I asked her to handwrite her story about the relationship as an 'obituary'; an obituary always has a beginning and an end. I wanted her to her to create a direct, visceral relationship with her account by writing it out. She was free to say whatever she needed, as no one outside therapy would see it, thereby increasing the intensity of the process. She should determine how long it should be, giving her control of the process.
>
> Jenny did this, and as suggested brought it to the next session. I asked her to read it aloud in her own time; particular points and themes were explored. This helped concretise and legitimise her anger and the other feelings she had struggled to articulate.

As a second "assignment", an ordeal, I asked her to find a time when she could go somewhere isolated but safe with her "obituary". She should read it aloud as many times as she needed until she no longer felt overwhelmed by her pain in its inchoate rawness. She was then to burn it; ashes to ashes, with all the primitive socio-cultural associations of burial, annihilation, and finality, leaving it behind physically and emotionally by her action. I had instructed her to find somewhere beyond the city boundary as part of the "ordeal", to heighten her commitment to the process and sense of completion. This becomes a "sacred" space outside the "profane" space of the city. It is physically beyond her familiar, a liminal place for her. I gave her structure, specific directions, and an experience of ordeal for her healing.

At the next session I asked Jenny to describe what she had done. This was further to "fix the moment", reinforce her sense of control and celebrate her completion. She recounted the whole process in considerable detail. She paused, then added: "Then I took my jeans down and peed on the ashes."

This is a complex ritual involving;

- A transformative experience of letting go.
- Active performance.
- A symbolic burial, initiating her journey from victim to survivor.
- Incorporating aspects of "redemption" and purification as she cleansed herself of feelings of toxic self-loathing, anger, and impotence.
- A deeply primitive act of annihilation, irreversibly reinforced with her potent body fluids.
- An irrefutable definition of her "before" and "after".

The basics of ritual are here. By standing over and urinating on the ashes of the relationship, she used the potency of her body fluids and their physical symbolism for total obliteration. In this annihilation we see an ending of time, fixing the event and that painful part of her history as now past. It opened the possibility of a "new time" and future. The consequences of her ex-partner's infidelity continued to live with her but a more self-assured Jenny began to emerge. It "*drove* out the sense of helplessness and despair associated with her situation" (Barfield 1997, p. 411).

The "obituary" was a "one-off" ritual. It took planning. It incorporated powerful performative elements of privately writing it, publically reading it aloud, repeatedly reading it aloud in a chosen "sublime" place, annihilation, and finally fixing it in a particular moment by then recounting it in therapy. In her "reporting back" she symbolically replayed the physical and emotional beginning of her new life. It was a rite of passage.

We know that "major rituals … aspire to annihilate measurable temporality … to redress the failures of the present 'time' … and to restore the primaveral past as paradigmatic reality" (Turner 1982a, p. 228; See also Turner 1982b). Jenny's journey from her familiar urban everyday context to "un espace sacré" (Eliade 1965, p. 26; see also Eliade 1969) was charged with potentiality, a transformative experience. I suggest that in "the ritual of psychotherapy" there exists an instant of potentiality that can only be resolved actively as change. The problem or crisis is momentarily *detached* from the moment before, is not yet *attached* to the instant after, and hovers in a fragile, liminal in-between (Stoller 2009).

Such an instant is frequently experienced as being out of time by the patient. Change occurs in the spontaneous detached-not-yet-attached instant. Plato's "instant" is a conceptual framework for grasping the fleeting moment for potential change; "in no time at all" while *simultaneously* "the one partakes of time".

A simple example captures some of this. Jane had never allowed me to hold her coat as she left, since to do so requires turning one's back with the second sleeve and becoming completely vulnerable, an impossibility for her, with a life-time of physical and sexual abuse. She describes her experience of this moment in the research post therapy interviews.

> **H.J.** "There was the issue about whether you could let me hold your coat to help you put it on. What happened there?"
>
> **Jane.** "When I couldn't let you do that, I thought, like, how difficult can that be? When it happened it was really good. After, I wondered 'Why did I get myself in a mess' and the next time it was back to square one. There was a point before when it was totally impossible. Then, like a binary system it was suddenly OK. You distracted me enough for me to do it, so that I wasn't exactly paying attention, because you got me thinking somewhere else, so I did it without me psyching myself up for it. I was concentrating on what you were talking about and not on what was about to happen. Somehow, for a moment I was not quite there, and then it was done. And it was good."

Jane realises that my structured, carefully timed distraction of her conscious attention placed her momentarily in a different temporal space. When she "was not quite there" in temporal terms, in spatial terms she could allow me to hold her coat, but without being aware. This took place "outside therapy" in the waiting room, a liminal in-between space between the consulting room and the outside world, between the *sublime* space of therapy and the *mundane* outside world. Boundaries, physical and temporal, are important (Jenkins 2014), but while it is simpler in some ways to attend to physical space, time (and timing) is more intangible. Later, putting her coat on with help became one of her "piece of cake" achievements, part of the humour that helped make the previously unspeakable more survivable.

Simple though it was, I planned this as a performative event with an element of "intentional ordeal" (Haley 1963). Not defining this as "ritual" or "therapy" made it less daunting. Part of the distracting involved my active playfulness, thus changing the frame. The act of helping Jane with her coat becomes "sacred" in this specific context. Therapy occurs as much in the accumulation of informal small events as in more formal, conscious interventions.

Rites of Passage: Temporal Phases in Therapy

In this section I suggest a way to think about therapy as a temporal process, taking the literature on rites of passage. Psychotherapy and rites of passage have much in common. In systemic vocabulary, psychotherapy is concerned with "second order change" (Bateson 1955, 1971; Hoffman 1985) and the same intended outcomes, as for Jenny above.

Gennep (1960) described three phases of a rite of passage: *séparation* (separation); *marge* (transition) the liminal phase; and *agrégation* (incorporation). Rites facilitate the passage to the "sacred" ("sublime" or "ideal") and back to the "profane" (mundane). "The sacred is not an absolute value but one relative to the situation. The person who enters a status at variance with the one previously held becomes 'sacred' to the others who remain in the profane state" (Kimball 1960, p. viii–ix). DiNichola speaks of the patient who comes for help: "People in this situation are liminal: at a threshold 'betwixt and between' the old world they know and the new one they are experiencing. … this is an ambiguous state" (Di Nichola 1993, p. 53).

In a filmed interview on ritual (Timişoara, 2011) Andreea describes the morning of her wedding, about to become a pastor's wife and her impending change of status through this rite of passage:

> **H.J.** "So, we must come back to the wedding. As Andreea the pastor's wife, you lose something of your identity in a sense.
>
> **Andreea.** "Yes, I did. My independence, complete independence. Yes."
>
> **H.J.** "So, what you're telling me is that the marriage for you, and maybe for him, meant letting go of certain things, of independence, of doing what you would like when you like."
>
> **Andreea.** "Yes, when I was thinking of rituals, I have a brainstorm, which was this exactly, what a ritual marks the end of something, the beginning of something else. You give away and you receive."

As Andreea says, a "rite of passage" is dynamic, an active process, whose function is "to transform one identity into another" (Kapferer 1983, p. 179). It facilitates an intended move from one state to a newly appropriate one.

Working in the In-Between

We can take this three phase thinking about the in-between and the liminal further. Anthropologist Edmund Leach draws attention to the betwixt and between moments *between* the betwixt and between, from pre-liminal to liminal, and from liminal to post-liminal. Such boundaries are artificial distinctions for the otherwise continuous (Jenkins 2014). In the no-man's land *between* boundaries lie ambiguity and uncertainty.

> A boundary separates two zones of social space-time which are *normal, time-bound, clear-cut, central, secular*, but the spatial markers are themselves *abnormal, timeless, ambiguous, at the edge, sacred. …* The crossing of frontiers and thresholds is always hedged about with ritual, … (Leach 1976, p. 35).

The uncertainty of the *limen* often evokes discomfort. I suggest that in this dynamic liminal tension, transformational events readily happen *between* therapy sessions. The interval *between* sessions becomes an active marginal time of potentiality, what Turner, quoted earlier, termed "the ritual 'pupation' of liminal seclusion – at least in life-crisis rituals" (Turner 1982b, p. 81). Jane described an in-between instant where the therapist intentionally blurred the boundaries. We read: "You distracted me enough for me to do it, so that I wasn't exactly paying attention, because you got me thinking somewhere else, so I did it without me psyching myself up for it." Similarly, time between sessions can become an in-between moment where the patient is "distracted" by their everyday life, and thus being "not quite there" allows the unexpected and the unplanned. Milton Erickson actively used the in-between of sessions in many ways for the patient to behave differently (Haley 1973, 1985). The well-known face-vase-face figure captures some of the ambiguous nature of boundaries (Fig. 4.6).

Lines define lip, mouth, nose, throat, vase, vase stem, forehead, a bowl. The lines simultaneously "frame" inside and outside: this is face; this is vase (*vide*, this is play; this is therapy; this is fight, this is not fight; this in instruction, not instruction), or this is *not* face, *not* vase, creating a fluidity of constantly morphing realities.

When considering what to focus on—faces or vase—perhaps the question always is: what is the story, the story of therapy in and outside the session. In the image of

Fig. 4.6 Vase—faces gestalt

Lille Molle (Plate 4.2), what is the story? This image has its own story. Originally the small dwellings at the foot of the mountain had clearly defined windows, roofs with strong colour, walls that stood out more. All this distracted the viewer. Surely the story is the mountain rising sheer out of the water, the clouds and the fjord even? By subduing the human habitation the story changes, but it is and always should be: both-and.

In this context Fig. 4.7 proposes a rites of passage dynamic of psychotherapy. The overall duration of therapy is liminal. Focus may be on one area, but always in the context of other, less immediately dominant areas; the huts in the shadow of the mountain, Lille Molle. It supposes treatment as a unity as if ritual were internally homogenous without variation or rhythm *within* its structure.

Treatment is *liminal*, a sublime period; transformation is possible. Its chronological time and the phenomenological experience of time from within are different kinds of time. Therapy can be highly stressful. It represents *separation* from the

Plate 4.2 At the Foot: Lille Molle, Lofoten Islands. Hugh Jenkins 2013

Overall course of psychotherapy: stages:

Separation — Liminal / Transformative — Re-Incorporation

The overall context of psychotherapy as Separation-Liminal-Re-Incorporation (S-L-R).

Fig. 4.7 Psychotherapy: a rite of passage structure

mundane. For example, at the start of his second session John reflected about his experience of the first meeting. He had found beginning to confront his personal experiences and relationships "traumatising"; he had left the session "exhausted". Beginning therapy was a visceral ordeal in the physical, emotional, and psychological separation from the familiar, in the presence of the unknown.

As therapy ends a process of re-integration must be achieved, separating from the psychotherapist's continuing involvement. Casement (1985, 1990, 2002, 2006), Sandler et al. (1992), Sandler et al. (1997), and Yalom (1989, 2001, 2006) discuss separation and ending as critical, transformative, and integral aspects of treatment. Ending symbolises a moment of re-incorporation to the world of the everyday, leaving the sublime behind.

Each session, to which attention rightly is given, is potentially transformational. However, the "ignored instant" or time *between* sessions suggests another kind of temporal space *out of time* from the sessions, which themselves are *out of time* from the mundane everyday. This becomes a betwixt-and-between time *between* betwixt-and-between. Transformation may occur in that *in-between* period "spontaneously" from the session or through the psychotherapist's explicit intentionality through ritual or ordeal-like tasks, as Jenny experienced (Jenkins 1987). Just as the traditional shaman's activities are intentional (Stoller and Olkes 1989; Vitebsky 1995), so too are the psychotherapist's in psychoanalytic (Sandler et al. (1992); Sandler et al. 1997) and systemic fields (Palazzoli et al. 1980; Penn 1985; Tomm 1987a, b, 1988).

Jane describes her experience of in-between session periods and the effects of timing and length. It clearly was not an inert period.

> **H.J.** "What did you think about the time and spaces in between our sessions? How did you experience them at different times, stages of our meeting?"
>
> **Jane.** "After meetings it could be worse. I needed time to settle. Sometimes it was worse, or sometimes it was better. Everything was there and I couldn't ignore it, and it was as though it was happening then, but better for the same reasons because I could feel in control of the situation. But then it would go in the opposite way, and swing and feel as though I was losing control of it. The space in between was better to give time to sort things in my head in between."
>
> **H.J.** "What was important about the intervals?"
>
> **Jane.** "When it was a longer time, that was quite difficult. By the time we met, I'd managed to tuck it away again. To a certain extent, that made it difficult to come back to it. When there were longer intervals, there was a danger of pushing it away like I'd done before I came."
>
> **H.J.** "How much were the intervals part of therapy?"
>
> **Jane.** "I think it was very much in my mind, or at the back of my mind all the time. It was like it was all the time because the things we talked about here, I could use as a tool in between. Going first thing in the morning allowed me to get over it a bit and to focus on going to work. Evening sessions were more difficult because I'd get in a mess."

Interval time between was complex. It gave time to reflect, but also to act. For example, speaking to the police and later a lawyer to give her "evidence", were momentous tasks that required courage to break their power - in simpler societies we would call them spells (Stoller and Olkes 1989) - of believing she deserved all that was done to her was long, painful, and traumatic. Timing—early morning or late evening—had different consequences.

H.J. "What was important for you about the rhythm, pattern, and timing of the sessions?"

Jane. "I found the flexibility of spacing helpful. It was helpful because we both decided at the time, a consensus, and sometimes I needed a break from it. That was important. It allowed me to feel I was partly in control. It was a joint thing."

Collaborative agreeing of time intervals was important. Feeling in charge was especially significant for someone who had been and continued to be abused. The agreed variable nature of time *between* sessions gave Jane a sense of control and autonomy; *timing of sessions* had a significant impact on how she coped. She had responsibility for knowing what she needed when leaving an ansaphone message each Sunday evening to say whether she need a call back. Significantly "It was knowing you were there" and the importance of time constancy that was most important. A central premise for therapy was that eventually she would internalise that figure of constancy of the therapist and that would signal the end of the work.

Figure 4.7 re-configures this structure for each therapy session. Each session isomorphically mirrors the larger whole. The liminal space of each session is "boundaried" by a beginning (separation) and ending (re-incorporation). However, the intervals "boundaried" by and *between* each session have their own liminal quality and 'rhythm' (Hubert 1999): five times a week, weekly intervals, every 2/3 weeks. These are not inert periods in expectation of the next meeting. They are replete with potential for planned or spontaneous change. The example of Jenny's ritual of obliteration is an example.

Each S-L-R sequence represents an individual session, a particular separation from the mundane. Intervals *between* sessions embody a different kind of liminality. Session–interval–session becomes figure and ground in dynamic flux, each defining and re-defining the other, like the face–vase–face gestalt (Fig. 4.6). Each interval has its own S-L-R (Fig. 4.8). Interval–session–interval becomes an alternative counter-point sequence, like music's rhythms.

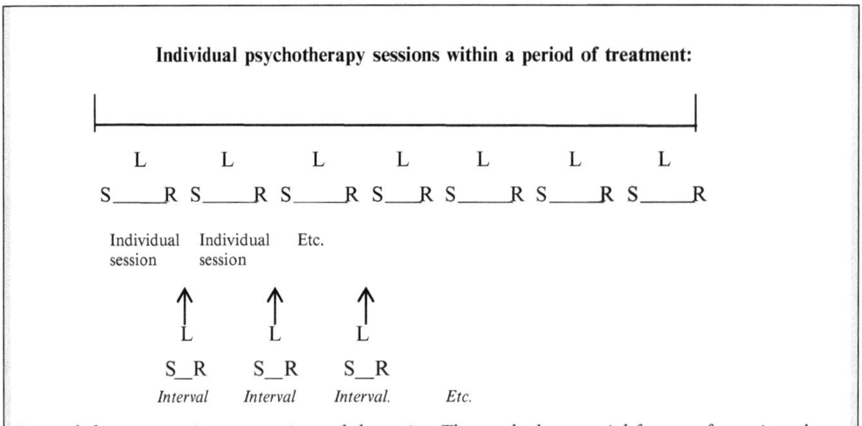

Intervals between sessions are active and dynamic. They embody potential for transformation, that occurs 'spontaneously' as part of the therapist's intentionality, or serendipitously.

Fig. 4.8 Each session is a microcosm of the larger gestalt of therapy

As we know in basic general systems thinking (von Bertalanffy 1968) the whole is more than the sum of its parts. So in deconstructing this rite of passage structure into its component parts something of the whole is inevitably lost. We must therefore return to the whole, to experience the tonality and totality of therapy.

Reflections

The analytic invariant of time and place over a long period of months or years is a sublime, liminal state, an experience of different kinds of time; of no time, "the anti-temporal character of ritual" (Turner 1982a, p. 237). Systemic therapy is likely to be more variable in frequency of sessions, planning longer intervals in between when the patient cannot immediately bring material back to treatment. Palazzoli and her colleagues (Palazzoli et al. 1978) discovered that this creates a different kind of tension, more likely to precipitate crisis (Jenkins 1989) and change in the family as they could not readily rely on the therapist to hold them. In effect, psychoanalytic and systemic models create different kinds of time during and between sessions.

Therapy through process and structure shares much with age-old healing traditions. What scholars have to say from their researches into ritual opens up ways to understand therapy, the nature of change, and the experience of being a patient. Of particular interest are ideas about the mundane/profane and the sublime/sacred; the nature of ordeal, and change or transformation.

The sense of uncertainty or imminent chaos as part of a liminal state, the sense of time slowing down and experiencing oneself out of time, are brought into sharp focus. The idea that the liminal is a dynamic phenomenon (Kapferer 2004), occurring in interstructural points (Turner 1967) provides powerful concepts for psychodynamic and systemic therapists. In order to cross thresholds (Leach 1976) we need structures and procedures to navigate these ambiguous areas.

This chapter has travelled a long way from 1971 and R.D. Laing, the period of the early ideas of Minuchin (1967; 1974) and Haley (1963; 1976) emphasising working in the present with family structure. Over the years I have re-connected with my concerns and interest in time, our experience of it, and its place in making sense of my life, the lives of my patients, and the inner world that psychodynamic models help articulate. If we are to be "systemic" as I understand the term, models that encompass the relational and interpersonal *AND* that provide ways to conceptualise the internal system of mind (Jenkins 1990; Jenkins and Asen 1992; Jenkins and Cowley 1985) are essential.

The peculiar nature of the Plato's "instant" may now have an extended duration in the liminal. It is not *chronos* that we experience or measure, but *kairos*. The inner process of what happens structurally and externally to the patient, or initiate, is they become "invisible" in this period of pupation (Turner 1967, p. 96). The therapist is architect and brick-layer, conductor and companion, immersed a-temporally while simultaneously holding other temporal foci in mind.

We have considered the internal structure of time, a thickness of the present; the present of past, present, and future things; that the "same logical point" marks pattern and can be an indicator for stuckness, a different take on Freud's "compulsion to repeat". From an archaeological view, Freud's work is profoundly time based, whether his idea that "there is nothing in the id that corresponds to the idea of time" (Freud 1933: Vol. XXII, p. 74) or the phenomenon of transference in analysis, the temporal confusion of the patient attributing to the analyst events, emotions, attitudes, from an earlier period and other contexts to the present of the consultation room; a simultaneity of different times. Such, in essence, was Dan's moment of rage as he crossed the boundary from talking out to acting out.

The timelessness paradox of ritual parallels psychotherapy. Traditional ritual emphasises stability and continuity, a loyalty to one's ancestors that requires change to ensure continuity. If in ritual it seems that the weighting tends to stability, in therapy the focus must fall towards change in a context of over-arching stability. In this dynamic tension the quality and perceptions of time may appear less obvious. As an aside, loyalty to ancestors and stability in the emerging field of psychoanalysis began early while Freud was still alive, and continues. This is well described in the letters of James and Alix Strachey (Meisel and Kendrick 1986). Fortunately it is less a debate in family and systemic psychotherapy today than 25 years ago.

If we lack ways to describe and take account of time and timelessness we are left with an "absence" that subtracts from understanding the experience of patient and therapist "meeting in the moment" (Jenkins 2005). In developing these ideas I have given importance to "the interval", not as the inert time-space of after and before but as dynamic, changing, elusive, and powerful, like human experience of time itself; like therapy and healing.

My explorations of this "meeting in the moment" that we call therapy (Jenkins 2005) through to asking to what extent philosophical and anthropological perspectives on time may assist to better understand the therapeutic encounter (Jenkins 2013), are part of a personal and professional journey. None of this makes claims for, not wishes to consider, new models of systemic psychotherapy; I have always avoided as much as possible the traps of orthodoxy (Jenkins 1985).

Time is and will always be fleeting, experienced in so many different ways. I began with an image of timeless time; the sun never setting but always against the backdrop of another winter and darkness. In the northern darkness the eternal constant changing of the Northern Lights (Plate 4.3) reminds us of our fleeting temporality on this planet; their presence unpredictable; their form ephemeral. From the light of summer when we "have all the time in the world" we return to darkness bathed in lights that can never be grasped. What sense is there to say: "While we have time" (*Dum tempus habemus*)?

So, to return to the beginning, which I trust is no longer the same beginning as at the start. *Dum tempus habemus* is a school motto I have carried in my head for over 50 years. But is only a part, for it continues; "*operemur bonum*", "let us do good".

Plate 4.3 Permanent impermanence: Northern Lights. Hugh Jenkins 2014

Surely this is an apt motto for every therapist, to be always aware of what little time we have and how best to occupy it: as smugglers of time perhaps?

References

Augé, M. (1995 [1992]). *Non-places: Introduction to an anthropology of supermodernity*. (J. Howe, Trans.). London: Verso.

Augustine of Hippo (1961) *Confessions*. London: Penguin Books.

Barbour, J. (2000). *The end of time: The next revolution in our understanding of the universe*. London: Phoenix Paperback.

Barbour, J. (2008). Bekjik de Noorderlicht-af levering 'Killing Time'. Regie: IJsbrand van Veelen. 7th April 2008. http://noorderlicht.vpro.nl/programmas/2848322/afleveringen/2380593/.

Barfield, T. (Ed.). (1997). *The dictionary of anthropology*. Oxford: Blackwell Publishing.

Baron-Cohen, S. (2003). *The essential difference*. London: Penguin.

Bateson, G. (1936/1958). *Naven* (2nd ed.). Stanford. Stanford University Press.

Bateson, G. (1955). A theory of play and fantasy. *APA Psychiatric Research Reports, II*. In: G. Bateson G. (1973) *Steps to an ecology of mind* (pp. 150–166). London: Paladin Books.

Bateson, G. (1960). Minimal requirements for a theory of schizophrenia. In: G. Bateson (1973) *Steps to an ecology of mind* (pp. 215–241). London: Paladin Books.

Bateson, G. (1964). The logical categories of learning and communication. In: G. Bateson (1973) *Steps to an ecology of mind* (pp. 250–279). London: Paladin Books.

Bateson, G. (1969). Double bind, 1969. In. G. Bateson (1973) *Steps to an ecology of mind* (pp. 242–249). London: Paladin Books. 242-249.

Bateson, G. (1970). Form, substance and difference. In: G. Bateson (1973) *Steps to an ecology of mind* (pp. 423–440). London: Paladin Books.

Bateson, G. (1971). The cybernetics of 'self': A theory of alcoholism. *Psychiatry*. 34. 1–18. In: G. Bateson (1973) *Steps to an ecology of mind* (pp. 280–308). London: Paladin Books.

Bateson, G. (1973). *Steps to an ecology of mind*. London: Paladin Books.

Beer, S. (1974). *Designing freedom*. Chichester: Wiley Publishers.

Boscolo, L., & Bertrando, P. (1993). *The times of time*. New York, NY: W. W. Norton.

Boszormenyi-Nagy, I., & Spark, G.M. (1973). *Invisible loyalties*. Hagerstown. Harper and Row [Reprinted (1984)]. New York, NY: Brunner/Mazel.
Bowen, M. (1978). *Family therapy in clinical practice*. New York, NY: Jason Aronson.
Byng-Hall, J. (1973). Family myths as defence in conjoint family therapy. *British Journal of Medical Psychology, 46*, 239–250.
Byng-Hall, J. (1980). Symptom bearer as marital distance regulator: Clinical implications. *Family Process, 19*, 355–365.
Byng-Hall, J. (1986). Family scripts: A concept which can bridge child psychotherapy and family therapy thinking. *Journal of Child Psychotherapy, 12*, 2–13.
Byng-Hall, J. (1988). Scripts and legends in families and family therapy. *Family Process, 27*, 167–179.
Byng-Hall, J. (1991). An appreciation of John Bowlby: His significance for family therapy. *Journal of Family Therapy, 13*, 5–16.
Byng-Hall, J. (1995). *Rewriting family scripts*. London: Guilford.
Canales, J. (2015). *The physicist and the philosopher: Einstein, Bergson, and the debate that changed our understanding of time*. Princeton, NJ: Princeton University Press.
Carter, E., & McGoldrick, M. (Eds.). (1980). *The family life cycle: A framework for family therapy* (pp. 3–20). New York: Gardner Press.
Carter, B., & McGoldrick, M. (Eds.). (1989). *The changing family life cycle: A framework for family therapy*. Boston, MA: Allyn & Bacon.
Casement, P. (1985). *On learning from the patient*. London: Routledge.
Casement, P. (1990). *Further learning from the patient: The analytic space and process*. Hove: Brunner Routledge.
Casement, P. (2002). *Learning from our mistakes*. Hove: Brunner Routledge.
Casement, P. (2006). *Learning from life: Becoming an analyst*. Hove: Routledge.
Combrinck-Graham, L. (1985). A developmental model for family systems. *Family Process, 24*, 139–150.
Damasio, A. (2000a). *[1994]) Descartes' Error: Emotion, Reason, and the Human Brain*. New York, NY: Quill.
Damasio, A. (2000b). *The feeling of what happens: Body, emotion and the making of consciousness*. London: Vintage.
Di Nichola, V. (1993). The postmodern language of therapy: At the nexus of culture and family. *Journal of Systemic Therapies, 12*, 49–62.
DSMIV. (2000). *American psychiatric association: Diagnostic and statistical manual of mental disorders (Text Revision)* (4th ed.). Washington, DC: APA.
Einstein, A. (1961). *Relativity: The special and the general theory*. New York: Wings Books.
Eliade, M. (1965). *Le Sacré et le Profane*. Paris: Éditions Gallimard.
Eliade, M. (1969). *Le Mythe de l'Éternel Retour*. Paris: Éditions Gallimard.
Eliot, T. S. (2001). *Four quartets*. London: Faber and Faber.
Freud, S. (1926). Inhibitions, symptoms and anxiety. *The standard edition of the complete psychological works of Sigmund Freud* (Vol. XX, pp. 77–175; James Strachey, Trans.). London: Vintage.
Freud, S. (1933). New introductory lectures on psychoanalysis. *The standard edition of the complete psychological works of Sigmund Freud* (Vol. XXII, pp. 3–128; James Strachey, Trans.). London: Vintage.
Freud, S. (1939). Moses, his People and Monotheist Religion. *The standard edition of the complete psychological works of Sigmund Freud* (Vol. XXIII, pp. 54–137; James Strachey, Trans.). London: Vintage.
Georgescu-Gorjan, S. (2012). *Asa grait-a Brâncuşi*. Craiova: Scrisul Românesc.
Goldbeter-Merinfeld, E. (1999). *Le Deuil Impossible: Familles et tiers pesants*. Paris: ESF.
Haley, J. (1963). *Strategies of psychotherapy*. New York, NY: Grune and Stratton.
Haley, J. (1973). *Uncommon therapy: The psychiatric techniques of Milton H. Erickson MD*. New York, NY: Norton Books.
Haley, J. (1976). *Problem-solving therapy*. New York, NY: Jossey Bass.

Haley, J. (1985). *Conversations with Milton H. Erickson, M.D: Changing couples* (Vol. 2). New York, NY: Triangle Press.
Hall, E. T. (1989). *The dance of life: The outer dimension of time*. New York, NY: Anchor Books.
Herr, J. J., & Weakland, J. H. (1979). *Counselling elders and their families*. New York, NY: Springer Publishing Company.
Hoffman, L. (1985). Beyond power and control: Toward a "second order" family systems therapy. *Family Systems Medicine, 3*, 381–396.
Howe, L. E. A. (1981). The social determination of knowledge: Maurice Bloch and Balinese time. *The Journal of the Royal Anthropological Institute, 16*(2), 220–234.
Hubert, H. (1999/1905). *Essay on time: A brief study of the representation of time in religion and magic* (R. Parkin & J. Redding, Trans.). Oxford: Durkheim Press.
Husserl, E. (1991 [1928]) *On the phenomenology of the consciousness of internal time (1893–1917)* (J. B. Brough, Trans.). Dordrecht: Kluwer Academic Publishers.
Jenkins, H. (1981). Can I (let you let me) leave? Therapy with the adolescent and his family. *Journal of Family Therapy, 3*, 113–138.
Jenkins, H. (1983). A life cycle framework in the treatment of underorganized families. *Journal of Family Therapy, 5*, 359–377.
Jenkins, H. (1985). Orthodoxy in family therapy practice as servant or tyrant. *Journal of Family Therapy, 7*, 19–30.
Jenkins, H. (1987). Task setting in family therapy. *Practice, 4*, 363–373.
Jenkins, H. (1989). Precipitating crises in families: Patterns which connect. *Journal of Family Therapy, 11*, 99–109.
Jenkins, H. (1990). Annotation: Family therapy – Developments in thinking and practice. *Journal of Child Psychology and Psychiatry, 31*, 1015–1026.
Jenkins, H. (2005). A talákozás pillanta. *Pszichotérapia (Hungary), 14*, 760–767 [Meeting in the moment: Reflections on the therapeutic encounter.].
Jenkins, H. (2006). Inside out or outside in: Meeting with couples. *Journal of Family Therapy, 28*, 113–135.
Jenkins, H. (2007). Continuities and discontinuities in a time of change: Reflections on time and change. In A. Neagoe & I. Radu (Eds.), *Continuities and discontinuities in a time of change: Family therapy and systemic practice* (pp. 11–26). Timisoara: Editura Mirton.
Jenkins, H. (2008). Making meanings: A family's multiple constructs of time. *Terapia Sistemica, 1*, 24–44.
Jenkins, H. (2012). *The time of the system: Standing on the shoulders of giants in systemic work with couples*. Invited lecture, Congresso Internationale SIRTS, Milan: La Coppia: Fascinazione, Delusione, Adattamento. Milano, 24 November 2012.
Jenkins, H. (2013). *Time: The silent guest at the therapeutic table*. PhD thesis, British Library, University of London. e-theses online service. www.ethos.bl.uk.
Jenkins, H. (2014). Crossing boundaries: Living in a liminal world. *Terapia Sistemica, 6/7*, 48–68.
Jenkins, H. (2015). When time stands still: an exploration of time in the process of healing. *Processi clinici tra vizi e virtù di pazienti e terapeuti: temi universali che ricorrono in psicoterapia*. Convegno Internazionale SIPPR. Caserta, Italy, 27–28 March.
Jenkins, H. (2015). Timeless time and change in Psychotherapy. *Psihiatria între teorie şi practică*. Congres Naţional al MARPR, Timişoara, 11–13 September.
Jenkins, H., & Asen, K. (1992). Family therapy without the family: A framework for systemic practice. *Journal of Family Therapy, 14*, 1–14.
Jenkins, H., & Cowley, J. (1985). Adolescents in crisis: On hypothesising with minimal information. *British Journal of Social Work, 15*, 351–362.
Kalsched, D. (1996). *The inner world of trauma: Archetypal defences of the personal spirit*. London: Routledge.
Kant, I. (2003/1781). *Critique of pure reason*. Houndmills: Palgrave MacMillan.
Kapferer, B. (1983). *A celebration of demons: Exorcism and the aesthetics of healing in Sri Lanka*. Bloomington, IN: Indiana University Press.

Kapferer, B. (2004). Ritual dynamics and virtual practice: Beyond representation and meaning. In D. Handelman & G. Landquist (Eds.), *Ritual in its own right* (pp. 35–54). Oxford: Bergen Books.

Keeney, B. (1983). *Aesthetics of change*. New York, NY: Guilford Press.

Kimball, S. T. (1960). Introduction. In: A. van Gennep. (1960 [1908]). *The rites of passage* (pp. 5–19) (M. B. Vizedom & G. L. Caffee). Chicago: The University of Chicago Press.

Laing, R. D. (1961). *The self and others*. Harmondsworth: Pelican Books.

Laing, R. D. (1965). *The divided self*. Harmondsworth: Pelican Books.

Laing, R. D. (1969). *The politics of the family*. London: Tavistock.

Laing, R. D., & Esterson, A. (1970). *Sanity, madness and the family*. Harmondsworth: Pelican Books.

Leach, E. (1976). *Culture and communication: The logic by which symbols are connected*. Cambridge: Cambridge University Press.

Leff, J. P. (1979). Development in family treatment of schizophrenia. *Psychiatric Quarterly, 31*, 216–232.

Leff, J. P., & Vaughn, C. (1981). The role of maintenance therapy and relatives' expressed emotion in relapse of schizophrenia: A two-year follow-up. *British Journal of Psychiatry, 139*, 102–104.

Leff, J. P., & Vaughn, C. (1985). *Expressed emotion in families*. New York, NY: Guilford Press.

Levine, R. (2006). *A geography of time: The temporal misadventures of a social psychologist*. Oxford: Oneworld Publications.

Lieberman, S. (1978). Nineteen cases of morbid grief. *British Journal of Psychiatry, 132*, 159–163.

Lieberman, S. (1979a). *Transgenerational family therapy*. London: Croom Helm Ltd.

Lieberman, S. (1979b). A transgenerational theory. *Journal of Family Therapy, 1*, 347–360.

Lifton, R. J., & Olson, E. (2004). Symbolic immortality. In A. C. G. M. Robben (Ed.), *Death, mourning, and burial* (pp. 32–39). Oxford: Blackwell Publishing.

Loach, K. (1972). *Family life*. Distributed by Optimum Releasing Ltd Artwork.

Malan, D. H. (1979). *Individual psychotherapy and the science of psychodynamics*. London: Butterworths.

McTaggart, J. M. E. (1927). The unreality of time. In: R. Le Poidevin R & M. MacBeath M (Eds.) (1993) *The philosophy of time* (pp. 24–34). Oxford: Oxford University Press.

Meisel, P., & Kendrick, W. (Eds.). (1986). *Bloomsbury/Freud: The letters of James and Alix Strachey 1924–1925*. London: Chatto & Windus.

Merleau-Ponty, M. (2011 [1945]). *Phénoménologie de la perception*. Paris: Éditions Gallimard.

Minuchin, S. (1974). *Families and family therapy*. London: Tavistock.

Minuchin, S., Montalvo, B., Guerney, B. C., Rosman, B. L., & Schumer, F. (1967). *Families of the slums*. New York, NY: Basic Books.

Palazzoli, M. S., Boscolo, L., Cecchin, G., & Prata, G. (1980). Hypothesising-circularity-neutrality: Three guidelines for the conductor of the session. *Family Process, 19*, 3–12.

Palazzoli, M. S., Cecchin, G., Prata, G., & Boscolo, L. (1978). *Paradox and counterparadox* (E. V. Burt, Trans.). New York, NY: Jason Aronson

Penn, P. (1985). Feed forward: Future questions, future maps. *Family Process, 24*, 299–310.

Perelberg, R. J. (Ed.). (2007). *Time and memory*. London: Karnac Books.

Plato. (1997) Parmenides. In: J. M. Cooper (Ed.), *Plato: Complete works* (pp. 359–397). Indianapolis, IN: Hackett Publishing Co.

Rappaport, R. A. (1999). Ritual and Religion in the Making of Humanity. Cambridge. Cambridge University Press.

Sandler, J., Dare, C., & Holder, A. (1992). *The patient and the analyst* (2nd ed.). London: Karnac.

Sandler, J., Holder, A., Dare, C., & Dreher, A. U. (1997). *Freud's models of the mind*. Madison, WI: International Universities Press.

Solms, M., & Turnbull, O. (2002). *The brain and the inner world: an introduction to the neuroscience of subjective experience*. London: Karnac Books.

Sophocles. (1984) Oedipus the king. In: *Sophocles: The three Theban plays* (pp. 159–251) (Robert Fagles, Trans.). London: Penguin Books Ltd.
Stern, D. (2004). *The present moment in psychotherapy and everyday life*. New York, NY: Norton.
Stoller, P. (2009). *The power of the between*. Chicago, IL: University of Chicago Press.
Stoller, P., & Olkes, C. (1989). *In Sorcery's shadow*. Chicago, IL: University of Chicago Press.
Szasz, T. S. (1972). *The myth of mental illness*. London: Paladin.
Tomm, K. (1987a). Interventive interviewing. Part 1. *Family Process, 26*, 3–13.
Tomm, K. (1987b). Interventive interviewing. Part 2. *Family Process, 26*, 167–183.
Tomm, K. (1988). Interventive interviewing. Part 3. *Family Process, 27*, 1–15.
Torrance, R. M. (1994). *The spiritual quest: Transcendence in myth religion and science*. Berkeley, CA: University of California Press.
Turnbull, C. (1990). Liminality: A synthesis of subjective and objective experience. In R. Schechner & W. Appel (Eds.), *By means of performance: Intercultural studies of theatre and ritual* (pp. 50–81). Cambridge: Cambridge University Press.
Turner, V. (1967). *The forest of symbols: Aspects of Ndembu ritual*. Ithaca, NY: Cornell University Press.
Turner, V. (1969). *The ritual process: Structure and antistructure*. New York, NY: Aldine de Gruyter.
Turner V (1982) Images of anti-temporality. In: E. Turner (Ed.) (1985) *On the edge of the bush* (pp. 227–246). Tucson, AZ: The University of Arizona Press.
Turner, V. (1982b). *From ritual to theatre: The human seriousness of play*. New York, NY: PAJ Publications.
van Gennep, A. (1960 [1908]) *The rites of passage* (M. B. Vizedom & G. L. Caffee, Trans.) Chicago, IL: The University of Chicago Press.
Vickers, S. (2007). *Where three roads meet*. Canongate: Edinburgh.
Vitebsky, P. (1995). *The Shaman: Voyages of the soul, trance, ecstasy, and healing from Siberia to the Amazon*. London: Duncan Baird Publishers.
von Bertalanffy, L. (1968). *General systems theory*. Harmondsworth: Penguin.
Yalom, I. D. (1989). *Love's executioner and other tales of psychotherapy*. Harmondsworth: Penguin.
Yalom, I. D. (2001). *The gift of therapy: Reflections on being a therapist*. London: Piatkus (Publishers) Ltd.
Yalom, I. D. (2006). *The Schopenhauer cure*. New York, NY: Harper Perennial.

Chapter 5
Steps to an Ultramodern Family Therapy

Juan Luis Linares

Synopsis Based on an interpretation of the history of human thinking as a succession of periods alternating objectivism and subjectivism, the author proposes *ultramodern family therapy* as a kind of dialectic overcoming of postmodern supremacy in the field. Complex love, understood as relational nurturing, becomes the core of psychological development, preceding language in a so precious role, and the therapist goes beyond the *non-expert position* to become *responsible* and *intelligent* in his/her interventions.

Between Objectivism and Subjectivism

Humans have likely been curious and concerned about the world around them since the dawn of the species. However, within Western culture the first clear evidence of this intellectual phenomenon is to be found in the ideas of the pre-Socratic philosophers. Thales of Miletus, the first of the founding fathers, and no doubt inspired by the largely aquatic world in which Greek culture developed, affirmed that everything came from *the humid*, from water. Modern science has certainly confirmed that there is an element of truth in this. And then there is the *atomic theory* of Democritus, another philosopher of the cosmos, of nature (Russell 1945). These sages looked at the world in which they lived and, struck by its infinite mystery, sought to capture and understand its essential nature. We might regard these as the first recorded steps towards objectivism in our culture, although even here there were also expressions of concern about the limits of human perception.

This concern acquired the status of a fundamental principle in the work of authors such as Parmenides, for whom the phenomena of nature and, therefore, cosmological explanations, formed part of the world of illusion, such that they constituted not the *truth* but merely the *opinion of men*. Although opposed to Parmenides in other respects, Heraclitus shared this idea of subjectivism, stating that *everything flows* and that we *cannot step twice into the same river*. Few statements in human

J.L. Linares (✉)
Universitat Autònoma de Barcelona, Spain
e-mail: juanlinares@telefonica.net

M. Borcsa, P. Stratton (eds.), *Origins and Originality in Family Therapy and Systemic Practice*, European Family Therapy Association Series,
DOI 10.1007/978-3-319-39061-1_5

thought offer a clearer expression of the precarious nature of reality, although Socrates himself was just as categorical in affirming that *all I know is that I know nothing*. In fact, what culminated in the ideas of Socrates was a line of reasoning that constituted both the strength and the weakness of the sophists, and which was essentially a movement in the opposite direction to that taken by the cosmological philosophers: reflection upon man himself and a questioning of his ability to know objective reality.

Objectivism and *subjectivism* have, of course, not ceased to ebb and flow throughout the history of philosophy. The marked subjectivism of Plato was followed by the realism of Aristotle, and for many centuries afterwards, neo-Platonist and neo-Aristotelian currents remained in evidence. In fact, the whole of Western philosophy may be understood in terms of this ebb and flow, with each new turn, in either direction, representing a superseding of the preceding current's principles, the incorporation of which enables new proposals of greater complexity to be made. Indeed, philosophers do not usually build their ideas by discrediting earlier writings, but rather they integrate the work of their predecessors and, generally speaking, start from what there is of importance for the development of their own thought.

The idealist and realist traditions continued through to modern times, marked by a staunchly objectivist positivism that captured the euphoria of the Industrial Revolution and its limitless faith in progress. This is the main source of modern ideology and it remains influential to this day. Indeed, in the case of psychology few alternative visions were proposed until the mid-twentieth century. On the one hand there was the Freudian illusion of a future in which psychodynamic ideas would be verified in the neurophysiological laboratory. On the other, the spirit of the times was ably captured by Pavlovian conditioning and the behaviourism of Watson, which together with psychoanalysis took command of the psychotherapeutic terrain of the day.

However, in 1927, the physicist Werner Heisenberg, who would later be awarded the Nobel Prize, had published a paper setting out his *uncertainty principle*, stating that there was a fundamental limit to the precision with which both the position and momentum of a particle could be known simultaneously. The implications for physics of this statement are not especially relevant to our argument here, but what proved to be of enormous importance beyond the confines of science was the idea of a *fundamental limit to knowledge*. Far from being a banal example of relativism, a conclusion that might be drawn from a literal interpretation of the statement, the uncertainty principle was philosophically important since it challenged the idea that objective knowledge was possible, leading it to become a source of inspiration for a new subjectivist turn known as *postmodernism*. The other key inspiration for this new vision was the Viennese philosopher Ludwig Wittgenstein, whose emphasis on the role of language has been seen by postmodernists as legitimizing their subjectivism.

The postmodern view that began to emerge around the turn of the twentieth century from the physical sciences, as a result not only of Heisenberg's work but also of Einstein's theory of relativity, paradoxically took more than five decades to reach the field of psychology and psychotherapy. However, when it did so, it had a notable effect on the two main models of the day. Lacan, for whom both man and the patient are *revealed in language*, issued a challenge to Freudian psychoanalysis and, like the good structuralist he was, replaced history with structure. For its part, *cognitiv-*

ism transformed behaviourism, such that thought and consciousness became as important as—or even more important than—behaviour as an object of study and intervention in psychology.

Yet the changes did not stop there. Gestalt therapy, psychodrama and the various therapies generally referred to as *humanistic* all highlighted the importance of the emotions in their respective models, shifting the focus to one of the more subjective aspects of the human mind. Importantly, this shift also saw the emergence of family therapy.

Postmodernism and Family Therapy

Given the conditions that led to its emergence it would not be inaccurate to say that family therapy was postmodern from the outset. Indeed, the idea that there is no single relational reality awaiting objective discovery, but rather that relational realities are constructed through subjectivity is probably the guiding premise of systemic (or as some would have it, post-systemic) postmodernism. The emphasis on the relational is, of course, essential if one is to avoid falling into a form of relativism that is incompatible with scientific and therapeutic activity. Furthermore, the family, with its multiple protagonists, roles and conflicts, is par excellence a place in which different subjectivities construct diverse relational realities. Indeed, even the novice and most inexperienced therapist soon learns that in a family it is impossible to determine who is right or with whom "the truth" resides.

However, family therapy was subsequently shaped by a further two postmodern influences, constructivism in the 1980s and social constructionism in the 1990s. Both led to a much more radical set of relativist proposals, in the name of the individual and of society, respectively, and in both cases this was to the detriment of the family. It is hard to understand what can only be regarded as an exaggerated adherence to an ideology that ended up undermining—and in some cases, openly questioning—the very model from which it sprang, and in order to do so we perhaps need to begin with two questions. Why did this occur in family therapy and not in other fields of psychotherapy? And why was the effect particularly felt in the USA and in those parts of Europe with which it shares a cultural affinity, notably the UK, Germany, the Netherlands and the Scandinavian countries?

The first question has already been answered in part. Family therapy was postmodern from the outset because, by definition, the bringing together of different family members inevitably evokes their different worlds and realities, ruling out the possibility that one of them can be regarded as the "true account" and the others as "false". The titles of two books by Paul Watzlawick, a key exponent of the Palo Alto approach to communication theory, say it all in this respect: *How real is real?* (Watzlawick 1977) and *The invented reality* (Watzlawick 1984). However, this work must have lacked a sufficiently pure postmodern pedigree, since in the 1980s, and coinciding with the rise of constructivism, authors such as Keeney (1982) and Dell (1982) launched a stinging critique of Watzlawick and his Palo Alto colleagues, dismissing them as *pragmatists* and arguing that improvisation was the only legitimate source of therapeutic creativity. The new *aesthetics of change* was undoubtedly a stimulating proposal, but it also paved the way for a frivolous kind of "anything goes" approach. Whatever the case, controversy was assured, with Watzlawick (1982) himself reacting to the discrediting of his ideas, and others counter-attacking by defining the proponents of the aesthetic approach as being under the sway of the *fashionable mind* (Coyne et al. 1982). Postmodernism, then, has long and established roots in family therapy, and it should therefore come as no surprise that later generations have been fed on a diet comprising "more of the same".

Constructivism in family therapy drew upon the work of authors such as von Foerster, von Glaserfeld and Maturana, who, coming from fields outside psychology and psychiatry, were enticed into becoming the epistemologists of the new systemic—or post-systemic—theory. The core theoretical idea here was *second-order cybernetics*, which highlighted the impossibility of observing from outside a system with which one is interacting; and since involvement with the system was inevitable, so was self-observation. Given that instructive interaction was also impossible, a system, which is determined structurally, could not be known objectively. Knowledge, according to this view, is merely structural coupling, which enables two systems to interact without either becoming distorted.

Constructivist family therapy adopted these ideas as principle and proposed an intervention based on improvisation and conversational practices. Circular and reflexive questioning (Tomm 1987) became the order of the day for therapists who, rather than impose their own reality on the patient or family, aimed to help them discover their own answers: *"What does your sister usually do when your father gets home and your mother greets him by telling him everything that's happened while he's been away?"* Through interventions of this kind the constructivist therapist seeks to introduce the possibility that the patient might avoid becoming triangulated, but does so without tackling triangulation head on.

Unfortunately, however, the radical shift continued from a reasonable questioning of the possibility of objective observation of a relational process in which one is participating to the complete denial of the role of expert and the extolling of improvisation as the supreme form of therapeutic intervention. Unsurprisingly, abuses were committed and family therapy began to lose favour in the clinical setting, a place where it had once promised so much. However, the coup de grâce to "radical constructivism" (as it was termed by one of its exponents, von Glasersfeld) was delivered not by other sectors of the systemic world but by feminism. Feminists were incensed by—and severely criticized—the idea that different subjective views of a phenomenon such as domestic violence (i.e. the view of the abuser and that of the victim) might be regarded as equally valid. Thus, by the 1990s, postmodernism in family therapy had almost completely abandoned constructivism and had eagerly embraced the social constructionist cause.

What was the difference? As noted earlier, and as its name implies, social constructionism emphasizes the influence of society in the construction of realities, especially those that are expressed in the form of symptoms. Drawing on the work of Foucault (1961), the social constructionists argued that the dominant social discourse played a decisive role in the construction of pathology and, indeed, in maintaining power relations. Other key sources of inspiration included Vygotsky (1934) and Bakhtin (1984), Russian intellectuals from the Soviet era whose theoretical writings on the social origins of language were consistent with a certain Marxism even if much more subtle than the official Stalinist ideology that governed the USSR.

These sources of reference reveal how postmodern social constructionism was, in fact, a veiled form of psychotherapeutic neo-Marxism that had been passed through the filter of politically correct thought. The label "neo-Marxism" is fitting not only because social constructionism turned to Marxist authors at a time when their ideas had been discredited, but also because it bought into the basic premise that human ills derive from the power relations of society. There is, of course, nothing new here, since a similar position had been adopted in the 1960s and 70s by the *anti-institutionalism* of Basaglia (1968) in Italy and the *anti-psychiatry* of Cooper (1967) and Laing (1971) in Britain, both of which had a notable influence in the early days of family therapy. Moreover, the extraordinary appeal and richness of systemic thought in Italy can only be understood as an inheritance of Basaglia and the democratic psychiatry movement that was founded by his collaborators, exponents of the critical Marxism of May 1968.

However, the Marxism of the social constructionists is veiled because, aside from the fact that Marx is never explicitly acknowledged as a source of inspiration, the references to Marxist or crypto-Marxist authors are made using the date of publication of their English translations, such that Foucault, for example, becomes a philosopher of the 1980s. The problem with this confusing anachronism is that it overlooks not only the previous experience of the critical movements that are being referred to, but also, and more importantly, their limits, which 30 years ago drove many of their followers towards systemic family therapy. To put it another way, the enormous influence that social oppression had with respect to mental disorders was already known back then, but what also became apparent was that this in itself did not solve the problem of madness. And yet here we were, years later, being sold the same idea as if it were something original, while all the time continuing to ignore the problem at hand.

A further point of note is that the Procrustean bed of politically correct thought also, paradoxically, infused the field of postmodern therapies, leading to the rejection of practices and ideas that were considered disrespectful or directly oppressive. This new form of censorship repudiated any kind of diagnosis, even if it was based on strictly relational criteria, and also rejected prescriptions and any form of intervention carried out from the position of expert. The only valid strategy, one regarded as a liberating practice, was the *therapeutic conversation* based on creative improvisation.

There are two fundamental branches of social constructionism: the *conversationalist*, which emerged from the Galveston Institute through the work of Goolishian and Anderson (1992), and the *narrative*, whose main proponents are Michael White (1989) from Australia and David Epston (1989) from New Zealand. These two branches share a basic political position, although the narrative therapists are more open to the use of technical resources and, therefore, are less radical in their rejection of the role of expert. For example, a key practice in narrative therapy is *externalization*, which, by locating the roots of the problem outside the subject, enables it to be tackled more effectively. This is well illustrated by White's awarding of a certificate to a young patient for managing to "*outwit sneaky poo*". The aim here is to *deconstruct* imposed and oppressive narratives, redirecting the discourse towards liberation from both symptoms and the power relations associated with them.

Ultramodern Family Therapy

The excesses of postmodernism and the sensation that its influence is waning raise the question of what might take its place. In response to this situation, Marina (2000) did not hesitate in proposing what he termed *ultramodernism*, a proposal that the present author has already explored in terms of its applications to the field of family therapy (Linares 2001, 2006).

The first point to make is that the ultramodern family therapist has no qualms about accepting the role of *expert*. However, this is not any kind of expert, since the ultramodern therapist is happy to submit his or her expertise to the family's judgement and at times even to that of the patient in a relatively independent way. It is important that family members are aware that the therapist "knows", and also that he or she will not use this knowledge to tyrannize them or impose upon them realities that they are not ready to accept. This is delicate ground, since the therapist must both demonstrate his or her knowledge and ensure that it is used wisely. An example would be the therapist who firmly resists the family's invitations to "tell us what we should do or show us where we are going wrong".

Ultramodern therapists must be—and show themselves to be—responsible, at the same as asking for *responsibility* on the part of family members, a responsibility that will be measured and proportional to the therapist's position in the system. Unlike the postmodern therapist who, as a mere partner in conversation, might occasionally be tempted to declare no responsibility for the family's future, the ultramodern practitioner does assume the responsibility that is inherent to expertise. Yet this does not imply we return to formulations of blame, as in the idea that "there is no such thing as a resistant family, only an ineffective therapist". For there are resistant families, and to an extent they all are, while some are simply impossible. What the exercise of responsibility does is rule out omnipotence, and all therapists are aware that there are limits to their knowledge and their good practice.

As for the responsibility that is required of family members, this is both obvious and replete with nuances. All those involved in a dysfunctional game must take responsibility for the consequences of their actions, albeit in different ways. If it is accepted that physical maltreatment has criminal consequences for the adult perpetrator, then why should psychological and relational maltreatment, often more harmful than its physical counterpart, be exonerated a priori from any kind of moral responsibility? A successful therapy involves a process of change that the therapist should guide by encouraging a healthy dose of self-criticism, even not hesitating on pointing out mistakes and misunderstandings. This also means that the therapist should avoid an inquisitorial attitude and adopt a position of warmth and understanding. Children should also be helped to understand the relational meaning of their actions, although care needs to be taken to avoid creating a situation in which children become more the protectors of adults rather than vice-versa.

Although the ultramodern turn implies a recovery of a degree of objectivism, it is far from a return to modern positivism (Linares 2012). Thus, while there is a place for the diagnosis of psychopathology, this is reformulated as providing a set of *guiding metaphors*. Bateson dismissed diagnosis as *dormitive*, not without reason if one considers how deviant behaviour was labelled by psychiatric nosology prior to its questioning by the critical movements of the 1960s and 70s. These were tautological diagnoses, of the kind that defines the alcoholic by his disproportionate love of drink, or the psychotic by his tendency to become delusional and agitated. Yet even then, amidst the propaganda and critical soul-searching, the so-called anti-psychiatrists could not avoid, albeit in hushed tones, the expression of a dual epistemology in the face of complex problems (e.g. "*OK, but ... is this person psychotic?*").

Family therapy has inherited something of this attitude, and the time has come to move beyond it towards a decisive redefinition of diagnosis in relational terms. This could be done in the same spirit that inspired the original formulation of the *double bind* theory, which established a certain linear relationship between this communicational phenomenon and schizophrenia, one that was subsequently denied in the interests of the by now sacred circularity. As if it were not obvious that circularity does not negate linearity but, rather, incorporates it on a higher level of complexity! At times, the desire for innovation shown by leading authors leads them to renounce certain proposals in the face of later ideas, the risk of this kind of revisionism being that something of value gets lost along the way. This happened to Freud (1915–1917) and his *theory of trauma*, and also to Bateson (1972) and his double bind, two ideas which, following criticism of their linear aspects, became seen as constructs that were too abstract and of little use, such that both of them eventually fell out of favour. This seems unjust when one considers the enormous potential of their original formulation.

Ultramodern family therapy, therefore, sees a place for *linearity*, without, of course, overlooking the value of circularity. The Copernican paradigm of the universe, which we still use to navigate the world, is barely three centuries old, and there can be no doubt that this heliocentric model is incredibly useful in terms of understanding time zones and for orienting ourselves during intercontinental travel. Yet we Europeans do not visit Australia very often and we are still happy to say that the sun rises and sets, which is a perfectly valid statement in the context of our everyday experience, even though it corresponds to the Ptolemaic paradigm that held sway for eighteen centuries prior to Copernicus, and which considered that the sun and stars rotated around a spherical Earth that sat at the centre of the universe. What's more, when moving around our immediate surroundings we continue to make use of a pre-Ptolemaic model that, since time immemorial, had argued that the Earth was flat. If, when going out to buy bread, we become preoccupied with the Earth's sphericity, then we are unlikely to make it to the end of the road!

Thus, linear causality is needed for many everyday interactions, even if the broader framework of circularity provides the essential dimension of complexity. Does anyone really believe that the way in which parents treat their children has no determining influence on the latter's developing personality? However, given that the family is a complex ecosystem, children's behaviour can also modify the way in which their parents treat them.

Highlighting that there is a problem with the way in which some parents treat their children psychologically must cease to be a taboo for family therapy, just as recognizing and pointing out *physical maltreatment* has. Many years have passed since the North American associations for relatives of people with mental illness felt attacked by family therapy, and with their counter-attack produced a trauma from which the systemic world in the USA has yet to recover. Since then, therapists have learned a great deal about how to treat relatives who feel blamed, and at the same time public opinion has taken on board the evidence regarding maltreatment of children by their parents, and the importance of society being prepared to do something about it. *Psychological maltreatment* is the intermediate step between the blocking of processes of relational nutrition and psychopathology, and it is the therapist's job to establish "good treatment" of the child, and not, of course, to enter into an inquisitorial combat designed to "stamp out any kind of maltreatment".

The ultramodern therapist must recover the best systemic tradition of using oneself, taking on board the need to love patients and their families, including aggressors, who should also be seen as victims of the terrible chain of maltreatment. The therapist "feels" in therapy and his or her emotional experience is a legitimate and decisive therapeutic resource. Of course, he or she will also make use of the rich and varied range of therapeutic techniques that have been developed within the systemic tradition, including behavioural prescriptions, which have unfortunately fallen into disuse in postmodern circles, where they are dismissed as being manipulative or disrespectful. Maturana, who is cited in support of this position, argues that interactions based on simple instruction are impossible, and that this is merely the arbitrary imposition of one subjectivity over another. However, a behavioural prescription is not an *instructive interaction* if, following the same author, it is offered from the position of *structural coupling*, that is, from a respectful acceptance of the other's subjectivity. Indeed, if a prescription is to be valid and potentially useful, it must be offered from within the relational horizons of the people at who it is aimed, who must be capable of carrying it out without becoming disturbed or experiencing even greater suffering. In fact, the same goes for all therapeutic interventions of whatever kind. If a supposedly respectful conversational proposal falls beyond the limits of the family culture, then it will at best be irrelevant to them.

If therapists can adopt and act in accordance with these ideas, they will find not only that they are speaking an ultramodern language, but also, and more importantly, that they are developing their *therapeutic intelligence*.

Ultramodern family therapy is an invention that seeks to be provocative, and it should not be regarded as a new banner under which territorial claims can be made. Its central message is that we should put an end to postmodern dogmatism and throw open the windows of the systemic world to fresh and demythifying air that brings with it all that is good in the psychotherapeutic tradition. Both these things are necessary if family therapy is to become relevant once again in the mental health field, to become a family therapy that puts forward novel and stimulating ideas and which ceases to regard itself as the flag bearer of the eternal revolution in therapeutic thought. What a humble revolution this has been, one in which in fifty years of trying has neither taken the Bastille nor conquered the Winter Palace!

When the German government examined a proposal to offer psychotherapy as part of state-funded healthcare, systemic family therapy was not recognized as a scientifically robust model since it was unable to provide a body of "evidence-based" research on a par with that presented by psychoanalytic and cognitive-behavioural therapists. It took the German systemic movement 10 years to put together a dossier of evidence that, only relatively recently (2008), led to official recognition being granted. This highlights how playing a relevant role in the field of mental health implies, among other things, being able to speak a language that is not so far removed from that of other practitioners as to lead to one's work being overlooked.

As for therapeutic intelligence, this is not a God-given gift whereby geniuses and fools are determined by fate, but rather it is what results from the development of simple resources that are inherent to the human condition. As in the case of *emotional intelligence*, this new "discovery" enables complex phenomena (great successes, spectacular changes) to be understood with simple and modest means. I trust that readers appreciate that therapeutic intelligence is within their grasp, whatever bureaucratic obstacles or administrative barriers may block the way. For all it takes are common sense, intellectual honesty and a reasonable amount of training.

Final Reflections

Table 5.1 summarizes some of the fundamental characteristics of the model that has been set out in the previous pages, and highlights certain differences with respect to the most well-known postmodern models.

Table 5.1 Some differences among models

	Postmodern, intrapsychic and critical models	Ultramodern family therapy
Construction of reality	Individual/society	Individual/family/society
Maltreatment and psychopathology	Discontinuous and dichotomous	Linked through psychological maltreatment
Diagnosis of psychopathology	Rejected	Relational diagnosis as a "guiding metaphor"
Linearity	Rejected	Integrated within circularity
Basis of psychological life	Language	Complex love/relational nurturing
Role of "expert"	Denied	Principle of "responsibility"
Therapy understood as …	"Collaborative" conversations	Intelligent interventions

Above all, it is perhaps worth restating that ultramodern family therapy is precisely that, a family therapy. However, it takes the individual and society as two fundamental points of reference: the individual because he or she is the indisputable subject of law and the legitimate participant in any relational game, as well as, in the context of a book about therapy, the carrier of symptoms; and society because it constitutes a higher-level system to which the individual belongs and which over-determines and contextualizes relational and psychological phenomena through an organization and a mythology that establish the two faces of culture.

The models that are usually referred to as intrapsychic—and, in the systemic tradition, constructivism—focus on the individual as the constructor of realities, whereas the alternative critical movements (anti-psychiatry, anti-institutionalism, etc.) and their epigone, social constructionism, attribute this function to society. Obviously, the latter also end up working with the individual, since society has a terrible habit of not turning up for sessions!

From an ultramodern perspective, both these aspects are inescapable, but the therapeutic emphasis continues to be placed on the family. This might seem to be patently obvious given that we are talking about family therapy, and it would be were it not for the fact that many supposedly systemic professionals no longer regard the family as worthy of their attention. In fact, however, the best investment a therapist can make is to approach the family as a privileged system, an essential intermediary between the individual and society.

The ultramodern therapist has no problem accepting that psychopathology (*individual*) is the complex outcome that results from the blocking of love by relations of power (*society*). But this process, which represents the essence of psychological maltreatment, takes a wide variety of forms that depend on the *family*. And that is why this text, and my therapeutic practice, are focused on the family in its dual role as generator of love and transmitter of power.

Psychological maltreatment has been defined here as the real problem that all therapeutic models in the mental health field need to address. This is especially true of family therapy, which as a relational model is better equipped to address relational phenomena of this kind. Far from being a less important appendix to physical harm, psychological maltreatment is what lends the former its real destructive power, enabling aggressive behaviour of generally minor severity to become capable of damaging the development of personality to the point of madness or annihilation.

In addition to clarifying what maltreatment entails from an epistemological point of view, what I am proposing also has important practical implications. On the one hand it closes the discontinuity between maltreatment and psychopathology that has so often dominated therapeutic intervention in the mental health field. For what sense is there is recognizing physical maltreatment and accepting the need to tackle its social origins, while simultaneously denying psychopathology or reducing it to a kind of trivial epiphenomenon about which we need only "converse" in an improvised and collaborative way?

On the other hand, by making family patterns of psychological maltreatment (triangulation, deprivation, chaotic relations) the fundamental object of intervention, two things become apparent: first, that it is useless—or even impossible—to make social control the priority, and second, that what is needed are specific 'scripts' that can guide and direct the therapeutic "conversation". Combating the disconfirming triangulation that underlies a psychosis is not the same thing as tackling the disqualifying deprivation that accompanies a major depression. And while social control will continue to be necessary when the individual's physical wellbeing is in danger, it will be secondary to a set of psychotherapeutic strategies that address the patterns of psychological maltreatment that underpin the problem.

It should be obvious by now that there is a place here for the diagnosis of psychopathology, not, however, as a way of labelling deviant behaviour, but rather as a system of guiding metaphors that facilitate our understanding of complex and dysfunctional relational phenomena. Let us call time on dual epistemologies, which, when all is said and done, are merely forms of dual morality. For it is senseless to deny the legitimacy of diagnosis and at the same time enquire in hushed tones of embarrassment whether "the patient might be psychotic". Ultramodern family therapy resists the anti-diagnosis propaganda and argues instead that the most effective way of deconstructing conventional psychopathology is to achieve a deeper understanding of its relational bases.

Consequently, ultramodern family therapy does not dismiss or raise its eyebrows at the idea of linear causality. On the contrary, it embraces the idea, although only after incorporating it within the higher level of complexity that is provided by circular causality. Once again, this has a number of important practical implications.

If I have my pocket picked in a crowded street I am likely, before reflecting on the injustices of social inequality that drive so many to crime, to report the incident to the police. There will then be time to reflect sufficiently on the matter so as to prevent myself and those to whom I recount the event from drawing crude and racist conclusions such as "it's all the fault of immigrants!" Likewise, as an ultramodern therapist I will first try to disrupt the pattern of psychological maltreatment that is generating the symptom, since I am aware that the parents or those who exercise the parental functions hold the primary responsibility for triggering the problem, even though its subsequent maintenance and development depend decisively on other participants, notably the patient. If, out of an obsession with hypersystemic circularity, I attribute the same responsibility to them all, then I will completely undermine the therapy, and the patient, above all, will suffer as a result.

It barely needs stating that language is a key element in defining the human condition, and also that it plays a decisive role in the therapeutic relationship. The ultramodern approach recognizes that language defines us as humans, but it considers there to be an even more decisive element in the process: love. We do not love one another because we are capable of speaking, but rather we speak because we are driven by that infinitely powerful relational force that is love. Of course, this is a complex love that goes beyond the strictly emotional and includes both cognitive and pragmatic ingredients. What I refer to as "relational nurturing" is nothing other than the subjective experience of receiving love in all its complexity, in other words, of being the object of loving thoughts, loving feelings and loving actions.

Just as love is a complex phenomenon, so too is the way in which it becomes interrupted by relations of power. And what results from this are the two sides of the human condition: the capacity for love and the ability to do harm.

Therapy, likewise, is a process that can restore love, freeing it up as far as possible from interference and blockages. To this end, the therapist will use his or her own loving subjectivity, projected outwards in thought, feeling and action of this kind. And once again, the vehicle for this process of enormous significance will be language.

Denying the role of expert has become a mark of identity among postmodern therapists, under the pretext that one must not invade the personal space of patients and families with authoritarian clichés. The defenders of this position tend to overlook the fact that what clients are looking for is precisely that, an expert. This debate may never be settled and is likely to become dull and fruitless, and so the ultramodern position appeals to common sense and to the simplest and healthiest tradition of non-authoritarian therapists, experts in mobilizing the resources of their clients more than in imposing their own.

The spectre that haunts the deniers of expertise is real and may readily manifest in medical authority, allied to relations of power. It is clearly present in modern medicine, as well as in pseudoscientific psychiatry that dons the cloak of biologism. However, the need to critique these perversions of the therapeutic relationship does not mean we should throw the baby out with the bathwater. The reassuring expert who is able to draw from people the potential that they themselves have been unable to develop is a blessing for the system, as are the empathic suggestions and advice that he or she may offer. To dismiss such an expert as disrespectful or authoritarian is, therefore, terribly unfair.

Ultramodern therapists, therefore, do give opinions, advice and prescriptions, although not from an entrenched position of supposed objectivity, but rather through an awareness of the responsibility that derives from being personally involved in human problems that require of them both a capacity for empathy and a legitimate use of their own internal resources.

Therefore, and to conclude, I wish to express my profound disagreement with the postmodern mythology that regards "collaborative conversation" as being the essence and ultimate meaning of therapy. Of course we must converse, and of course this must be done in collaboration! Yet this is so obvious as to be banal. Those therapists who do not converse (and strange though it may seem, they do exist), or those who do so in a non-collaborative way discredit themselves or remain a trivial presence—or in the worst case scenario become caught up in a "universal history of infamy" worthy of Borges. Yet being a therapist requires more of a person than that he or she avoids becoming infamous or trivial.

The kind of intelligent therapeutic intervention that is sought by ultramodern systemic therapists incorporates collaborative conversation but does so in conjunction with scripts or road maps that give some direction when conversing. These scripts or maps are developed using material derived from two basic sources. The first is the person of the therapist him or herself, the expression of his or her most legitimate subjective experience. Therapists must be as fully aware as possible of their professional profile, or to put it another way, of their internal resources in terms of narrative skills, emotional intelligence and practical spirit. And at the same time as therapists aim to draw upon these resources without wasting or undermining them, they must also seek to develop them further, filling in gaps and honing their skills where necessary.

The second source of material is, of course, the family and the patient, those who have inspired the guiding metaphors on which the relational diagnosis is based. One does not converse or collaborate in the same way with a psychotic patient, with the partner of someone with major depression or with a multi-problem family. The former must be helped to emerge from the disconfirmation brought about by triangulation, the second to counteract a position of rigid complementarity, and the third to establish a relational core that will begin to bring some order amidst the chaos.

Thus, therapeutic intelligence is defined, as were the best Hollywood classics, by detailed and creative scripts, in this case, scripts that link the subjective experience of the therapist with the particular characteristics of families and patients, and which draw the best out of all of them.

References

Bakhtin, M. M. (1984). *Problems of Dostoyevsky's Poetics: polyphony and unfinalizability*. Minneapolis: University of Minnesota Press (First Russian edition, 1929) (Ed. and trans. Caryl Emerson.).

Basaglia, F. (1968). *L'istituzione negata. Rapporto da un ospedale psichiatrico*. Turin: Einaudi.

Bateson, G. (1972). *Steps to an ecology of mind*. New York: Ballantines Books.

Cooper, D. (1967). *Psychiatry and anti-psychiatry*. London: Tavistock Pub.

Coyne, J. C., Denner, B., & Ransom, D. C. (1982). Undressing the fashionable mind. *Family Process, 21*(4), 386–391.

Dell, P. (1982). Beyond homeostasis. Toward a concept of coherence. *Family Process, 21*(1), 21–41.

Epston, D. (1989). *Collected papers*. Adelaida: Dulwich Centre Pub.

Foucault, M. (1961). *Histoire de la folie à l'âge classique. Folie et déraison*. Paris: Gallimard.

Goolishian, H., & Anderson, H. (1992). Strategy and intervention versus nonintervention: A matter of theory. *Journal of Marital and Family Therapy, 18*, 5–16.

Keeney, B. (1982). Not pragmatics, not aesthetics. *Family Process, 21*(4), 429–434.

Laing, R. (1971). *The politics of the family and other essays*. London: Tavistock Pub.

Linares, J. L. (2001). Does history end with postmodernism? Toward an ultramodern family therapy. *Family Process, 40*(4), 401–412.

Linares, J. L. (2006). Complex love as relational nurturing: An integrating ultramodern concept. *Family Process, 45*(1), 101–115.

Linares, J. L. (2012). *Terapia familiar ultramoderna. La inteligencia terapéutica*. Barcelona: Herder.

Marina, J. A. (2000). *Crónicas de la ultramodernidad*. Barcelona: Ed. Anagrama.

Russell, B. (1945). *History of western philosophy*. New York: Simon and Schuster.

Tomm, K. (1987). Interventive interviewing: Part II. Reflexive questioning as a means to enable self-healing. *Family Process, 26*(2), 167–183.

Vygotsky, L. (1934/1986). *Thought and language*. Cambridge, MA: MIT Press.
Watzlawick, P. (1977). *How real is real?* New York: Vintage.
Watzlawick, P. (1982). Hermetic pragmaesthetics or unkempt thoughts about an issue of family process. *Family Process, 21*(4), 401–403.
Watzlawick, P. (1984). *The invented reality*. New York: Norton.
White, M. (1989). *Selected papers*. Adelaida: Dulwich Centre Pub.

Part II
Models and Concepts

Chapter 6
From Networks to Resonance: The Life Journey of a Family Therapist

Mony Elkaïm

Synopsis This chapter recounts the path of a psychiatrist who has specialized in family therapies since 1968. The author describes his work as the manager of a mental health centre in the South of Bronx in the USA as well as his instrumental contribution to the establishment of the international network for "Alternatives to Psychiatry" and to the founding of EFTA. He then relates his main contributions to the field of family therapy such as network practices, the application of I. Prigogine's theory on systems far from equilibrium to family systems, the introduction of a new model for couple therapy as well as the development of "resonances" and "assemblages" concepts.

The Life Journey of a Family Therapist

This chapter describes the path of a psychiatrist who has had a keen interest in family therapies since 1968, specifically, my own journey of life. I had been extremely active in the student movement at the Free University of Brussels (ULB) during the events of 1968. Back then, people were beginning to call into question a number of established values and works by David G. Cooper (1967) and Ronald D. Laing (1970) had a considerable impact for practitioners working in the field of mental health. The practice of family therapy was perceived as a tool to give mentally ill patients back their humanity. Indeed, apparently incoherent behaviour began to be perceived as the metaphoric experience of a reality felt to be intolerable, with mentally ill patients confusing their metaphoric experience and reality. The patient was the seat of his suffering but no longer its sole source. Other contextual and relational parameters came into play.

In light of this, while studying psychiatry, I started to offer family therapy sessions in the fields of both adult and child psychiatry. In doing so, I learned a whole series of aspects that had been discovered by family therapy pioneers in the USA and that I rediscovered through my own practice.

M. Elkaïm (✉)
5, Square des Nations, 1000 Bruxelles, Belgium
e-mail: monyelka@gmail.com

M. Borcsa, P. Stratton (eds.), *Origins and Originality in Family Therapy and Systemic Practice*, European Family Therapy Association Series,
DOI 10.1007/978-3-319-39061-1_6

Having completed my psychiatry studies in Brussels, I pursued my interest in the link between family therapy and the social, cultural, economic and political context, taking up a fellowship in social and community psychiatry at the Albert Einstein College of Medicine in New York. It was there that I had the pleasure of collaborating with Israel Zwerling, Harris Peck, Chris Beels and Andrew Ferber. And above all, I was lucky enough to meet Albert Scheflen (1968) and work regularly with him. His research helped me to broaden my interests, not only in the field of non-verbal behaviour or the importance of the urban context, but also to consider an alternative epistemological perspective (Elkaïm and Scheflen 1973).

Having completed my fellowship in social and community psychiatry, I managed a mental health centre in the South Bronx, on behalf of the Albert Einstein College of Medicine. In 1973, realizing the need for training specifically tailored to therapeutic intervention in the context of the urban ghetto, I founded the Lincoln Family Therapy Training Program in New York. This family therapy school delivered training courses at the Lincoln Hospital. Students who followed the programme obtained credits from New York University and the course was ratified by a diploma awarded by the Albert Einstein College of Medicine, Department of Psychiatry. The training prepared mental health professionals for the specific demands of working within the challenging environment of the South Bronx. It was through this school that, in 1974, I organized a national conference in New York on the theme "Training Family Therapists for the Urban Ghetto". Jay Haley, Marianne Walters, Albert Scheflen and Ross Peck were the principal speakers. A number of supporters of the European anti-psychiatry movement also took part in the conference, including Félix Guattari, Robert and Françoise Castel and Giovanni Jervis.

Back in Europe, with the help of Félix Guattari, Françoise and Robert Castel, Franca and Franco Basaglia, David Cooper and Ronald Laing, I established the International Network for "Alternative to Psychiatry". This network, which I coordinated until 1981, organized conferences with thousands of participants, both mental health workers and the "psychiatrized" alike, in Brussels, Paris, Cuernavaca, Trieste and San Francisco. Throughout these years, in the context of this network, mental health practitioners continuously shared the results of the original approaches they were trying to implement in their respective countries. It was an era that generated a wide body of research and publications in the field linking mental health and sociopolitical contexts (Elkaïm 1977, 1980, 1981a; Onnis and La Russo 1979; Marcos 1980).

The friendship I forged with philosopher and psychoanalyst Félix Guattari and our collaboration within this network enabled me to take my practice beyond relational and sociopolitical aspects and incorporate a wealth of different aspects of all types. It was thanks to him that I created the concept of "assemblage".

For me, an "assemblage" is "the whole created by interrelated elements interacting in a given situation". These can be genetic or biological elements as well as ones linked to family rules or aspects of society and culture" (Elkaïm 1990 p. 142). Thanks to Guattari, I began to think less in terms of systems composed of individuals in interaction and more in terms of interrelationships of "assemblages".

It was at this time that I set about developing the network practices I had initiated in the South Bronx (Elkaïm 1987) at the "La Gerbe" mental health centre in Brussels. There were various types of network practices. They could involve regular sessions with a mentally ill patient and his/her relatives and friends as well as sessions with groups of people experiencing the same problems. It was in this way, for example, that groups formed by mothers who were head of the family and whose children were causing problems evolved over time to become support networks. In some instances, these networks led to the creation of small businesses jointly managed by participants in these sessions. Where we had schools in which numerous immigrant children were exposed to multiple problems, we held sessions with groups of parents, children and teachers. When patients with chronic mental illnesses were ostracized by their neighbours, we organized meetings with them and the residents of the building in which they lived. By negotiating with a union, we were even able to get patients with mental health problems into the workplace, securing jobs for them in Belgian supermarkets. Again with the support of "La Gerbe", we also worked with elderly people who were isolated and in declining health. This project, called "*La Mémoire Vivante*" (The Living Memory), allowed them to go out into schools and share aspects of their story and experience. The sessions were filmed and meetings with these "teachers" provided an opportunity for discussion with the support of team members. These elderly people were thus given the role of passing on knowledge, making them feel valued and bringing them out of their isolation. We were able to observe that their overall state of health improved significantly. The examples described above provide an idea of the multitude of actions undertaken to put the problems, experienced as being on an individual level, back into the socio-economic and cultural context in which they had arisen in the first place. The purpose of our interventions was to create support networks and modify as best we could the harmful parameters in play in these situations, with a view to offering those who saw themselves as patients an alternative future.

While continuing my activities at a mental health centre in Brussels, I then turned my attention to the work of Ilya Prigogine (Prigogine and Stengers 1984), winner of the 1977 Nobel Prize in Chemistry. I was ill at ease in a systemic context associated with the theories of von Bertalanffy (1968), in which stability reigned, whereas our practice is based on change. The work of Ilya Prigogine focused on systems far from equilibrium rather than systems in equilibrium as described by Ludwig von Bertalanffy. Not only did his work enable a better understanding of our therapeutic practice, but, by reintroducing the importance of chance, it also made it possible to think in terms of freedom, and hence responsibility and ethics. Transposed to the field of psychotherapy, Prigogine's work implies that the evolution of a therapeutic system can be completely modified by the amplification of some—apparently trivial—element arising in a given situation. Based on this premise, the therapist enters the system with the aim of moving it away from equilibrium so as to cause an amplification of the fluctuations until, by bifurcation or otherwise, the system's way of functioning changes. I was honoured to have Ilya Prigogine as a friend and, as a result of our discussions, new models were developed for family therapists (Elkaïm 1981b, 1985; Elkaïm et al. 1982, 1987).

In 1979, I established the Institute for the Study of Family and Human Systems in Brussels as a centre for research, training and the organization of international conferences. In the same year, I also founded the first French-language family therapy journal, "*Cahiers Critiques de Thérapie Familiale et de Pratiques de Réseaux*" (Critical Journals of Family Therapy and Network Practices). In 1981, this Institute began organizing regular international conferences in the field of family therapies. The principal founders of family therapy schools in the USA and different countries in Europe took part in these conferences. It was through these conferences that we were also able to establish an international network of family psychotherapists, which I coordinated. Many of its members were therapists from the anti-psychiatry school of thought. It was this informal network that led, in 1990, to the creation of the European Family Therapy Association (E.F.T.A.) that I had the privilege of chairing for many years.

It was also during this time that I forged friendships with some of the founding members of our profession, such as Donald Bloch, Jay Haley, Virginia Satir, Mara Selvini-Palazzoli, Carlos Sluzki, Paul Watzlawick and Carl Whitaker. Their support and the exchanges we had broadened my outlook and helped me enrich my practice. Furthermore, during these early years, I was able to count on the support of therapists such as Maurizio Andolfi, Théo Compernole, Jacques Pluymaekers, Edith Goldbeter, Paul Igodt, Juan Luis Linares, Elida Romano, Fritz Simon, Luigi Onnis, Maria Orwid and many others to ensure the development and reinforcement of EFTA. It was also at the start of the 1980s that I developed a new model for understanding couples undergoing a crisis and devised specific therapeutic approaches to deal with these situations. This model, based on the reciprocal double-bind concept, considers each of the partners as being divided between an "official program" and a "world view" that are opposed to each other. For example, somebody may, on the one hand, want to be loved and, on the other hand, fear that they will simply end up being abandoned if they are. The person is thus torn between and hemmed in by two contradictory expectations. The behaviour that each member of the couple reproaches his or her partner for paradoxically "protects" the world view of the person complaining while contradicting his/her conscious expectation. The publication of this approach to couple therapy (Elkaïm 1986) paved the way for new practices in a field in which systemic therapists were increasingly sought after. I also used the model to analyze some international conflicts, such as the Israeli-Palestinian conflict (Elkaïm 1994) and, later on, it helped me develop the notion of resonance in the therapist-patient couple.

Throughout the 1980s, I was lucky enough to be invited to annual gatherings in the USA by the "Gordon Conference on Cybernetics". Each event was an opportunity for us to come together in small groups for a few days and compare our research and practices. Humberto Maturana, Heinz Von Foerster and Ernst Von Glasersfeld were regular participants, among others. In addition, as a speaker at numerous conferences organized in the USA and Europe, I forged close links with fellow speakers such as Heinz von Foerster, Humberto Maturana and Francisco Varela.

Heinz von Foerster, the creator of second-order cybernetics, helped me to see the observer as a member of the system observed. The concept of the objective observer was thus called into question. But how can therapists carry out rigorous work when they are stakeholders in the human system within which they are intervening?

The answer to this question led me to introduce the concept of "resonance" in psychotherapy. The experience of the therapist is related to him or her but is not reduced to him or her. His/her experience is amplified by the human system in which he/she is participating to reinforce the world views of the other members of the system. Hence, if the therapist feels irritated by a patient, it is possible that the latter amplifies this sense of irritation in the therapist in order to reinforce his/her own belief that one cannot help but be irritated by him/her. The experience of the therapist, when appropriately analyzed, can help him/her hypothesize about the patient's world view, check the hypothesis and intervene to introduce some flexibility into the belief. My model of the reciprocal double-bind concept operating in couples' relationship problems can be found in this description. The role of the therapist then becomes that of someone who does not join in the game he/or she is invited to join. He/she recognizes that the patient has a legitimate right to demonstrate an unconscious expectation at odds with his/her official request but acts in such a way as to attempt not to reinforce the world views of the patient when they are deemed to be harmful.

Discovering that similar experiences may dominantly appear in situations in which different human systems are interrelated, I defined resonance as follows: "Resonances" are those special assemblages created by the intersection of different systems that include the same element. Different human systems seem to enter into "resonance" from the effect of a common element in the same way that material bodies can begin to vibrate from the effect of a given frequency (Elkaïm 1990, p. 138). This work on couple therapy, "assemblages" and resonances and the contributions that the work of Ilya Prigogine, Humberto Maturana, Francisco Varela and Heinz von Foerster made to my research were published by Basic Books in New York in 1990 under the title "If you love me, don't love me: construction of reality and change".

In this book, I focused on "singularities" which are elements intrinsic to a given therapeutic system, as well as on the role of chance and of personal history. For me, personal history is neither linear nor determining. In a critic of Whitehead and Russel's work on paradoxes, I endeavoured to show the usefulness of working within the self-referential paradox rather than trying to escape it, and I introduced the concepts of "resonance" and "assemblage".

In the interrelations between assemblages at play in a system, a specific element plays an important role, that of world view. As such, human systems can be analyzed as relations between world view systems rather than between individuals. The use of resonance analysis thus becomes a crucial tool not only for psychotherapies but also for supervisions (Elkaïm 1997, 2008).

I mentioned the debt of gratitude I owe to Heinz von Foerster, who was a close friend and constant support for many years, in a piece I dedicated to him in 2005 in the Kybernetes journal (Elkaïm 2005). (What's more, it was Heinz who advised me to go with the term "resonance" rather than the one I had hitherto been employing, namely "intersection").

Both Heinz von Foerster and Ilya Prigogine helped me to escape from a rigid systemic interpretation that carried the same risk as the structuralist approach. The risk then being that the individual may merely be seen as a person ensnared by the structure or system. These two researchers paved the way for the role of responsibility and ethics in systems (Elkaïm 2002a, b).

I'm also grateful to Paul Watzlawick who invited me to speak in Palo Alto on a number of occasions, and to help him with a summer school at Stanford University aimed at students interested in the approach of the Mental Research Institute (M.R.I.). His support and humour—he once suggested I replace the title of my book "If you love me, don't love me" with "For the love of me, don't love me!" were invaluable to me throughout the years when I was developing my theories on the application of the systems far from equilibrium theory to family therapies and when I was defining the resonance concept.

In the following years, I turned my attention to the systemic function of unconscious elements such as the dream. Elements of dream may have a function in the context of the human system in which they occur (Elkaïm 2002c).

I have also looked at the field of spontaneous order and the work of Steven Strogatz (2003) in particular. I considered to what extent resonance may be a specific case of spontaneous order. This interpretation of resonances opens up a new field of exploration (Elkaïm 2014).

I have also developed more specific tools for systemic supervision, such as "pictorial resonances". With this approach, it is possible to take a drawing produced by the person being supervised and analyze its resonances with respect to the situation presented (Elkaïm 2014).

A Supervision Using Pictorial Resonances

The following example illustrates ways in which a drawing inspired by a difficult clinical situation can be used in supervision using the concepts described above. It is based on one of a set of examples (Elkaïm 2007) and is drawn from live notes underlining the main points of that supervision made during a training day. I have proposed to the trainees on the systemic course to take a blank sheet, to reflect on a case they are following and which presents them with a problem, and then draw something that evokes this case.

In the situation of pictorial resonances the plan is not to analyze the drawing despite its wealth of material, it functions simply as a springboard to bring out the dominant therapeutic life of this specific situation. In this case Cloé (the name I have invented for this trainee) offered the drawing of Fig. 6.1.

ME: what have you drawn?

C: A young ado (adolescent) in an institution. He is outside his family which consists of his dad, his mum and his little brother.

ME: What is the dominant element of this drawing?

Fig. 6.1 The drawing of Cloé

C: The paradoxical relationship between the step-father (who is not his father) and his mother. Whenever one says something the other says the opposite. The mother says the ado is not the central problem at home and the step-father says the opposite.

ME: (I am struck by the fact that the father, the mother and the child have neither feet nor shoes while the ado has enormous boots!). What do you feel about the relationship between the step-father and the mother?

C: It's very complicated … they set off on debates that are difficult to stop.

ME: But what do you feel?

C: Powerlessness/Helplessness. It is difficult to find a place in there!

ME: Tell me some things regarding relationships where it is difficult to find a place.

C: My parents sent different messages during our upbringing; for example, my mother did not want us to smoke. My father smoked and felt that one could smoke …

ME: One could think here of the concept of "delegation" of Helm Stierlin who considered that we send our children on a mission. These delegations are legitimate, unless they are contained within a double bind; for example, if the father says to a child: "study and succeed" but at the same time says on another level: "have fun, the rest is not important". For Helm Stierlin a mother may also transmit A and the father transmits not-A.

What happened when your parents said contradictory things?

C: I went to my bedroom and listened to music to get away from that which I could not understand; there were also times when I came closer to my mother who was at home more often.

ME: It is as if you couldn't find your place: your mother said A, your father said not-A. It was a difficult situation and so you took refuge in your bedroom…
What is the usefulness for Cloé feeling this in the presence of this family? You see the ado is in his room! The younger brother seems to suffer less.
One finds oneself in a therapeutic system which tries to maintain its equilibrium and the homeostasis of its beliefs, of its constructions.
One could ask this couple: were there moments in your personal history where the situation did not let you find a place? Your feeling resembles information about them provided by a stethoscope, but it is necessary to verify your hypothesis.

One could see things another way: when for me, as Cloé, I feel that I do not have a place I perhaps receive an indication of what they experience in their lives … My client is the relationship, I am for each of them for it is the relationship that must change. I must see how to reinstate a place for the step-father and for the mother: so that they can thereby reinstate a place for the ado. They are going to be surprised to feel the recognition without one being wrong and the other right… Both are able to be recognized without having to force the other to be in the wrong.

ME to C: Do you have a place with me?
C: Yes!
ME: You can accept the idea telling you: what is the usefulness for them that I do not have a place? It is not therefore the time to take a place because it is first necessary that they can take their own.
Cloé, do you feel this is sufficient for you?
C: Yes!
ME: The goal of the supervision is not just to "understand" but to "feel differently" about the rapport with the patients, to change the affect. It is this that liberates our valences, our capacities.

Further Developments

With laws on psychotherapy practices beginning to emerge in Europe, I published a work describing various psychotherapeutic approaches (including family therapies) as well as their evidence-based results (Elkaïm 2007). Similarly, through my involvement with the European Association for Psychotherapy (E.A.P.), which I chaired and of which I am honorary president, I have endeavoured to enable various psychotherapeutic approaches—particularly humanistic approaches—to better develop and acquire greater research rigour. Indeed, recognition by European legislators of different psychotherapeutic approaches often depends on their capacity to present evidence-based data.

It is important to point out that this criterion of evidence-based results is challenged by a number of psychotherapists who suggest alternative criteria. What's more, some legislators appear to be sensitive to these criticisms. In Austria, for example, in addition to recognizing the analytical psychodynamic as well as the systemic and the cognitive-behavioural approaches, legislation recognizes thirteen approaches generally categorized as humanistic.

An important field is currently opening up for systemic approaches. Beyond institutions and companies where this approach is already developed, the contemporary socio-economic and sociopolitical situation, as well as the very serious issues raised by the refugee crisis, demand that we contribute to the public debate. Unlike the linear interpretation approaches that have often prevailed, it is time we were able to offer alternative approaches that can pave the way for other futures.

Rather than discussing who is right or wrong, what is becoming increasingly important nowadays is to understand how new assemblages can lead to bifurcations and change, and I believe that some of our concepts linked to the systemic approach could prove useful to analyze international events. With respect to the current situation in Iraq for instance, two of our concepts could be used easily. Indeed, what we see in systemic therapy is that the solution often becomes part of the problem and it seems to me that what is happening in families is transposable to the international arena. The invasion of Iraq as a solution to the threat, which the USA considered Saddam Hussein's regime to represent, played an important role in the assemblage which, subsequently, gave rise to the "caliphate" and the group known as ISIS.

Iraq also gives us an example of how a specific context can amplify dormant conflict or specific worldviews, as is the case for the Sunni–Shiite conflict which was dormant before being amplified by the consequences of the American invasion of Iraq. In France, the slaughter of the Protestants by the Catholics, which began in Paris on August 24, 1572, known as the St Bartholomew's massacre, was a bifurcation resulting from a number of complex factors moving the system away from equilibrium, an assemblage of religious, social and political elements. However, in the same way that some contexts can amplify conflicts, others can soothe them as happened later in the case of the Catholics and Protestants in France.

The ways in which our analysis of elements leading to conflicts can help to propose alternative paths leading to peace is a new field for us to explore.

References

von Bertalanffy, L. (1968). *General system theory*. New York: Braziller (rev. Ed.).

Cooper, D. G. (1967). *Psychiatry and antipsychiatry*. London: Tavistock.

Elkaïm, M. (1977). *Réseau—Alternative à la psychiatrie*. Paris: Union Générale d'Editions.

Elkaïm, M. (1980). Family system and social system. In M. Andolfi & I. Zwerling (Eds.), *Dimensions of family therapy*. New York: Guilford Press.

Elkaïm, M. (1981a). Broadening the scope of family therapy or from the family approach to the socio-political approach. In State of mind (Vol. 7, No. 4). Somerville, USA (This article was republished with some changes under the title "From the Family Approach to the Sociopolitical Approach" in The International Book of Family Therapy, F.W. Kaslow (Ed.), Brunner Mazel Publishers, New York, 1982).

Elkaïm, M. (1981b). Non equilibrium, chance and change in family therapy. *Journal of Marital and Family Therapy*, 7, 291–297.
Elkaïm, M. (1985). From general laws to singularities. *Family Process, 24*(2), 151–164.
Elkaïm, M. (1986). A systemic approach to couple therapy. *Family Process, 25*(1), 35–42.
Elkaïm, M. (Ed.). (1987). *Les pratiques de réseaux : santé mentale et contexte social*. Paris: E.S.F.
Elkaïm, M. (1990). *If you love me, don't love me: Constructions of reality and change in family therapy*. New York: Basic Books.
Elkaïm, M. (1994). The Israelo-Palestinian couple: From confrontation to joint construction. *Palestine—Israel Journal of Politics, Economics and Culture, 4*, 29–33.
Elkaïm, M. (1997). Reciprocal double binds, amplification of construction of reality and change in a training context. In T. Nelson & T. Trepper (Eds.), *101 interventions in family therapy* (pp. 198–204). Philadelphia, Pennsylvania: Haworth Press.
Elkaïm, M. (2002a). Therapists, ethics and systems. In R. F. Massey & S. D. Massey (Eds.), *Comprehensive handbook of psychotherapy* (Vol. 3). New York: Wiley.
Elkaïm, M. (2002b). At the boundaries of the systemic perspective in psychotherapy. In D. F. Schnitman & J. Schnitman (Eds.), *New paradigms, culture and subjectivity* (pp. 235–244). New Jersey: Hampton Press.
Elkaïm, M. (2002c). A systemic approach to dream. In A. Pritz & T. Wenzel (Eds.), *Mythos—Traum—Wirklichheit*. Vienna: Facultas Universitätsverlag.
Elkaïm, M. (2005). Observing systems and psychotherapy: What I owe to Heinz von Foerster. *Kybernetes: The International Journal of Systems and Cybernetics, 34*(3/4), 385–392.
Elkaïm, M. (2007). *Comprendre et traiter la souffrance psychique*. Paris: Editions du Seuil.
Elkaïm, M. (2008). The use of resonance in supervision and training. *Human Systems, 19*, 16–25.
Elkaïm, M. (2014). *Où es-tu quand je te parle?* Paris: Editions du Seuil.
Elkaïm, M., Goldbeter, A., & Merinfeld-Goldbeter, E. (1987). Analysis of the dynamics of a family system in terms of bifurcation. *Journal of Social and Biological Structures, 10*, 21–36.
Elkaïm, M., Prigogine, I., Guattari, F., Stengers, I., & De Neubourg, J. L. (1982). Openness: A round table discussion. *Family Process, 21*, 57–70.
Elkaïm, M., & Scheflen, A. E. (1973). *Antipsychiatrie: pour une révision épistémologique* (p. 18). Brussels: Mosaïque.
Laing, R. D. (1970). *Knots*. London: Tavistock.
Marcos, S. (1980). *Antipsiquiatria y politica*. Mexico: Editorial extemporaneos.
Onnis, L., & La Russo, G. (1979). *La ragione degli altri*. Rome: Savelli.
Prigogine, I., & Stengers, I. (1984). *Order out of chaos: Man's new dialogue with nature*. Flamingo: Bantam Book.
Scheflen, A. E. (1968). Human communication: Behavioral programs and their integration in interaction. *Behavioral Science, 13*(1), 44–55.
Strogatz, S. (2003). *Sync: The emerging science of spontaneous order*. London: Penguin.

Chapter 7
Families, Therapists and Nodal Thirds

Edith Goldbeter-Merinfeld

To my dear friend Gigi Onnis, now absent, but still present in my heart.

Synopsis Some families stabilize their functioning around one of their members, who acquires therefore an essential role in the conservation of the balance of the system.

This function tends to attribute to this "nodal third" a particular responsibility and specific expectations as for the way he/she will meet it.

The departure (through separation or death) of such a "nodal third" confronts the family with the risk of an important disorganization and makes difficult—even sometimes impossible—the mourning of the one who left.

The presented model is built on the working hypothesis (to verify beforehand) that the therapist sometimes sees offering the place of the now absent "nodal third" to seal the created empty space and to allow the eclipse of the impossible mourning. In its application, this model appeals to the echoes amplified around the sensibilities to absence.

Introduction

I started slowly to be interested by the absent when I met in 1978 a family composed by a father aged 70, a mother in her fifties and their teenaged son. My co-therapist and myself invited them to sit in the "family therapy room" of the underfunded Mental Health Centre where we worked. Furniture was second hand and the chairs were all different from each other. At one moment, the mother who was the one who requested the session because her son "was nearly becoming a bad boy" asked us to let him stay in the waiting room and then explained a family secret: her companion, "Pappy", was first married with a cultivated and elegant woman of the same age as him, "Mommy", who was sterile. She, the mother, was taking care of their household

E. Goldbeter-Merinfeld (✉)
Systemic Psychotherapy, Free University of Brussels, Brussels, Belgium
e-mail: edith.goldbeter@ulb.ac.be

M. Borcsa, P. Stratton (eds.), *Origins and Originality in Family Therapy and Systemic Practice*, European Family Therapy Association Series,
DOI 10.1007/978-3-319-39061-1_7

and only one time had sex with Pappy and became pregnant. They all decided that Mommy would take care with Pappy of the child, and that later, they will support his education and his cultural development (the old couple was more educated), that the mother will not work anymore for them but elsewhere. She rented a small apartment in the same building; nevertheless, the son slept every night in his mother's studio. Mommy died some months ago and the mother did want to regularize her situation and marry Pappy who was reluctant, invoking administrative reasons. Suddenly, the empty chair between Pappy and the mother caught my attention. Unlike other wooden seats, it was a chair covered with red velvet, worn and fastened with copper nails, a chair that has been repaired in the past. I then said: "it is as if Mommy is there". Pappy reacted immediately by saying: "Yes, and she will remain there!"

Progressively, I became more and more sensible to the possible significant absent inside family sessions and also, I discovered that it could happen that I, as a therapist, was sitting on their chair.

I began to use this perspective, first discreetly on my own, without speaking about it with colleagues or trainees. But an event helped me to open it to others: around the mid eighties, I invited Luigi Cancrini to give a workshop in our Institute in Brussels but he had to cancel it 2 days before. I was desperate: apart from our trainees, professionals from outside registered also to the workshop and I had no time to announce a cancelation. I tried to find someone who could replace him (the topic was on "Working with addiction in families"). But none was free and anyway, everyone is unique and irreplaceable. So, I decided to propose to the people arriving to the workshop to be reimbursed or to remain with me who will present "Coping with the absent in the system". The majority of them decided to remain and I presented the new-born model expressing and using also the experience I went through when I learned that Luigi would be "absent"!

I started later on to present the model outside the country, first in 1987 in Roma, at an international conference on "Couples in crisis", and I published in French my first article presenting the model in 1990 (Goldbeter-Merinfeld 1990). My work was than translated in several languages (Italian, Spanish, Greek). In 1995, I presented my doctorate at the Univesité Libre de Bruxelles on "Tiers pesants et tiers légers: une nouvelle approche de la famille et de l'intervention thérapeutique" and published a book in 1995 (Le deuil impossible. Familles et Tiers Pesants.) that was later on translated also in Spanish and Italian.

This topic grew up conjointly with my involvement first in the *European Network of Family Therapy* that became *EFTA* in 1990 (in which board I belonged until 2013).

I must add that I became also sensitive to those absent as full family members because of my own family history: my parents emigrated from Bessarabia in the late 1920s to study in Belgium, and then remained during the war and did not see again their family of origin (partly dead during the war, partly «prisoner» of the communist regime). I knew my grandparents only through stories and some photos. Nevertheless, I never felt them as absent but as a floating intermittent presence (Goldbeter-Merinfeld 2013).

This lead me to conceive that the absent forms part of our families, whether silent or secret, weighty or light. When I mention the weight, I refer to a triangular conception of relations, each dyadic bond being seen as part of a triangle in which the "third one" could be *light*—this means that its impact is temporary—or *weighty* if he became the unavoidable reference, being present physically or just through words and feelings. This weight is at the same time heavy for the two first persons and for the third him/herself. That's the reason why I call him weighty third ("tiers pesant") but some English speaking colleagues told me that it was not so convenient to use the expression "weighty", and as "heavy" did not contain the idea of the personal weight for the weighty third himself, I decided to choose the adjective "nodal" even if it does not express perfectly the content I have in mind.

My goal here is to present a model that offers a different perspective of the therapeutic system and that provides guidance on how to organize the therapeutic work, in particular looking around for absent *nodal thirds*. It attaches at the same time, starting from the experience of the therapist, to make him/her[1] think about his place in the system and the potential discomfort it brings him, thereby attracting the attention of all members to their own place simultaneously with that of absent members. The work of mourning to which this approach can lead, will help to make the position of everyone in the family more flexible.

I propose therefore to consider the meaning of a therapeutic session from other elements than those derived from the direct analysis of the demand. The first meeting between therapist and patients can be seen as staging the opening of the family system to allow the introduction of a new third party: the therapist.

We often forget that such a share of intimate content of the family life with a foreigner (the therapist) is something very unusual, special. What gives to a family the courage but also the energy to meet a therapist for the first time?

I use the word "family" for families, as for couples or individuals. I consider that in any case, people come with their family, as silent, secret ghosts floating in the session, or as real physical presences. Moreover, the limits of what we label as a "family" are arbitrary and leave open questions about who to include: how many generations, only people still alive, only people living in the same home. So, to abbreviate the speech, I will use most often the term "family", regardless of the size of the system and whatever the number and rank of the generation are present.

Nevertheless, if we consider that we always meet "incomplete families", what about the absent parts? Do we have to go back to Adam and Eve, to take into account all the distant cousins to different degrees? How to choose persons who could be "significant" in the present family choreography even if they are absent and not evoked at first? And if we work with such a perspective, how could we give places, seats, to these missing people?

All during my already long journey in the practice of psychotherapy, I became more and more sensitive to those aspects and I developed an operating model that includes the dimension of absence.

[1] I will refer to the therapist as he/him to avoid to put to much weight on this text.

Basic Framework

The concepts underlying the model of the *nodal third* emphasize the *triangular* relationship and it includes *second-order cybernetics*, considering that the therapist is included in the system he observes. Therapeutic intervention can therefore be based on the analysis of the function that the therapist is supposed to fulfil in the therapeutic system in order to efface absences that are too difficult to confront. It therefore employs the unique *resonances* emerging in the meeting between the therapist and the family which consults, a concept introduced by Mony Elkaïm (1990, see also Chap. 6 in this volume), highlighting the possible intersections between the construction of the world of the family and that of the therapist about absence and the *nodal third*.

Indeed, the way that the therapist lives in the therapeutic system, particularly in regard to the feeling of being there and being offered a function in and by the family, is related to the amplification of common areas of sensitivity in the therapist and the family. In accordance with Elkaïm, I consider that this amplification (from the time it is confirmed) can be considered as having a function in the therapeutic system; beyond the meaning it has for each of the subsystems (family and the therapist(s)) that constitute it.

The model refers also to the work of Norman Paul (1986) about the *experience of absence*, *mourning management* and the *concept of replacement*. It therefore deals with the evolution of human systems over time, with elements favouring continuity and those creating discontinuity in their history.

The *Nodal Third* model refers also to a *transgenerational perspective*, even though I rarely invite the members of the extended family to sessions.

A child may become the identified patient, in turn filling the role of *nodal third*. Either the family will be content with this replacement, or continue suffering under a barely tolerable overload. It may finally be that the *nodal third* function is no longer satisfied in the same way as before, which leads to reintroducing a lack of balance in the system. The goals of consulting are both calming intra-family pain (explicitly linked to the problem of the identified patient and not to the absence of previous *nodal third*) and the search for a "better" *nodal third*.

One can imagine that in a number of cases, a whole series of attempts will emerge to undo the pain or malaise that appears at the departure of the *nodal third*. These attempts tend very often to obscure any resolution of mourning, as they are the sign of the refusal of the absence of the *nodal third*. A symptom may occur in one of the members of the system, denying the absence and taking a part of the place of he who is no longer there; or a new person can also be introduced into the system, with the vain hope that the other will be forgotten. This newest member can be one more child or an adopted child, a lover or a mistress, an individual or family therapist, or even an object of addiction (alcohol, drugs, gambling, work, activism, sect, etc.).

The functions of these "replacements" should replicate those of the previous *nodal third*: if a couple is created with at least one member who is in individual therapy, the couple can live "its" relationship with an individual therapist "in the middle of the marital bed" for 5 or 10 years; it is likely therefore that the therapist has taken without his knowledge, the place of the *nodal third* in this couple, even in the family. The termination of the individual therapy, even if it is preceded by a work of separation, as it should be, almost always hides the fact that it does not take place exclusively between therapist and patient but between therapist and the patient's family (the latter in part of course). We regularly see the appearance of discomfort in couples after termination of individual therapy followed by one of its members in a long and intensive manner. Emotional equilibrium was built on the triangle for years, and the remaining dyad is unbalanced; it is not prepared to live the unusual distance that is established, it will then turn to another *nodal third*: another therapist for the same person, or for the spouse this time, a lover or a mistress, a new child, etc.

Time, History and Construction of the Therapeutic System

When a family decides to ask for a therapist, it is explicitly linked to psychological discomfort. Making appointments, which takes place on the phone most of the time, is not the first step, however, in building the future therapeutic system, nor, on the other hand, is the answer made by the therapist that has his agenda under his eyes. This first contact is "for identification purposes" in the sense that it brings together (even if it is only orally) on the one hand, a therapist who has a name, gender, and a certain age, and on the other hand, an individual who also has a name, a sexual identity and is a member of a generation, but also of a family. The future therapeutic encounter is based on a web of individual contracts and interactions, explicit and implicit, conscious and non-conscious. All these contracts are constructed from elements before the start of the game and they introduce time as history in the system; this history will have an impact on the present and the future of the therapeutic process.

Despite that the therapist will begin his work by setting the boundaries of the therapeutic system (Goldbeter-Merinfeld 1994a, b), the history of this system exists already before the physical meeting of its members, in the same way that a child exists for his family well before her birth or even conception. This story will build on the biographies of the subsystems involved in this meeting: family, or therapists, the institution to which they belong, the psycho-medico-social mediators that have already played a role in this family that are sometimes even the instigators of the consultation.

I find it useful to reflect with those that call us as therapist, on the meaning of this kind of call (possibly confidential) with respect to the therapeutic system being so created, to which belongs his family (I inform myself of their identity) and myself. I then evoke the forms that different possible interventions could take (requests to be seen alone, in secret, as a couple, with children without a spouse, with all the family, etc.). To immediately address this helps to open a relational space that may be frozen and to prepare for myself (if I physically enter later) a more comfortable position because more spacious. At the same time, it could broaden the personal spaces of family members; in fact, the reactions of the family to the suggestion to consult together is often (pleasantly) unexpected for the appellant, as well as for their family; the request appears to be a form of opening.

The family comes to the consultation with a story in which the therapist is already unwittingly involved, covering everything that happened from when for the first time, the idea of going to consult dawned. They constructed a destiny in which the role of the therapist is already more or less clearly marked. One thing is "certain": the presence, at least temporarily of the therapist in the family interrelationships. In addition, it is preparing for the meeting as a milestone.

For his part, the therapist, a prisoner of his routine and his conception of the therapeutic role, evolves in another time. He knows nothing of this family "history", and his representation of their common future remains unclear.

He will therefore spend a period of partial synchronization between the time of the revitalized family and the routine time of the therapist. The latter can refreeze time, or otherwise maintain its flow, including introducing a crisis. In the latter case, he will favour a dynamic time, non-routine, making more important the space between meetings than the time spent in therapy, considering that the essential role of these events lies in their catalytic function. The sessions remain "events" and should not necessarily take place at regular intervals, but will rather agree with a process of evolution in the family, which is inherently unpredictable. It is obvious that the relationship that each has with time will also affect the speed of exchanges during the sessions, as well as their own pace. Interviews become events for a transition to a future, so stimulating the life of the system.

If the therapist contributes to the petrification of the time, he will soon be no age (or gender) in the eyes of family members, in short, he could became ready to enter the role and function of the missing *nodal third* of the family like Proteus. He will be available at any time, or receive the family at regular intervals, to which an end (another inherently dangerous event in such a case!) cannot be considered. The time is stopped; you cannot design a future other than the present. The therapeutic relationship seems built for eternity, interdependence within the therapeutic system is intense; the separation seems to be a non-existent concept.

In short, everything happens as if the evolution of the therapeutic system is organized at *the intersection of three histories*:

- That of the family with the future therapist that begins at the emergence of the idea to consult (which can even happen before there is a consensus in this regard, as we saw),
- That of the therapist who adopted this function (or profession) very early in his family of origin, long before he began to be trained and to practice. But, in his family, he did not succeed to solve forever the situation he was sensitive to, and did not reach the goals he had set and he felt invested by his own family of origin. So there are the side feelings of incompleteness, of lack of achievement. He had to accept that he can never successfully complete his mission in his own family, but it is difficult for him to mourn this mission. In addition, he may be found again in the same situation if he finds it impossible to meet the expectations of the family, because at the same time, it is impossible to replace the absent.

- That which will be built from the first meeting of all the people involved in the therapeutic system.

It is at the intersection of these histories that areas of singular resonances can emerge. They will interpenetrate and rebuild within the relational network of the therapeutic system.

Beginning the Session

It starts by setting always from the beginning more chairs than the previous number of participants (therapist included) at the session. As the family seats first in the room, it always arouses in me the question of what seat I will myself choose. Families let some chairs free, which one do I have to occupy? In fact, with the perspective I have presented, one or more of the empty chair(s) may belong to absent third(s). My point is that it is important to let this absent keep his seat rather than taking it for us as if it does not matter.

When people sit not close to each other but occupy the space by letting free here and there some chairs, I begin the session still standing, asking to the family where I am supposed to sit (which means often close of whom, between who and who, etc.) and after they show one free place (they agree most of the time of this answer), I ask, again still standing "Why there?" Most of the time, it is possible to discover that it is because this would have been the place of someone who is not there anymore (break, departure fare away, death) and that he/she is now missing a lot.

I than mention that as the place proposed to me belongs already to someone else (a nodal third?), I will respect this. Is there another place where I can sit? Usually in such a case, the family insists gently for me to accept the first place they offered to me … and if I persist with my refusal (always repeating the same "justification"), they let me free to choose whatever other seat.

As soon as a session starts like this, emotions arouse because the first free chair is not anymore unoccupied. It became "The" absent person and in my words a *nodal third*.

Limit of the System

The system is thus designed here as always incomplete, even after the introduction of the therapist. This changes the perspective of the role of the therapist who cannot become an omnipotent even deified "stopgap", and also the attitude concerning the number of people who "should" participate in a systemic therapy session; in fact, the system will never be "complete". Another way of looking at things is to consider that the presence does not take place only in a physical way, and a series of floating members, ghosts of the family, are also taken into consideration during the sessions.

Triangular Relations

It is crucial to make thirds "exist" (see Goldbeter-Merinfeld 1990, 1994a) in this framework, based on two assumptions:

1. All relationships are triangular; the absolute symbiosis being the case of a perfect and impossible figure in fact, is one that defines that merger as a relationship between two people so that any third party is excluded, the latter participates (by his exclusion) in the designation of the relationship between the two partners of the triangle. Still, there will be at least allusion, if not explicitly a call to the third, to regulate the distance between two partners.
2. The therapeutic relationship should never seek to be self-sufficient or autarkic; it would be presumptuous, dangerous, (or even impossible), for the therapist to attempt to impose a break between the patient and his relational universe. Similarly, the brief intrusion of the world of the therapist manifested for example in phone calls interrupting therapy sessions are a "reality" that it is normal to have to integrate into the therapeutic relationship. Otherwise, the therapist could build an artificial world that would be far from allowing the patient to live a more fulfilling day in the context in which he belongs. This attitude denotes more, the existence in the therapist of a worldview where "others" are dangerous, and where only extremely intense dual interdependence constitutes the necessary conditions for an acceptable survival.

However, if you are sensitive to the content and even the "external side" of the relationship, we can always remark the evocation or even the presence of thirds: they can actively intervene in the relationship triangle, or appear as officially passive spectators but whose presence is essential.

Bowen observed that dyadic tension can lead to the introduction of a third that contributes to stabilizing the relation in a triangular pattern. But one might consider, unlike Bowen (1976b) who idealized the dyad and considered it as the goal of his therapy that it is as if the relationship strictly of two persons did not exist, as if it had always held "three". Although a link between two individuals is so intense that one might call it fusional or symbiotic, it is then defined by the inability to include someone, by the exclusion of all others. Therefore this person participates in fact, even if external to the equilibrium of this relationship.

My reading differs from that shown above in the sense that I cannot imagine the existence of a purely dyadic relationship. The third is always necessary, he is "intrusive" or interventionist, whether passive or resolutely introduced by one member of the dyad, or is excluded dramatically: we all know the intense bond between spouses who are supported by their common desire to exclude from their privacy the "invasive stepmother", who is nevertheless essential in the regulation of emotional distance in the couple. It is in relation to her that conflicts, marital reconciliation and the degree of intimacy of the couple is regulated.

The Third in the Face-to-Face of Individual Therapy

When a patient asks to see us alone, the systemic therapist must appreciate the meaning that would be the orientation towards individual therapy or instead proposing a family interview. The choice is sometimes "forced" if the patient seems very isolated. If, however, he lives in a couple, family, or is not far from home, the assessment of the future "physical" border of the therapeutic system is based on an exploration of the human environment and an estimate by the therapist, based on mutual resonances (Elkaïm 1988; Chap. 6, this volume) that appeared during the initial meeting.

Nevertheless, it is conceivable that each carries within himself significant companions still alive or already dead, with whom a frequent or distant relationship is maintained.

Opportunities to use these absent thirds appear only if we want to include them in the consultation. The system boundaries are open, as well as the range of interpretations.

It is possible that therapists seek to create with the patient a very intense relationship, excluding any third party, insofar as it allows them to be in the same position as that of the *nodal third* they occupied in their family of origin, exclusive ally of a family member in coalition against another member experienced as dangerous; as this scheme can also resonate with maps of the patient's family, the interlocking can be achieved without there being strictly a therapeutic work.

The therapeutic process as part of the "individual" therapy could yet join as a dynamic co-evolution of the therapist and the patient developing from the mutual co-evolution of the world of each one in a framework including *nodal thirds* as an important part of this process: the representations of these will probably be re-sculpted in the context of the therapeutic encounter, and the reframing of their functions may be as critical as any other reframing in the evolution of the therapeutic system.

It should be added that if the therapist works alone, he is not however isolated sitting face to face with those who consult him. He "takes" with him, besides his family, his supervisor, colleagues, even his theoretical gods—Freud, Lacan or Bateson—who certainly participate very often in psychotherapy sessions!

Nodal Third and Light Third

By the term ***nodal third*** I refer to someone whose presence (physical or evoked) is almost essential to "good" balancing of relationships within a system (Goldbeter-Merinfeld 1990). While everyone can be a third for two others, in a manner unwitting rather than consciously or even voluntarily, the *nodal third* is assigned or takes a specific and permanent feature as the third in relationships in the family.

The departure (in any form) of a *light third* is easy to live with: the system quickly finds another partner to fulfil this function. In contrast, given the "need for his function", it is difficult for the *nodal third* to leave, as it is for the rest of his family to bear his absence, whatever its form: death, brutal rupture or gradual distancing. The other members of the system are faced with a grief that is difficult to support if they do not change their inter-relational organization. A profound transformation of the state of the system, that is to say a second order change is often impossible, since the emergence of a *nodal third* system is the result of a difficulty to introduce another mode of operation. But also, we know that bifurcations in the evolution of a system are not totally impossible when it is far from equilibrium (Elkaïm et al. 1987).

Ackerman (1967) had already noticed that in dysfunctional families, some members take on emotional roles that rigidify their manner of interaction, both within the family and outside. Among these roles, he identified those of the black sheep, the genius but also the saviour or healer. I tend to consider these roles, from the moment they "stick to the skin" of their actor, makes them the *nodal third*, since the emotional balance of the system can no longer occur without risk of an upheaval for which it may not be prepared. These *nodal thirds* are essential guarantors of the system of protection, regulators of affective distances and emotional balance among its members.

Supernumerary seats offer therefore many advantages:

1. Of course, we can interpret building on the structural grid of Minuchin (1974), as a concrete demonstration of the emotional distance between two members of the system.
2. They involve the recall of the choice of the place we are facing as therapists. This emphasizes that such a choice is not random and pushes us to consider the possible meanings. This reflection can orient the first contact with patients: one can ask a family where it would be better that we sat and why, at the same time returning to the seat remaining vacant.
3. Empty seats dramatize absences by making them "tangible" and pointedly remind the family as well as the therapist that *the system is (always) incomplete*, there are those absent who are present and they have the right to be there.

   This form of construction highlights differently absences of members invited to the consultation; I will not necessarily refuse to receive a part of the system on the grounds that I only work with "the whole family, or nobody". "*The whole family*" *is never there*. This does not mean we cannot refuse the opportunity to receive those present if deemed inappropriate in relation to the direction given to the therapy, but the reasons given will be other than those concerning the impossibility "by definition" to address an "incomplete" system.
4. To see empty seats helps us to keep in mind the question of the meaning of our place and those places in the system. If for example, we feel that a couple repeatedly requests our arbitration we can tell them about this impression to check if they adopt this view and then ask them why do they have such a need, since when, who filled the function of arbitrator previously, what happened to that person, etc.

The moment a ghost appears, it means that we cease to embody it and we can strengthen this movement by interviewing partners into the place that would be occupied by the absent if that party was still there. It may be that they mean precisely the chair on which we sit; standing to change places is a dramatization of the absence of the third, his "irreplaceability", and allows displacement of the definition of our own function in the system: *instead of masking the absence by taking over its function, we will confront the therapeutic system with the mourning not performed and initiate work to resolve this grief.*

Mourning and Ghosts

The mourning after the departure of the nodal third, even more his death, is often pathological. Set aside the experience of a lack, of a vacancy, absence, and the myriad of feelings that are attached to it, as well as those of abandonment, guilt, hatred and resentment which is in itself an understandable protective reaction. But, the "freezing" of the grieving process that is thus established will weigh on and even block other processes necessary for the development of family members and the whole system. It is crucial that the therapist does not reinforce this judgment by helping to hide the absence by the place and the position he will occupy in the system.

Long before I developed the model of the *nodal third*, I had my attention drawn to the complexity of the work of mourning that in my opinion is still influenced by the emotional and socio-cultural context. On the other hand, whether we can bring it to an end, stop along the way, or are stuck in its entry, ignoring the need, grief is a process that concerns everyone. Whether it concerns the departure or death of ones loved or hated, we all, at one time or another, are faced with the experience of absence.

Many clinicians have noted the large number of families who visit shortly after the death of a loved one. They come to us frequently for various types of symptoms, both behavioural (enuresis, running away, a drop in school performance) and psychiatric or psychosomatic, which have emerged or are amplified shortly after the death of close ones. Not only do they make no connection between the death and the onset of the problem, but also, this first event is not even mentioned in the list of the family changes around the time of the emergence of the symptom.

Paul and Grosser (1965) formulated from such observations the hypothesis of a direct link between inadequate response to object loss and crystallization of symbiotic relationships in the family. Everything happens as if it took erasure of the loss to preserve the balance of the system. However, when the fact is stressed, strong emotions arise, often followed by attempts to avoid dwelling on the subject, and return instead to the "symptom-card" that led to the consultation.

Among family therapists, Norman Paul (1967) has built a therapeutic model (which will be discussed later in this chapter) where mourning is central. According to this author, grief is a psychological process triggered by the loss of a beloved object, which, when successful, is associated with the abandonment of the object.

As in the Scottish legends, ghosts mark the return of a dead person who was not actually buried according to the rites. The unresolved grief allows the ghost to become a full member of the family system.

When the grieving process cannot be initiated and the system freezes around a *nodal third* ghost we observe that:

- The dead is often idealized or demonized, but is never mentioned as a simple human being with the strengths and weaknesses of everyone.
- Unresolved conflicts with the deceased interfere in current relationships within the family.
- The facts surrounding the death are often confused, uncertain or unreal.
- Survivors never speak of the deceased, or they talk as if he were still alive.
- And finally, if the family members are encouraged to talk, they do so with a significant emotional intensity, suggesting still open wounds.

In some families and in some cultures, the child usually receives the name of a dead grandparent and filiation flows as a cycle in some way, the ancestors being perpetuated through the living. These cases of memory maintained consistently and deliberately will not necessarily lead to pathological situations and do not imply an inability to perform mourning.

The child can maintain, thanks to the ghost that he partially reincarnates, some type of emotional flux in the family, awakening in it the same feelings as those raised by the deceased ghost to which he gave asylum (Bank and Kahn 1982; Walsh and McGoldrick 1991; McGoldrick and Walsh 1991). These emotions can both express love, security, dependency; or hatred, even a death wish for the replacement, the desire to crush it, a feeling of suffocation, etc. Add that these children often receive the name of their grandfather, brother or sister, for which they were designed "as replacements".

Selvini-Palazzoli et al. (1978) discuss the case of the ghost of a grandfather reincarnated as Ernesto (10 years), who is described as follows: "He walked stiffly, slightly bent forward in a rigid manner, a little bent forward, taking short and hesitant steps like those of a very old man." Seated between the parents at an equal distance from both, he responded to all questions talking "staccato" in a high nasal voice. He used difficult and obsolete words alternated with expressions, which sounded as if they came from an early nineteenth century novel. For example, he interrupted his father once with the following phrase: "It is advisable that I now intervene with a clarification so that these gentlemen will not be deceived by appearances".

Acknowledging the presence of an absent at the meeting mobilizes each one differently: the members of the family are faced with their unique relationship with the absent; at the same time different possibilities of grief open up to them, individual time resumes its importance with respect to systemic time. In this context, the therapist must be ready to assist members of the family to develop both a collective family mourning and individual grief. He must provide a container for the intense emotions, underline the legitimacy to free patients from guilt; the dead will take back a place to be human, i.e. an imperfect person who has made mistakes as well as good actions, and finally each can separate from him. He will acquire at this time his status as an absent recognized and not clandestine. The living will, therefore, have to manage their lives based on themselves, in a responsible manner.

The last step will be for the therapist to become himself an absent recognized by the system. It therefore seems to me essential that the therapist himself be armed to mourn his family, which brings us to its own systemic history.

This phase of therapy is often an important moment in that it conveys to every member of the therapeutic system (including the therapist) the sense of his place, and therefore the difference (of his unique individuality) compared to other people present … and absent.

Anticipating what was the specific function of the *nodal third* is often almost palpable when we are sensitive to how the family interacts with us and the place where it puts us: does it submit all conflicts to us by seeking a form of arbitration? Does it leave one of its members to try to establish a special relationship with us? Is it expected that we share a family secret (that is to say, a "false secret", something that everyone knows but about which the group is forbidden to speak) with one of its members, or to join in a coalition with one against the other, or that we wear the rags of someone who only can be rejected and thus strengthen the cohesion of the rest of the group? It is often interesting to ask who fulfilled this specific function that is expected of us before problems occurred. The therapeutic encounter does not necessarily reflect the expectation of change but rather the desperate search for a way to undo a recent and unbearable change.

The therapist as a Professional *Nodal Third*

Beyond *singularities* (Elkaïm 1981), a constant emerges in the history of (systemic) therapists. This constant appeared to me in thinking with my students (training in systemic family therapy) about their own families of origin. All started, very young, to help other members of their own family: they refereed conflicts, supported the "weak" against the "crushing", deviated tension onto themselves, sometimes being Identified Patients, acted as a buffer in relational situations they considered too tense. They also had the feeling of not having achieved the desired result and somehow lacked finesse or skill. It was as if they had then selected studies that permitted them to improve their skills.

They abandon with difficulty their role of support, repairman, and unconditional ally, buffer or, conversely, scapegoat, the officially responsible for any intra-family tension. They feel they have a mission that they should bring to an end.

In addition to loyalty, a special sensitivity, probably built on a few fragmented successful attempts to help the family and the stubbornness to go through with this mission, will make some of these family *nodal thirds* choose studies and training to enable them to improve their capabilities previously only developed within their families. These psychologists, doctors, educators, psychiatrists, social workers, nurses, etc., will become *professional nodal thirds*. The choice of a profession in the field of psycho-medico-social assistance is a sign of a vocation solicited early (Goldbeter-Merinfeld 1990). Having started very early to play an active role in the regulation of intra-family relationships, the therapists were somehow *nodal third* in their family. They felt invested with responsibility of the reorganization of the emotional balance of his family of origin, even if all the other members also contribute to the protection of the homeostasis of the system. Their roles could be alleviated due to this more responsible participation assumed by the *nodal third*.

Having not helped enough their own family so it could do without a *nodal third*, they choose to be trained as professional helper, and often followed their own therapeutic path. Even though they have finally learned that they cannot be the therapists of their relatives, and even if they ostensibly work in this direction, they will have difficulty to trust another therapist … and they seek at the same time "to repair their own family" among the other families. They are looking for other systems that can offer them a place of *nodal third*.

These therapists will therefore be affected by the expectations of patients, because they vibrate at the same time with their own areas of sensitivity related to the evolution of the *nodal third*.

During the establishment of the therapeutic system the meeting will be organized between a *nodal third* professional in search of a (his?) family, and a family in search of a (its?) *nodal third*. The dance around the establishment of a systemic time will occur silently. The issues will be the restoration of a previous state, where the family had no lack and where the therapist helped his family of origin, or the emergence of a present and a future. Thanks to the *shifted-space* built from discrepancies of respective expectations of all members of the therapeutic system (which do not "fit" perfectly), the revitalization of time is likely to occur. In this space can appear "asynchronies:" the flow of words, the gestures of the therapist and family members are sometimes discordant, differences in relation to time creates hiatuses, as happens when the family, or otherwise the therapist are late or do not come to finish the session "together".

If, however, this regulating function becomes essential to protect the balance of the system, it can be a permanent attribute of the role played by one specific person. The term *nodal* then highlights the pressure that this function exercises on he who fills it and it reduces some of his freedom by pushing him to maintain vigilant attention to the plight of other members of his family. This qualification also reiterates the need for the *nodal third* to be firmly implanted to support the family structure so that everyone can rely on him. This word *nodal* has therefore in no way a negative component or any other value judgment. During a prolonged period of turbulence, it is as if a *nodal third* is required to guarantee the stability of the system. His absence from the system, for any reason whatsoever (departure of a grown child, separation, death), places the family in front of a double danger: the protection of its security is no longer guaranteed and therefore, mourning the third is impossible, his departure being unacceptable. The emergence of a symptom and the designation of a "patient" may constitute a negative feedback. The identified patient occupies a double space with the weight of his symptoms, which are somehow the ghost of the absent. But the response of the system is not always sufficient and, moreover, it is very expensive in suffering. One may then ask if the family does not expect that the therapist take the place of the *nodal third*, feeling in turn the unbearable loss experienced in the system.

One might ask to what extent the request for consultation in systemic therapy (and often patients are unaware what specific reference model their future therapist uses), beyond the reason given of the real suffering experienced over a problem that is ostensibly hard to bear, is not an attempt to find someone that will take the place of a *nodal third* now absent. Indeed, the application can be reinterpreted as a call for a new player to enter the intimacy of the system and fill a certain function. Even if there is a desire or hope to remove the symptoms, but associated with the desire to come back, to find a somehow "lost paradise" where the actual absent was still present, even if the story does not convince us that what happened was blessed harmony. It is time that therapists realize that their patients do not necessarily seek "happiness", and even much less what each of us considers happiness to be!

Everything happens as if, before the first meeting or the first call, the therapist has a form of identity, or a predetermined role for the family.

During the establishment of the therapeutic system a meeting will be organized between a *professional nodal third* in search of a (his?) family, and a family in search of a (its?) *nodal third*. The fit may therefore be perfect! There would be no change, but rather a restoration of a previous state: where the family had no lack and when the therapist helped in his original environment.

"Fortunately", most of the time an unfitting space is created beyond these common resonances: if they allow the meeting to take place and make sense to all, this lack of fit constitutes an area of freedom. These resonances and this discontinuity seem to me essential for the emergence of therapeutic work because they guarantee both the possibilities of building a common understanding of the world and the opportunity to bring various changes.

If he uses this reading perspective, this means that, far from claiming neutrality, the therapist must be aware of the sensitive points his patients touch in him and then verify that there is a resonance and not an outright invasion by his own concerns that have emerged independently of the relationship with the other. He may then guide the session on these issues that are significant for everyone.

The Concept of Resonance (Elkaïm)

It should be noted that this approach has as its explicit starting point the experience of the therapist, verifying the presence of a possible *resonance* (Elkaïm 1988, 1990, see also Chap. 6 in this volume) especially around absence with the experiences of the clients, and if this is the case, the amplification at the intersection of common maps, to open easier routes for those who look at them. This reading also permits being attentive to the personal comfort of the therapist who, rather than simply asking what is his place in the process, or taking a back seat, will specifically use himself as a tool to enable everyone to think on an isomorphic way to his own approach to his own place and his relationship with others, including with the absent *nodal thirds*.

On the other hand, the therapist must also be able to remember that this family is not his, even though the common *resonances* are a prerequisite for the meeting to take place (Elkaïm 1993). At the same time, the imperfect nature of the junction that will occur between the therapist and the family creates a space of freedom for all members of the therapeutic system. Of course, every encounter between a family and a therapist is unique and singular; possible assemblages therefore also may occur in a unique and special way. Absence and replacement are broad categories for me, almost universally known but every time lived and amplified in a specific way.

The Therapeutic Intervention

Therapeutic intervention involves oriented work of changing a state of suffering and disability into a lighter state, which can be described as "well-being", with all that this term includes in subjective evaluation on the part both of the patient and the therapist. Systemic therapy involves the definition of a relational space in a field of social and emotional constraints. It essentially calls for the transformation of this space into a place of greater freedom, freedom of thought, action, of living. In other words, it is necessary to use external constraints in such a way that they do not prevent the emergence of areas of possibility within the system.

During therapy, it happens that empty seats move, are "undressed" of their function, and the system, freed from the necessity of the presence of a *nodal third*, opens to the outside with many floating thirds. In brief, our presence becomes unnecessary and we're heading towards the end of the therapeutic encounter.

It seems fundamental to me not to blindly engage in therapy, or if it has been done anyway, to consider the set of resonances which favoured this relational movement. Indeed, an application of therapy can be understood, I repeat, as the introduction of a new third party. If a woman asks to be seen only to talk about her marriage and her husband ignores her approach, my reading is that it is as if she was looking for a secret ally to maintain the status quo in an unsatisfactory enough way to justify the relationship with the therapist, since it is woven of confidences and requests for advice and protection of the patient. At the same time, the husband would remain excluded from this analysis (although profound) of his couple! The therapist may be the "secret" partner of the couple, sleeping in the middle of the marriage bed, and allowing it to avoid any common problem that concerns the difficulty of discussing their entire relationship.

One could explain to patients seeking advice the sense that such an intervention might take and how, orienting differently, it could instead create the feared but expected changes at the same time. Did the woman ask the therapist to take the place of her mother, to whom she previously confided all the intimate problems of her marriage? Did she ever feel that her mother helped to improve her marital relationship in any way, or did she benefit from her parent's expression of an unalterable support while offering to her the reaffirmation an undying loyalty? Does this means that the essential dyadic relationship in her life had always been the relationship with her mother, as if neither she nor the patient had ever been married? Now does she want to marry the therapist and again leave the legitimate husband in the role of a remote intruder?

The therapist is therefore not merely a therapeutic operator. Whatever his theoretical reference model, technique and skills, he would do well to consider the meaning of a response in one way or another to a legitimate request whose consequences are sometimes beyond the partners involved.

What the therapist amplifies has a meaning and a function not only in relation to his own history, but also from the history of the therapeutic system to which he belongs. Feelings in the therapist are therefore an indication of a specific bridge between him and the family he treats. When the therapist is flexible with respect to the themes and core beliefs that weave this link, the therapeutic situation may change in a sense different from repetition.

This reflection on the possible *resonances* between the place "offered" to the therapist and that which he held (and still holds) in his own family can refer to a particular intervention, but it will most certainly affect the life of the therapist. Therapy is a process of evolution of the therapeutic system in which each actor will be touched in his trajectory so that he can be brought to reconsider, or to change it. The psychotherapist is, I repeat, one of the actors.

The therapist should be able to become "lighter" in the history of the family, in order not to remain forever the *nodal third* replacement or not again confront the family with his own unbearable absence one day, which would lead to a tireless search for new therapists. I have often received such "professional patients" who, after an impressive past in psychotherapy at the same or at different therapists over a number of years, come to consult one more time. They invoke either the same problem that led them to see the others above, or they come for another reason. I would be tempted, in these cases, to work on the place and function of these previous therapists, as well as expectations regarding my presence in the system. Perhaps there is no desire to change the situation; it is possible, but the therapist is apparently essential to the preservation of a unique equilibrium in which he will find his own comfort. Is there still therapy in this case? Or is it necessary to try to change it to establish a therapeutic relationship that seems fruitful to him?

It is important to note here again how intensive therapy involves at the same time the frequent presence of the psychotherapist, strengthening the systemic running around or in function of a *nodal third* (even if all members of the system do not meet the therapist) and how, after the end of psychotherapy, the system may be in crisis if it does not find alternatives to the *nodal third*. This could be taken as an indicator of the lack of the work of separation and mourning done by the entire system upon the termination of a therapeutic relationship experienced by one of its members.

How to manage this separation depends on the personal resources of the therapist as well. He is touched here in his own way of living separations, to take his distance and no longer regard himself as an indispensable *nodal third*. If he continues to play this role in his own family, getting out of this type of function in the intervention system will be difficult, but could be done with the help of the family who consults him. The impact will be felt in the different systems in intersection (Elkaïm 1990): the family who consults, the therapeutic system, the institution and the family of origin of the therapist. Thus, any therapy involves a kind of co-therapy, that is to say, a mutual process helping to change different systems together, in which each partner or subsystem can in turn or jointly be more of an inductor or active.

Clinical Example

I would like to illustrate this with a recurring phenomenon at the beginning of therapy with these couples: while the first appointment was clearly for the couple, one partner is on time and we are left alone to wait the arrival of the other "who is nevertheless usually never late", before moving into my office. When the latecomer arrives, he seems surprised (disappointed?) to find that the consultation did not start without him. "You should not wait, you could start without me!" he says frequently. I will say that I consider that the couple is something that is important to each of them, it would give me the feeling of disrespect to one of the partners, if I began the meeting by acting as if what could be said about their relationship by each of them could be out of their presence, as if the absent was not concerned and could not respond and give his point of view.

The couple then takes its place, leaving more often an empty chair between the two partners (Fig. 7.1):

During the first interview, it appears that the "problems started" within the couple when one spouse (who arrived on time) broke off an affair he had had for years. He announced it to his spouse (who arrived late), and who had not agreed to be informed in this way of this infidelity. Since then, the couple has been in perpetual conflict around settling unmanageable scores. It was not necessarily the sudden discovery of the infidelity that tipped the balance, especially as the "innocent" had not really been so fooled.

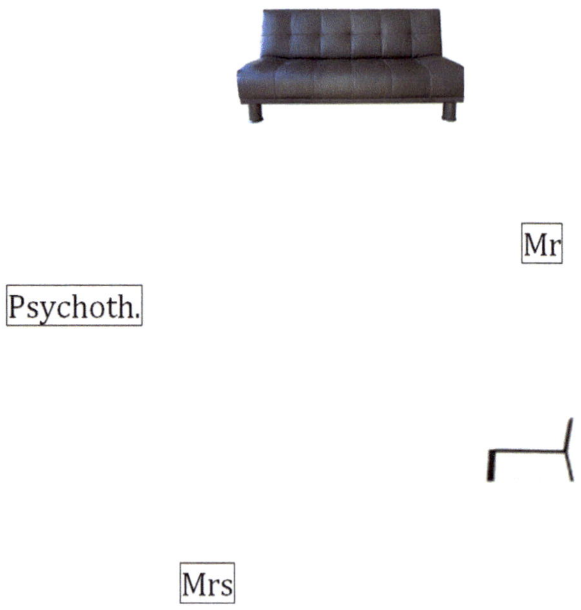

Fig. 7.1 Seating positions of the members of the couple (Mr and Mrs) and of the therapist (Psychoth.) during the therapy session. A couch and a chair remain unoccupied

Everything happened as if there has been an attempt to replace the triangle they left recently by a similar isomorphic triangle: from a situation where one spouse had a special relationship outside of the couple, while his "innocent" partner was officially excluded, we moved to an arrangement where the first to arrive would have established a "privileged" relationship with me, while the laggard would be excluded. I can, reflecting on the place of the third offered to me by the couple, enter through a unique door in their problems. Each of them came punctually to subsequent sessions.

I would add that I am struck by the non-verbal behaviour of patients with respect to the empty seat at the meetings: one partner may casually pose his arm on the unoccupied chair, even sometimes caressing it. The other will push out of the common area; give a kick to the base of the legs. The empty chair comes alive and becomes an almost living character.

Chairs as Metaphors

The presented approach allows the metaphoric and symbolic to join in an intense emotional experience and its application gives a sense of "palpable emotional reality" (Goldbeter-Merinfeld 2014).

Using chairs as metaphors of an absent member of the family gives to these chairs a special quality: they became a representation of the reality but at the same time, everyone knows that it is not the accurate reflection of this reality. It therefore encourages imagination, free association, and movement at a new level. This new ground, by the interaction of its components with the new figure that is inserted therein, affects the meaning and experience of what we represent (Goldbeter-Merinfeld 2012, 2014).

Metaphor is often associated to the poetic to the extent that it is to escape the mind of a real and a literal and objective conception of reality. Its use induces a movement and thus we can already perceive its usefulness in psychotherapy: we are often dealing with situations or jelly families stuck, frozen in a heavy relational game woven with pain and discomfort. Metaphors can reinstate the movement, life … and all of a sudden, it happens that it acquires a real dimension. Whether using words or tools, the therapist will thus promote the emergence of unexpected performances. One wonders to what extent it does not also induce trance as it takes us into a second state in which the real is "as if" and where the "as if" becomes real … There is a change of consciousness … the epicentre of attention moves from a narrative describing a true story, to a narrative touching another area which offers the strange feeling of expressing the same thing but it is different, a different similarity, which in turn arouses emotions. We have a new way of seeing "reality".

That is what creates the shock, surprise and tipping some rooted certainties, conditions essential to a therapeutic step. One enters a creative process … that occurs when normal patterns of associations are interrupted. It can be a psychic shock, sensory or emotional experience overflow.

The creative moment is therefore a bifurcation in the configuration of the usual consciousness of someone, it reflects its experiential change. The fact that metaphors can disrupt our experiences in depth prevents us from reduction to a simple illustrative and clarifying proposal, a figure of speech. There's as if an injection of a new real ….

The metaphor that appeals to emotional places through chairs is therefore a proposal for a representation of reality, but it is based on something new and allows therefore the exploration of new terrain, from which arises a therapeutic effect.

Conclusion

Using the concepts of *nodal* and *light thirds* involves the consideration of how to live with distance, departure, death, trust in other people's resources and awareness of the non-indispensability of our presence, be it active or passive. It implies both a personal recognition of our expertise, but at the same time a form of modesty, humility before the evidence that others may develop similar qualities.

The model presented here does not pretend to be an objective explanation of reality. This reading is not for me the only possible construction of the "therapeutic reality", since as many different realities as there are intersections of family and therapeutic maps (Elkaïm 1988) can emerge in the consultation. But this construction may make sense when particularly intense vibrations occur around the theme of absence, amplifying one another in the encounter between patient and provider, offering the therapeutic system a common metaphor that refers each member to this process that is universal but nevertheless so unique every time. With reference to Bateson (1971), I could say that this reading offers for me, at the same time, "a structure that connects" and a "difference that makes the difference."

References

Ackerman, N. W. (1967). Prejudice and scapegoating in the family. In G. Zuk & I. Boszormenyi-Nagy (Eds.), *Family therapy and disturbed family* (pp. 48–57). Palo Alto: Science and Behavior Books.

Bank, S. P., & Kahn, M. D. (1982). *The sibling bond*. New York, NY: Basic Books.

Bateson, G. (1971). *Steps to an ecology of mind*. New York, NY: Ballantine.

Bowen, M. (1976). Theory in the practice of psychotherapy. In P. Guerin (Ed.), *Family therapy* (pp. 42–90). New York, NY: Gardner Press.

Elkaïm, M. (1981). Non-equilibrium, chance and change in family therapy. *Journal of Marital and Family Therapy, 7*(3), 291–297.

Elkaïm, M. (1988). Résonance. In J. C. Benoit & J. A. Malarewicz (Eds.), *Le dictionnaire clinique des thérapies familiales et systémiques*. Paris: ESF.

Elkaïm, M. (1990). *If you love me, don't love me: Constructions of reality and change in family therapy*. New York, NY: Basic Books.

Elkaïm, M. (1993). Co-constructions, systèmes et fonctions. *Cahiers Critiques de Thérapie Familiale et de Pratiques de Réseaux, 15*, 253–256.
Elkaïm, M., Goldbeter, A., & Goldbeter, E. (1987). Analysis of the dynamics of a family system in terms of bifurcations. *Journal of Social and Biological Structures, 10*(1), 21–36.
Goldbeter-Merinfeld, E. (1990). Le tiers absent du système. *Cahiers Critiques de Thérapie Familiale et de Pratiques de Réseaux, 11*, 83–90.
Goldbeter-Merinfeld, E. (1994a). Le tiers absent dans le système. In M. Elkaïm (Ed.), *La thérapie en changement* (pp. 103–109). Paris: Les Empêcheurs de Penser en Rond.
Goldbeter-Merinfeld, E. (1994b). Tiers pesant et tiers absent dans le système. *Thérapie Familiale, 15*(4), 373–380.
Goldbeter-Merinfeld, E. (2012). De la chaise à la métaphore, de la métaphore à ... *Cahiers. Critiques de Thérapie Familiale et de Pratiques de Réseaux, 48*, 129–134.
Goldbeter-Merinfeld, E. (2013). Légendes familiales et thérapeutes. *Cahiers Critiques de Thérapie Familiale et de Pratiques de Réseaux, 51*, 35–42.
Goldbeter-Merinfeld, E. (2014). La métaphore comme tiers et le tiers pesant en psychothérapie. *Cahiers Critiques de Thérapie Familiale et de Pratiques de Réseaux, 53*, 67–83.
McGoldrick, M., & Walsh, F. (1991). A time to mourn: Death and the family life cycle. In F. Walsh & M. McGoldrick (Eds.), *Living beyond loss. Death in the family*. New York, NY: Norton.
Minuchin, S. (1974). *Families and family therapy*. Cambridge: Harvard University Press.
Paul, N. L. (1967). The role of mourning and empathy in conjoint marital therapy. In G. Zuk & I. Boszormenyi-Nagy (Eds.), *Family therapy and disturbed family* (pp. 186–205). Palo Alto: Science and Behavior Books.
Paul, N. L., & Grosser, G. H. (1965). Operational mourning and its role in conjoint family therapy. *Community Mental Health Journal, 1*(4), 339–345.
Paul, N. L., & Paul, B. (1986). *A marital puzzle*. New York, NY: Gardner Press.
Selvini-Palazzoli, M., Boscolo, L., Cecchin, G., & Prata, G. (1978). *Paradox and conterparadox*. New York, NY: Jason Aronson.
Walsh, F., & McGoldrick, M. (1991). *Living beyond loss Death in the family*. New York, NY: Norton.

Chapter 8
Fascinating Interfaces and Systems: Integrating Biology, Psychology and Social Sciences in Teaching, Therapy and Coaching

Theo Compernolle

Synopsis To help people and families who do not function optimally, as a therapist or a coach, you need to be "Always confident but never certain". You need to be a confident leader of the process. To be confident you need a therapeutic map to quickly find your way in the ever new and ever changing territories that these individuals and families represent.

Once you become certain however, you become dangerous, because you are no longer open to feedback. Therapists become certain when they treat the map as if it were the territory. They also become certain when they believe in their intuitions. Although all kinds of unscientific psychobabble claim the contrary, it's better not to follow your intuitions. Research on the role of intuitions in decision making shows that they are 50/50 bets, unless these intuitions are learned under specific conditions (Kahneman and Klein 2009).

Every therapeutic strategy is nothing but a hypothesis, inspired by your therapeutic map, but that needs to be tested in a continuous learning process of trial and error.

In this chapter the author describes his therapeutic maps at different levels: the level of epistemology, the level of methodology and the level of technique. He suggests an eco-psycho-somatic approach to therapy to better integrate relevant knowledge from different scientific domains and to pay special attention to what goes on at the interface between them.

T. Compernolle (✉)
Compernolle Consulting, Tervurenlaan 19, 1040 Brussels-Etterbeek, Belgium

CEDEP European Centre for Executive Development, Boulevard de Constance, 77305 Fontainebleau, France
e-mail: office@compernolle.com; theo.compernolle@insead.edu

M. Borcsa, P. Stratton (eds.), *Origins and Originality in Family Therapy and Systemic Practice*, European Family Therapy Association Series,
DOI 10.1007/978-3-319-39061-1_8

Therapy in the Heart of an Eco-psycho-somatic Model

As you see in the references and acknowledgements, my contribution to this book is also the story of a fascinating professional journey.

As a medical student I was always very interested in the interface between different fields of knowledge, especially psycho-somatics. Later, working with families I used what's sometimes named a socio-psycho-somatic model.

Working in Philadelphia with families from the ghettos and being confronted with the awful living conditions in which many of these families had to survive, I converted this into my own Eco-Psycho-Somatic model (Compernolle 1980a) (Fig. 8.1), initially mainly for teaching. As a family therapist I choose the word Eco because it comes from the Greek word OIKOS=house and because it creates a link with the dire material and economical context of these families while including the social aspects. At the same time I was working with patients from very wealthy families and a family from the mafia, which further enriched my ideas about "ecological" factors.

There are four interfaces and the fascinating heart of the model is where the three domains interface. Reflections about problems, challenges, pathology, solutions and collaboration can be widened and deepened by putting them in the heart of the model.

The model was used for research and teaching not only about therapy but also about for example: Paediatrics (Compernolle 1980a), Anorexia nervosa (Compernolle 1981b), Alcoholism (Compernolle 1981a), Stress in schools (Compernolle 1987),

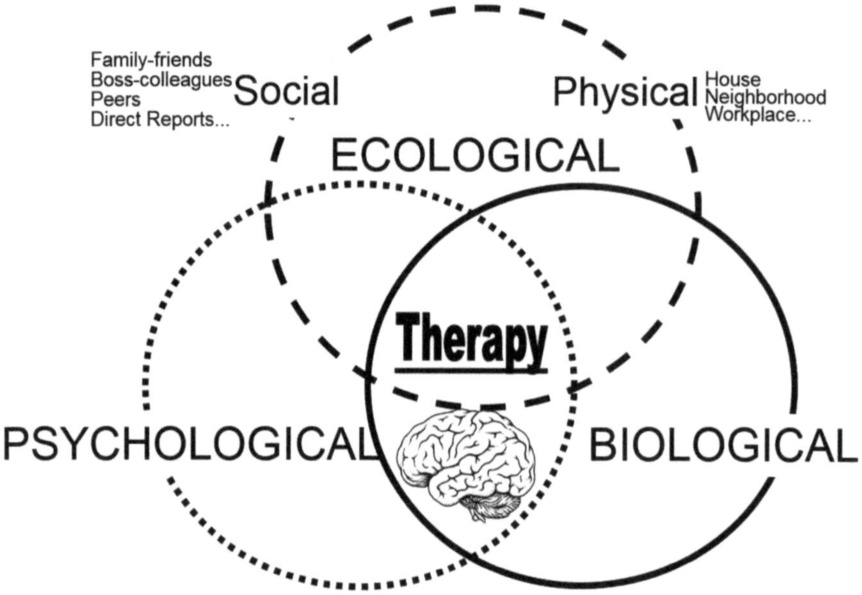

Fig. 8.1 An eco-psycho-somatic model for therapy (Compernolle 1980a)

Stress at work (Compernolle 1993, 1999, 2000), Family Businesses (Compernolle 2002), Executive coaching (Compernolle 2007), Knowledge work (Compernolle 2015a) and Open offices (Compernolle 2015b).

Distinguishing Epistemology, Method and Technique

Quite some family therapists tend to equate "system" with "family", thus thinking that a "family approach" is the same as a "systems approach" and vice versa. They forget that an individual, the brain, a single cell, an atom or society are systems too. One can work with a family using a non-systemic, reductionist model: isolating the family from its context, seeing the family as the cause of the symptom. On the other hand one can very well do individual therapy using a systemic method: seeing the individual as only one level of organization, interacting with other levels, itself being constituted of interacting parts etc. (Compernolle 1980a, b, 2007, 2015a, b; Spronck and Compernolle 1997).

The early descriptions of the Palo Alto group (Watzlawick et al. 1967), for example, about schizophrenia and the double bind, were not "systems oriented" at all, but very reductionist isolating the family from its context, thinking in linear cause—effect relations etc. This was a family view but not yet a systems view, neglecting everything that was known about schizophrenia at other levels.

Jay Haley (Haley and Hoffman 1967) as another example had a systemic view on the family of a person with schizophrenia when he describes the interactions of the person suffering from schizophrenia with the other family members. At the same time he is very non-systemic reductionist when he saw schizophrenia as only a family problem, without taking into account existing knowledge on other levels of organization and especially the role of biological and genetic factors.

The structural therapy model was an exception that helped to integrate not only knowledge from family therapy with knowledge from medicine and child development, but also to integrate the roles of paediatricians, teachers and street workers, collaborating with family therapists, specifically for the treatment of children and adolescents with diabetes, severe asthma and anorexia nervosa.

Epistemology

In the area of epistemology, the people who influenced me most were Ackoff (1974), Ashby (1956), Bateson (1972), Emery (1970), Maruyama (1997), Miller (1978), Miller and Miller (1995), Prigogine (1999), Rapoport (1984), von Bertalanffy (1969) and Guntern (1981).

I try to avoid the word "Systems theory" because von Bertalanffy (1969), who coined the word, originally used the German word "Lehre", which does not have an English equivalent and was translated as "Systems theory". It would have been better

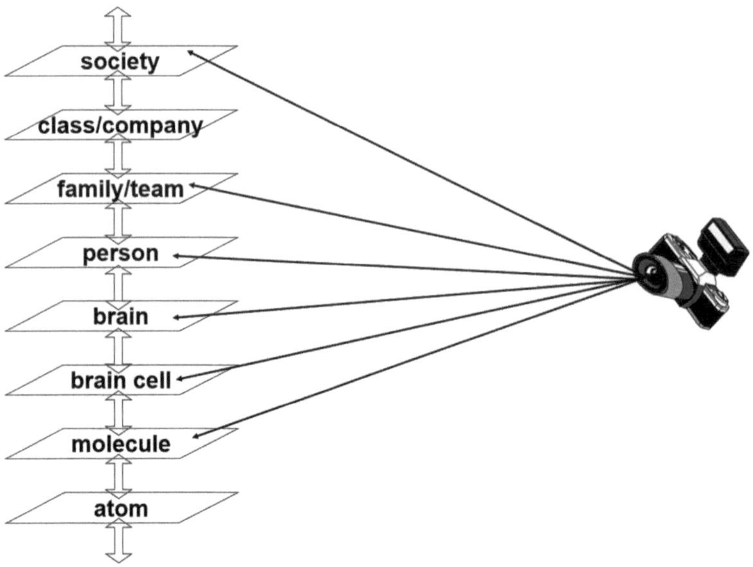

Fig. 8.2 The systems vies as a zoom-lens

translated as "view", "epistemology" or even "philosophy" because this is not a theory in a scientific sense, e.g. being testable and refutable.

To use Miller's (1978 p.9) definition in his classic "Living systems": "General systems theory is a set of related definitions, assumptions and propositions, which deal with reality as an integrated hierarchy of organizations of matter and energy *and information*" (*and information* added by myself).

To use a metaphor: The systems view is like a zoom lens keeping us aware of the fact that one can always zoom in and out to different levels of an organization, *without losing focus*. Each level is a subsystem of the next level above and a suprasystem for the next level below (Fig. 8.2). For example, one can zoom out from the biological level of the brain cell, to the brain, to the human individual, to the team (or family), to the company … and then reverse the process. With a systems orientation, one is continually aware that different observations at each level, lead to different theories, different hypotheses, different research and different interventions. Going from one level to another does not imply an increase or reduction in complexity; each level has its own complexity.

The level you choose to study and to intervene in depends on your interest, training, goal, knowledge, tools, capacities, power etc.

It is impossible to predict the behaviour of a system at one level with only knowledge about its parts at the lower level, because we also need to understand the interactions, or the relationships, between the units. In other words, the system is something altogether different from the sum of the parts. For example, one cannot predict the quality of a couple based on knowledge about the individual partners from before they married. The behaviour of couples and individuals are governed by different rules. The whole is not the sum of the parts, it is something totally different.

The other side of "the whole is different from the sum of the parts" is that "the part derives properties from the whole that it does not have itself in any other context". A simple example from linguistics: it is totally impossible to know the meaning of a word or a message without knowing the context (see also Bateson 1972). In systems thinking, linguistics, cybernetics, mathematics, sociology, economy, chess, genetics, embryology, philosophy etc., these properties are often called *Positional Value* or *Extrinsic Properties*.

This is a very fundamental concept that got someway lost in family therapy. It is also very useful for training and teaching family-therapists, especially to remind them that many crucial behaviours and emotions do not at all find their cause "deep inside" but are influenced, if not determined by the context, e.g. the family. These characteristics cannot be discovered outside the family, even not with the most extensive testing, nor in many years of psychoanalysis.

Imagine you want to study the value of the white knight in a game of chess, concentrating on only the knight, you will miss the most important features. You may study thousands of individual knight pieces, and learn a lot about wood, plastic, ivory, realistic and abstract representations. You may even delve down into its molecular and atomic composition, but you will learn nothing about the value of the knight in a chess game. You can move one systems level up and study the knight in an actual game, but only looking at the knight. You will discover the interesting fact that knights jump over other pieces and that they always go two steps ahead and one to the side or the other way around. Very interesting, but you still know nothing about the value of the knight in a game. It is only when you study the knight in an actual game, all the time taking into account its relationship with all the other pieces on the board, that you will learn something about the value of that knight in that game. You will then also discover that the value of the knight changes with every move by the other pieces. The knight obtains his most important qualities from the positions of all the other pieces on the board.

Another example of extrinsic qualities: nobody, not even using the most sophisticated psychological tests and analysis, can determine my qualities as a teacher for large audiences in any other way than by observing me while teaching. As a teacher, I derive properties from the teaching situation that I do not have in any other situation, and certainly not in a one-on-one test situation. Going into the other direction: nobody can discover my qualities as a teacher by studying my brain as a whole, the cells of my brain, the chemicals they produce, the molecules, the atoms.

The only way to discover the qualities of the whole system as well as some of the most important extrinsic properties of the parts is by studying it as whole, taking into account the relationships between the interacting units. That is one of the reasons why I like so much Minuchin's (1974) technique of enactment, where in the session one tries to elicit interactions in the family as close as possible to what's going on in the family at home.

In my current work with executive teams, the systems lens keeps me aware of the fact that one can study a phenomenon, such as leadership or the functioning of a senior leadership team, on many different levels, making observations on a particular level leading to a hypothesis valuable for that level only and interventions specific for that level (Compernolle 2007).

Working a lot with "psychosomatic" disorders, S. Minuchin and his team at the Child Guidance Clinic in Philadelphia were very aware of the role of neurophysiological processes and we collaborated closely with the paediatricians of the Penn University Hospital. It was very different from the reductionist approaches in other family therapy schools where one tended to see the family level as the most important if not the only level. For me this integration of the biological, psychological and social systems was one of the major reasons why I choose Structural Family Therapy as my preferred method. Another reason was that having drawn a structural map, the issue of cause and effect, guilt and blame, becomes irrelevant.

Causality

Ideas about causality lead the behaviour of therapists much more than they think. We are so used to thinking in terms of cause and effect, that we forget that causality is only a concept. We think that it is self-evident that an event now causes another event later, or that the problem we observe now must have a cause in the past (Fig. 8.3). In addition, from a reductionist view of the cause–effect relationship, one tends to look for the one and only cause that explains the effect in a straightforward, linear way.

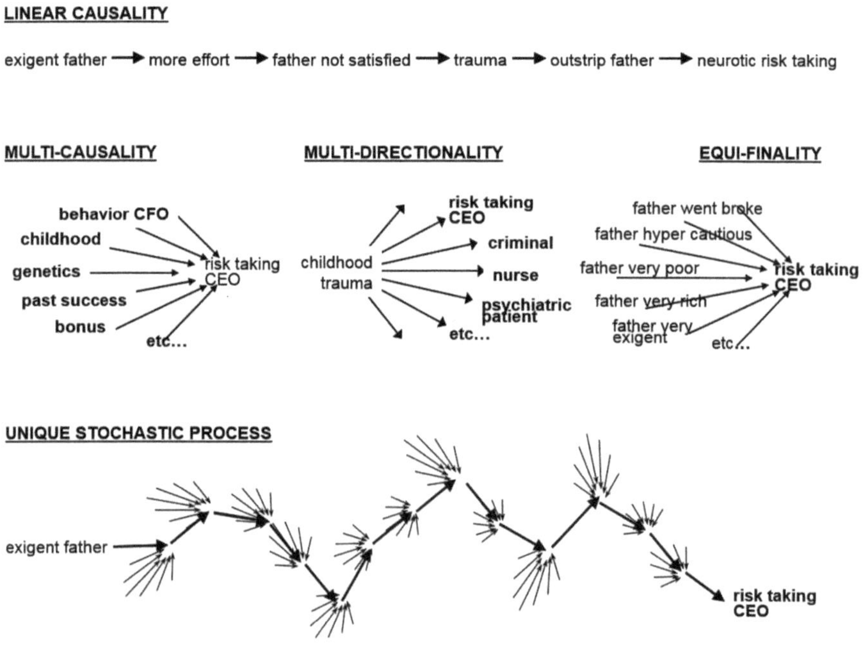

Fig. 8.3 Different kinds of causality

Theories of linear causality underlie approaches like psychoanalysis and traditional behaviourism. Thinking in a linear, causal model, the effect will be found if the cause is discovered and the cause will be detected if a particular effect is manifest. This leads to a model of chronological homogeneity or linear causality, where A (cause) leads to B (effect) directly and in one way only.

In single case studies, for example, one may repeatedly find a distant, punishing father in the history of narcissistic leaders. Within a linear causal model, therapists will therefore tend to see this type of father–child relationship as a cause of behaviour in adult life (Fig. 8.3). When they do not find any trace of such a father–child relationship, they will still keep to their cause–effect theory and conclude that this relationship has been pushed away into unconsciousness, rather than doubting their theory.

Families involved in these relationships too are usually not aware of the way their behaviour is influenced by interpersonal patterns of interaction. They too use a linear causal model, ascribing the cause of the problem, the blame, to other people. This sometimes leads to a power struggle about the cause, not only between family members but also between therapists and family members.

In the first half of the twentieth century, scholars and therapists realized that human behaviours and interactions cannot be fully understood, nor adequately changed, if they are seen as a link in a linear chain of events. It was recognized that, at any point in time, the actual situation is the result of many concurring influences. This is the notion of "multi-causality" (Fig. 8.3). Each of these concurring influences has a different and changing impact, because it is also in its turn influenced by many other factors. At every step in the chain, multiple directions can be taken, leading to a process wherein randomness and chance play a major role (Fig. 8.3).

Multi-causality leads to the notion of multi-directionality, in other words, any given starting point can lead to very different pathways (Fig. 8.3). Bifurcations appear all the time. All branches are possible, but only one of them will be taken, depending on the influences at that point.

This is one of the reasons why prospective studies often cannot reproduce the results of retrospective studies and why one should be very careful with their conclusions. Sometimes, a "cause" found in retrospective studies doesn't have a significant impact at all in prospective ones (Dutra et al. 2009). One should not forget that when one finds, for example, that 20 % of children who suffered from a particular childhood event develop mental problems, this may be a very significant number, but that 80 % developed normally. Hence, the "cause" is always only one of the many influences that determine the outcome.

The cause–effect reasoning sometimes becomes problematic in therapy. First when therapists think that "*a* cause" they sometimes find in retrospect, such as oedipal triangulation or sexual abuse, is "*the* cause" and if one does not find that "cause" it must have been repressed. Secondly when their focus on the supposed cause prevents them from seeing and dealing with other or more important influences.

On the other hand, in different people the same behaviour and attitudes are the result of totally different histories. For example, in different people epileptic seizures, which often look like carbon copies of each other, can be the result of totally different events, such as a childbirth trauma, an infection, a car accident or a drug. In the same way, the reckless behaviour of a CEO can be the result of an extremely demanding father, a permissive father, a risk-averse father seen as a loser, a culmination of very gradual increases in risk-taking reinforced by positive results, an all-or-nothing attitude in situations of being cornered, boredom in the job, etc.

This is called "equi-finality" (Fig. 8.3) or to put it more simply, many roads lead to Rome. In the context of such chronological heterogeneity, looking back for the "real" cause in a chain of events does not make any sense whatsoever.

Ascribing a cause that starts a chain of events is totally random: this is sometimes called making an arbitrary interpunction. When, for example, two children fight, parents sometimes try to find out who started the fight. When one analyzes a video of an actual fight, it becomes clear that every behaviour seen as the "cause" of the fight by one child, is preceded by more or less subtle behaviour by the other child that "caused" this "cause", and that the event sometimes even was influenced or "caused" by (not so) subtle behaviour by the parents themselves or other influences in the context.

Here the traditional notion of cause and effect completely loses its meaning. In cases like the one described above, the term "circular causality" is sometimes used, indicating that in interactions between people, while a source may trigger an effect, this in turn has an impact on the source. But even that way of thinking is of limited help, and if one uses this model to simplify complex interactions, one should never forget that it's just a simplification, a very simple map, a concept, not reality.

By the way, the systems view also made me realize how extremely reductionist medicine is. All the time physicians and researchers look for *the* cause of a disease and every time they find there is never one cause but always a system of many factors, at different levels, that together make the difference between health and disease. They forget that bacteria do not "cause" a particular infectious disease. The disease is always the result of many factors such as the virulence of the bacteria, the number of bacteria, prior exposure to the bacteria, the specific immunity of the person, her general immunity, her general health, her levels of stress, her age etc. As a result many people who are infected with a bacterium never get ill, or can be cured without attacking "the cause" with antibiotics, but by improving the other influences.

Guilt, Blame and Pathology

Linear cause–effect theories, when dealing with people, unavoidably introduce guilt and blame in the discourse. When parents are seen as the cause of disturbance in their children, they get the blame, to the extent that the most terrible things have been written, for example in psychoanalytical literature, about the mothers of children with autism or anorexia nervosa.

The mere description by a therapist of problem behaviour or problematic relations in terms of cause-free, blame-free and guilt-free patterns of interactions can provoke a deep relief and free people to behave differently.

Moreover, when the therapist does not use a linear causal model, he manifestly does not blame anybody himself. This has a very fundamental impact on his relationships with his clients. Therapists who think linearly and reductionist in terms of cause and effect, cannot avoid looking for culprits. A therapist using a linear model will try not to blame anybody, but merely by thinking in terms of cause and effect, he *is* blaming. Analysis of videotapes we made in training-situations of therapists who were used to a reductionist linear thinking model, clearly showed that the blaming often happened in subtle, non-verbal and verbal ways, of which the therapists were unaware. For example, at the beginning of the training program, a very emotionally intelligent French child-psychiatrist, whose psychodynamic model made him think that the psychopathology of the mother was the cause of anorexia nervosa, was unaware of the fact that in a session with the family whenever the mother started talking he would spontaneously cross his legs, lean back and cross his arms. When he uttered statements of support to the mother, at the end of the sentence his tone of voice went up, making it sound like question, as if he doubted what she said. Even a simple affirmative "Yes" sounded like "yes?". He was shocked when we analyzed the video of that session. Notwithstanding this experience, he later unknowingly behaved similarly with the mother of an autistic child. Of course he did not want to blame, but he was blaming because his model made him see these mothers as the cause of the problem. It took some time, but his spontaneous behaviour towards mothers changed when he progressively became convinced that the behaviour of the mother was also "caused" by the daughter, the son and the father in a rigid pattern of interactions.

Hence the best result a linearly thinking therapist can hope for is not to *appear* to be blaming. In reality this is very difficult, if not impossible. The client will leave the session with a feeling of being blamed even if not a single blaming word has been spoken.

The blame of therapists is often wrapped in the notion of pathology. However, from a systems point of view, whether behaviour can be labeled pathologic or pathogenic depends on the social space in which it takes place and the arbitrary choice of the systems level and boundaries. A particular behaviour can be considered constructive or positive within the realm of one system or one level, but at the same time destructive and negative in the context of another system or at another level of organization.

Being a scapegoat, for example, can be very destructive for the child concerned, but at the same time it can be positive for the survival of the couple or the family. Becoming indifferent can be life-saving psychological flight behaviour for an individual in a disturbing, stressful work situation, preferable to suffering from a heart attack or burning out. On the level of the team or the company, however, it is a big problem if many people become indifferent.

The systems oriented therapist or coach no longer deals primarily with hypotheses about possible causes in the past, but with patterns of interaction in the present, at different systems-levels, in which the search for *the* cause is no longer relevant. At that point the therapist does not need to try not (to appear) to blame people, she *is* no longer blaming.

One of the reasons I like "Structural Family Therapy" (Minuchin 1974) is that S. Minuchin's way of trying to draw maps of a family helps to describe the relationships without implying cause–effect, hence without implying guilt and without blaming.

The Level of Methodology

From a systems point of view many very good hypotheses (explanations) co-exist on different levels at the same time. Observations (research) and hypotheses for example about the continuation of violence on the level of the family does not exclude very different observations and hypotheses on the level of the individual, society or even about the neurobiology of violence.

Templates and metaphors developed as part of a particular method help us to understand and communicate about the complex reality. They focus us by simplifying.

A first issue about our models is that too often practitioners and researchers in family therapy, psychotherapy and coaching think and behave as if their theories and metaphors are reality. They treat the map as if it were the territory (Korzybski 1933; Bateson 1972). Freud, for example, developed some of the most beautiful metaphors in psychology. The Oedipus triangle was certainly fascinating and inspiring for many. Problems arise when such metaphors are treated as if they really exist, and even more so when they are taken as universal "truths". The same is true for family therapists who think "boundaries" between people really exist. Therapists forget the original "as if". They do not say "it is *as if* unconsciously…" but "Unconsciously she …", not "it is *as if* there is a boundary…" but "there is a boundary". The metaphor, the concept becomes a thing. Indeed, when clinicians fight their turf wars, they actually forget that they are often fighting about metaphors more than about reality.

The systems point of view acknowledges that these concepts are extreme simplifications of reality and that is what they should be. If a map were a true representation of reality, it would actually lose its usefulness, to the point where a simpler map would be needed to understand the complicated map. Secondly, one can make very different maps that refer to the same territory, depending on the goal or interest. To get as quickly as possible from Amsterdam to Paris a very simple map showing only highways is sufficient. To visit Paris a detailed tourist map is required. To the engineer responsible for checking the pipelines buried under Paris all these maps are useless: he needs a custom-made map for his specific purposes. Thirdly, not all maps are reliable. Anybody can invent a new theory or a new psychotherapy method. Even a psychotic person follows his map, but usually his map is not sufficiently reliable to help him to find his way in the real world. Although all kinds of unscientifi psychobabble claim the contrary, it's better not to follow your intuitions. Research on the role of intuitions in decision making shows that they are 50/50 bets, unless these intuitions are learned under specifi conditions (Kahneman and Klein, American Psychologist 64(6):515, 2009). Therapists need scientific research to find out if a particular map is a trustable representation of reality. A fourth issue is that therapists often think that the success of interventions based on a particular method proves their theory. This is a common error. Homeopathic healers, for example, believe that water has a memory, and that a solution of one in a billion is therefore still effective. There are about 40 scientific ways to prove that this theory is completely wrong. In practice, however, homeopaths cure people with their solutions regardless of the theory being wrong because of the placebo effect. Therefore, the success of homeopathic methods does not prove that water has a memory and that a solution of one in a billion can have an impact. Prayer can help people to overcome major difficulties, but that does not prove the existence of God. Exorcism is sometimes a very effective method of treating major disturbances, but that does not prove the existence of the Devil.

In brief: clinical methods, metaphors and templates are helpful and necessary tools for a better understanding of a very complex reality, and as subsequent guides to our interventions. They help therapists to become confident guides. They trap us when we reify them, start believing they are "the truth" and become certain. Therapists should be confident but never certain.

The Level of Technique

In all the family therapy methods or schools, not only therapeutic maps were developed but also more or less *specific techniques*. The more a method is systemic, the easier it is to integrate techniques from other schools, even those developed in very reductionist non-family oriented methods of psychotherapy or medical practice. Another advantage of structural family therapy for me was that it was easy to integrate the techniques from other schools of therapy that I had learned before and after.

Some techniques work well on the brain level, others on the individual level, others at the family level, others a societal level etc. There is nothing wrong with intervening at those different levels as long as one does not proclaim the supremacy or superiority of one of those levels, certainly not the family level.

Therapists should give priority to techniques about which at least some outcome research shows that they make a difference. If they use a technique that has no support or if they creatively invent a technique on the spot, they should be twice as critical towards their interventions, and try to follow up on them while thinking about the issues mentioned above.

Conclusion

Systems "theory", or developing a "systems zoom-lens" will help a therapist or coach to integrate learning from very different disciplines and schools. Medicine, neurology, biology, psychiatry, psychotherapy, management, and family therapy for example are not in conflict with each other but they deal with different system-levels. On these levels one can make different observations, different hypothesis leading to different interventions. One can never totally understand what happens on one level only based on knowledge about other levels. One cannot, for example, fully understand what happens at an individual level with only knowledge about the family and vice versa. For the therapist this idea greatly widens her scope of observation and intervention.

The liberation from the reductionist cause–effect thinking eliminates the resulting paralyzing issues of guilt and blame. From a systems point of view, nobody is to blame, but everybody is responsible for the necessary change in the pattern of interactions.

Finally, this systems point of view jettisons most turf fights and power struggles between professionals from different schools and disciplines and improves collaboration.

Ideas about why people and families behave as they do are resolved when these ideas are no longer formulated as truths, but as simplified representations of a part of reality at a particular systems-level and as hypotheses to be tested all the time in the therapeutic process,. This does not mean that all methods and techniques are of equal value. We need research to find out how efficient and reliable they are.

Acknowledgements I am extremely lucky not only because in my career I got more than I strived hard for, but also because I have enjoyed so many fortunate serendipitous encounters with very inspiring people.

It was a fascinating journey. As a dwarf on the shoulders of giants, I did not become any taller, but it gave me a better view. It lead me from medicine, to neurology, to psychiatry, to psychosomatics, to behavioural therapy, to family therapy, to systems thinking combined with stress research, to executive coaching, consulting and teaching managers the directions of use of people and last but not least, working with families with a business. The last 6 years I did research about the brain and how we ruin our intellectual productivity and creativity by using our information and communication technology without knowing the directions of use of our own thinking brain.

It would take dozens of pages of references to mention the writings of all the writers who influenced my ideas mentioned in this chapter. I learned a lot in personal conversations and workshops too. The most important live learning happened with the following, more or less in chronological order: L. Van Trotsenburg, E. Wassenaar, R. VanDijk, above all S. Minuchin with whom I collaborated for 2 years and also G. Patterson, M. Erickson, G. Bateson, G. Guntern, J. Haley, C. Whitacker, many colleagues, team members, trainees, students and especially the sometimes very humbling learning from patients and their families.

Looking back, my journey through family therapy was an unremitting and sometimes tempestuous learning experience. I am very grateful to so many fascinating creative people who got, and still get, me out of my comfort zone again and again.

References

Ackoff, R. L. (1974). *Redesigning the future: A systems approach to societal problems*. New York: Wiley.

Ashby, R. (1956). *An introduction to cybernetics*. London: Chapman & Hall.

Bateson, G. (1972). *Steps to an ecology of mind*. Chicago: University of Chicago Press.

von Bertalanffy, L. (1969). *General system theory: Foundations, development, applications*. New York: George Brazillier.
Compernolle, T. (1980a). *Eko-psychosomatiek: de invloed van het gezin op het fysiologisch functioneren van het kind en vice versa. Academisch Centrum voor Huisartsgeneeskunde*. Leuven: Katholieke Universiteit Leuven.
Compernolle, T. (1980b). La thérapie familiale structurale, approche systémique par excellence. *Bulletin de thérapie familiale, 2*, 9.
Compernolle, T. (1981a). Het Alcoholisme Vanuit Een Systeemoptiek. *Tijdschrift Voor Psychiatrie, 23*(9), 522–532.
Compernolle, T. (1981b). Anorexia nervosa: een een eco-psycho-somatisch probleem. *Tijdschrift voor psychiatrie, 23*, 80–86.
Compernolle, T. (1987). *Stress op de middelbare school*. Leuven: ACCO.
Compernolle, T. (1993). *Stress: Vriend en vijand*. Tielt: Lannoo.
Compernolle, T. (1999). *Stress: Friend and foe*. Alkmaar: Synergo.
Compernolle, T. (2000). *Stress: Vriend en vijand* (2nd ed.). Tielt: Lannoo.
Compernolle, T. (2002). *Succesgids voor families met een bedrijf*. Tielt: Lannoo.
Compernolle, T. (2007). Developmental coaching from a systems point of view. In M. K. de Vries, K. Korotov, E. Florent-Treacy, & M. F. R. de Vries (Eds.), *Coach and couch. The psychology of making better leaders* (2nd ed., pp. 41–62). New York: Palgrave Macmillan.
Compernolle, T. (2015a). *Brainchains. Discover your brain and unleash its full potential in a hyperconnected multitasking world*. Brussels: Compublications.
Compernolle, T. (2015b). *The open office is naked*. Brussels: Compublications.
Dutra, L., Bureau, J. F., Holmes, B., Lyubchik, A., & Lyons-Ruth, K. (2009). Quality of early care and childhood trauma: A prospective study of developmental pathways to dissociation. *The Journal of Nervous and Mental Disease, 197*(6), 383.
Emery, F. E. (1970). *Systems thinking*. Harmondsworth: Penguin.
Guntern, G. (1981). System therapy: Epistemology, paradigm and pragmatics. *Journal of Marital and Family Therapy, 7*(3), 265–272.
Haley, J., & Hoffman, L. (1967). *Techniques of family therapy*. New York: Basic Books.
Kahneman, D., & Klein, G. (2009). Conditions for intuitive expertise: A failure to disagree. *American Psychologist, 64*(6), 515.
Korzybski, A. (1933). *Science and sanity: An introduction to non-aristotelian systems and general semantics* (pp. 747–761). New York: Institute of General Semantics.
Maruyama, M. (Ed.). (1997). *Context and complexity: Cultivating contextual understanding*. New York: Springer.
Miller, J. G. (1978). *Living systems*. New York: McGraw Hill.
Miller, J. G., & Miller, J. L. (1995). Applications of living systems theory. *Systemic Practice and Action Research, 8*(1), 19–45.
Minuchin, S. (1974). *Families and family therapy: A structural approach*. London: Tavistock Publications.
Prigogine, I. (1999). *Letters to future generation. The die is not cast*. Retrieved from http://www.unesco.org/opi2/lettres/TextAnglais/PrigogineE.html
Rapoport, A. (1984). *General systems theory: Essential concepts and applications*. Cambridge: Abacus.
Spronck, W., & Compernolle, T. (1997). Systems theory and family therapy: From a critique on systems theory to a theory of systems change. *Contemporary Family Therapy, 19*(2), 147–175.
Watzlawick, P., Beavin Bavelas, J., & Jackson, D. (1967). *Pragmatics of human communication; a study of interactional patterns, pathologies, and paradoxes*. New York: Norton.

Chapter 9
Systemic Theory and Narratives of Attachment: Integration, Formulation and Development over Time

Arlene Vetere

Synopsis I am interested in explanation—how we can explain relationships and their dilemmas and satisfactions, both ordinary and extraordinary. Clearly we can describe life's joys and sorrows, despair and trauma responses, but we need to explain how they come about, if we are to be able to help people cope and to live more satisfying lives. For me, systemic theory provides a reflexive framework to map pattern and process and communication and meaning-making in our relationships. It is a process model and helps separate the person and the relationship from the problem. But it does not directly speak of content. From the early days of my training in family therapy I turned to theories of content, namely attachment theory and attachment research, narrative theory and trauma theory. For me, theories that purport to capture our life experiences in our intimate relationships need to have face validity and the explanatory power to help me understand what is happening to me and to others, and very often this involves multiple theories and hypotheses. Thus the task of explanation becomes one of integration, formulation and critical reflection. In my view, we have an ethical responsibility to draw on available theories as resources to aid understanding, and to integrate them in a way that all involved agree makes the best sense, and the best plan for action. Clearly no explanation is ever sufficient, and needs to be flexible to incorporate new information, and open to critical appraisal, or to be open to change in the face of non-confirmation. But it needs to be useful—useful to all involved in the therapeutic process.

Introduction

Therapeutic work in Europe takes place in a mix of public, private and charitable social and health care settings. Clients and their professional practitioners inhabit and move between contexts of cultural and ideological diversity. Collaborative

A. Vetere (✉)
VID Specialized University, Oslo, Norway
e-mail: drarlenevetere@hotmail.com

M. Borcsa, P. Stratton (eds.), *Origins and Originality in Family Therapy and Systemic Practice*, European Family Therapy Association Series,
DOI 10.1007/978-3-319-39061-1_9

practices, in therapeutic exchanges and inter-agency working, often informed by systemic theory and the wish to bypass the power hierarchies implicit in many social relationships, contribute to the multi-layered spirit of practice in our modern social and health care networks (Anderson and Gerhart 2006; Anderson and Jensen 2007). The complexity of change processes for individuals, relationships and groups of people is recognised and supported by collaborative working and demands a more theoretically integrated approach, across all social and health care disciplines (Vetere 2006; Vetere and Dallos, 2003). Trust, engagement and clear straightforward communication with clients and with colleagues are the common factors in relationship repair and healing and underpin effective help and assistance (Vetere 1993). So, for example, paying utmost attention to relationship building, communicating with clarity and honesty, understanding family members' appraisals and concerns and responding to their values and goals is the platform on which we approach and develop our understandings and explanations for distress and troubled relationships.

Per Jensen (2007) has researched the narratives that connect a therapist's personal history to their professional practice through their preferences for some theories and practices over others. In a powerful example from my own childhood, my father was killed by drunk drivers in a road traffic accident when I was 11 years old, and he was 42 years old. He was driving home and never made it. My mother's response was catastrophic. At first she turned her face to the wall. When she emerged, she was changed. Irrevocably and unrecognisably. I knew then I wanted to be a psychologist. I needed to understand and to explain in order to know how to go on.

It is in knowing how to go on, and in taking the feedback, that we find our best opportunities to learn—to explore, to illuminate, to process, to re-process and to transform (Stratton 2005; Vetere and Stratton 2016). In this chapter I shall draw out some theoretical pointers from attachment, narrative and trauma theories and show how they can be integrated in systemic therapeutic practice by using "formats for exploration" (Dallos and Vetere 2009). This integrative approach has been profoundly influenced by my collaboration with Jan Cooper in our family violence intervention project (Cooper and Vetere 2005), and with Rudi Dallos in our Attachment Narrative Therapy work, cited above. To both of them, I offer my gratitude.

Integrative Practice

The integration of large and well researched systems of thought—attachment theory, narrative theory, trauma theory—with systemic theory and practice provides a powerful explanatory model for understanding and healing the sources and maintenance of distress in relationships—the attachment threats, relational traumas and unresolved hurts, losses and disappointments that constrain relational empathy, listening and trust. These are poignant and challenging conversations with our clients and need to be rooted in relationships of trust and for me, attachment theory points the way.

Attachment theory is a lifespan developmental theory of the social regulation of emotion in families (Bowlby 1982). Initially Bowlby integrated cognitive neuroscience, object relations theory, evolutionary biology and systems theory to develop attachment theory. Safety and protection is at the heart of attachment thinking and emphasises our need for a secure base, i.e. knowing that we can turn to others for comfort, support and assistance when needed (Bowlby 1988). Modern empirical developments of attachment theory emphasise the development of our attachment strategies in response to attachment threat, i.e. a continuum of styles of self-protective and defensive processes, activated when we fear rejection and abandonment, or we have been rejected and abandoned (Crittenden 1998). These strategies are thought to develop in childhood in the context of family relationships, and to continue into our adult relationships. These strategies can become overlearned through processes of reinforcement or they can be subject to change with "corrective" experiences in relationships that provide a context of felt security. Examples of such protective strategies include the following, for example, a strategy of deactivating emotional arousal and avoidance of the expression of the need for reassurance can develop in the context of caregiving when a growing child's needs for comfort and reassurance are not met, or the child learns that their expressions of distress and need are overwhelming and distressing for their parent or caregiver. Thus the child learns that they cannot rely on emotion as a guide to behaviour because the expression of emotion cannot reliably elicit comfort or caring. At the other end of the continuum, if the child's requests for comfort and reassurance when distressed are unpredictably responded to, so for example, sometimes they are scooped up and comforted and reassured, and sometimes they are left crying in the corner, this unpredictable responding from the parent or caregiver leaves the child unable to trust what people say or to predict what people will do. The child learns that persistence on their part can sometimes elicit a response from the parent but consequently the child is not helped to understand or regulate their affect. The child develops a chronic level of unregulated and unprocessed arousal and preoccupation and may learn to develop coercive strategies to attain parental attention and concern.

Children who receive more or less contingent and predictable responses to their requests for help and comfort are helped to internalise strategies for calming and self-soothing and to develop a range of coping responses when unhelpfully physiologically aroused that may also include forms of de-activation, withdrawal and avoidance, and preoccupation and persistence. Here the child has a broader repertoire for coping and can balance their use of strategies for affect regulation. Over developmental time, and in response to the above, beliefs and expectations grow about our acceptability to others and whether we are deserving of others' comfort and care—sometimes called internal working models. These beliefs about the self and others can follow us into adulthood if they remain unchallenged by others or by emotionally safe "corrective" experiences. From a systemic perspective, children are often making close connections with more than one caregiver and may well develop different attachment strategies with different family members (Crittenden et al. 2014). This potential plurality in learning and responding can contribute to children's adaptability and resilient responding.

Thus strategies can be seen as "fall-back positions" of safety and self-protection when we are distressed, worried and fear rejection in our relationships. Within this theoretical framework strategies are not seen as right or wrong, pathological or healthy, more as whether they are helpful or unhelpful, and that is most often determined by the relational context and cultural meanings.

Practitioner based developments of attachment theory include the work of Susan Johnson and colleagues with Emotion Focused Therapy, an integration of attachment theory with systemic theory and practice (Johnson 2002). In particular, Emotion Focused Therapy emphasises the signal importance of identifying and healing attachment injuries (or relational traumas) in intimate relationships, i.e. the unresolved hurts and resentments that are re-evoked every time there is a misunderstanding and disappointment in a close relationship. Johnson and colleagues have deconstructed the process of carefully tracking and acknowledging family members' hurt and distress in their relationships, to enable a process of affirmation, apology and healing that resolves hurt, loss, resentment and disappointment.

The implications of attachment theory research for systemic psychotherapy are clear and helpful:

(a) Naming and regulating emotions. Understanding and communicating our emotional responses in a straightforward and clear way helps us navigate and resolve difficult moments of potential misunderstanding and hurt in our relationships and begin the process of repair and recovery. For example, in my therapeutic work with couples and families where hurt and misunderstanding prevail, we track a recent episode of conflict and disappointment, slowly and carefully, looking for the attachment triggers that escalate the interaction into unhelpful physiological arousal. An attachment threat of rejection or abandonment can result in an angry and defensive response. It is hard for family members to be curious at these times as to what else the angry person might be feeling, such as sadness, shame and fear. Thus a slow and careful process of de-construction enables the hidden feelings to emerge in a context of compassion, supported by good listening.
(b) Standing in the emotional shoes of the other. Empathy and compassion, for the self and for the other, fosters accessibility and responsiveness in relationships, the building blocks of trust (Gottman 2011). The ability to listen to the other, and to stay engaged, when they are hurt and upset with something we have done or not done, is a difficult and challenging task—this is the task of relationship therapy to help people listen to each other and to feel deeply heard and understood. This enables a de-escalation of unhelpful physiological arousal and a feeling of calmness, necessary for more satisfying and effective problem solving in our relationships (Schore 2012).
(c) Comforting and self-soothing. Our ability to seek comfort, to give comfort and to accept comfort is at the heart of attachment theory. Attachment injury occurs when we have a high need for reassurance and comfort and the other does not realise this and does not provide it. Many of the people I work with in therapy were never comforted, soothed and calmed as children, and in growing up they have learned to rely on psychoactive substances to help them regulate their mood and to escape unbearable feelings of sadness, shame and fear (Vetere 2014).

The emphasis on the importance of comforting and safety in relationship suggests both the benefit of exploring the development of current relationship problems in earlier family of origin attachment experiences, and of the continuing legacy of such experiences for our understanding of ourselves and others. We have developed a systemically informed format for exploring intergenerational patterns of comforting in families that can include these prompt questions: "When you were upset or frightened as a child, what happened?" "How did you get to feel better?" "Who helped you to feel better?" "How did they do this?" "What have you learnt from this for your own family?" "What do you want to do the same?" "What do you want to do differently?" "How do people comfort each other in your own family/relationships?" "How do you comfort your children?" "How do they comfort you?" "What do you hope your children will learn from you about comforting for their future relationships?" and so on (Dallos and Vetere 2009).

(d) Information processing. When we fear rejection or are threatened with rejection and abandonment, we become preoccupied with our own anxious affective state, and either try to dismiss and minimise what is happening in an attempt to persuade ourselves everything is fine and we do not care, or we become overwhelmed with anxiety and unable to regulate ourselves, at the extremes of our experience. Either way it is difficult to think reflectively and to problem solve in these circumstances. We tend to fall back on "old" solutions even if we know they do not work to help us. Our information processing slows down, particularly for negative affective material. And most worrying of all, our ability to read relational cues is impaired. In the face of such overwhelming emotional reactivity and distress it is sometimes very hard for therapists to stay calm, necessary for therapeutic holding and containment. Goldner (2014) has written of the extreme emotional and cognitive challenges for therapists when working with couples "on the brink" that can sometimes lead to secondary trauma for the therapists and a form of physiological countertransference, i.e. pounding heart, dry mouth and trembling limbs.

(e) Transformations in representational systems. This for me is the most exciting development in modern attachment theory and draws on memory research and the research work of Tulving in particular (1987). Memory research suggests we hold memories in different representational systems, and thus our attachment experiences, memories and meanings can be held in separate representational systems, or they can be integrated into coherent narrative accounts of ourselves, our relationships and what has happened to us. Narrative theory suggests we need a degree of felt security in our relationships to link our thoughts, feelings and actions into coherent narrative accounts so that others may know what has happened to us, and so that it may be safe enough for us to reflect on what is happening to us and what has happened to us (Bruner 1990). The complex layering of attachment memories can be seen in:

- Procedural memory—memory for how we do things, for example, riding a bicycle, showing affection, having an argument, and so on;

- Sensory memory—visual images of those we love, what touch feels like, how they smell and taste, and so on;
- Semantic memory—our cognitions, beliefs, values, and attitudes about love, emotion, relationships with significant others, and so on;
- Episodic memory (sometimes called autobiographical or narrative memory)—memory for what happens to us in the form of episodes, stories, narratives, that integrate action, feeling and thought;
- Integrative memory or reflection—our ability to think about our thinking, to reflect on how we integrate thought, feeling and action, and an on-going ability to monitor our speech and thought—often called meta-cognition, meta-communication, reflective self-functioning, and so on (Fonagy et al. 2002). Thus the form and content of our narratives of attachment both express and also construct our attachments. The re-organisation of our attachment strategies requires reflection and integration across our different representations of our attachments. And this requires emotional safety or the co-construction of the secure base in therapy: affirming and clarifying family members' experiences, modelling acceptance, slowing down the therapy to give people time to process information, offering comfort in response to difficult emotional experiences, and exploring the meanings of powerful human emotions.

When working therapeutically with couples and families, sometimes family members become upset and unhelpfully physiologically aroused during the meeting. At these times we can ask—"What is happening for you right now?" This allows the family member to respond from their preferred representational system at a time of distress and attachment threat. So they might say, "I think …", "I feel …", or "I want to do …". This information allows us then to meet them in their preferred position. If we ask, "What are you feeling?" "What are you thinking?" "What do you want to do?" we are inviting them into our preferred representational system.

Understanding family members' preferred strategies for self-protection when they are upset allows us to tailor our therapeutic ideas and responses to help us engage them in what is always a challenging process of understanding, illumination, processing and change. So, for example, for someone who prefers a semantic positioning at this time, a cognitive behavioural approach (CBT) might be most helpful with engagement, and helps them feel safe, but needs to move to more of an emotion focus to help them explore and process warded off emotional responses and experiences. This is needed to help them integrate their thoughts, feelings and actions, as a precursor to reflection and thus more effective problem solving. In another example, someone who becomes overwhelmed with unregulated emotion when perceiving an attachment threat, i.e. positioned within a sensory representational system, would benefit from a CBT approach to help them calm and think about their dilemmas, options and choices and so on, so that they can begin to empathise with the other. Initially though, an emotion focused response would build the therapy alliance. The theoretical goal in all this work is to help people integrate their experiences and reflect upon them, whilst developing empathy and compassion for self and other.

Systemic psychotherapy practice over time has developed an array of interventions that support family members in either calming and soothing so they can begin to think about what is happening, or help them take emotional risks and explore warded off, painful emotions and unresolved losses and hurts that need to be processed to enable healing and repair in relationships. For example, enactment, role play, internalised other interviewing and emotional sculpting can all help encourage the expression of feelings, and similarly, the use of genograms and lifelines, circular questions, scaling questions, letter writing and tracking circularities can all encourage the expression of cognitions. (Dallos and Vetere 2009; Dallos and Draper 2010 for a full description of the above systemic interventions.).

Change and Re-organisation: Corrective and Replicative Scripts

John Byng-Hall was probably the first British family therapist to incorporate attachment theory into mainstream systemic practice in the UK, with a specific focus on corrective and replicative scripts (1995). These are thought to be a cluster of intentions, feelings and actions which have developed from our childhood experiences and represent what we have learned, for example, how to look after ourselves and look after others, and what we want to apply in our own contemporary lives. Byng-Hall suggested that family members make comparisons across the generations in terms of similarities or differences between how are own parents (and grandparents?) were with each other and with us (their children) and how this is repeated or altered in the next generation. For example, in the context of family care giving, a replicative script is an intention to repeat the things that were good about our childhoods, such as, my parents were warm and caring and I had discipline, and I learned respect from it.... In another example, a corrective script is an intention to do things differently, perhaps better than my parents were able to do things for me as a child, or to have a different kind of marriage than my parents had.... A few aspects of their interpretation of their own experience of being parented may well dominate currently so that some other aspects may be unthinkingly replicated. Importantly this allows us to work in a positive therapeutic frame with the family because we may construe the intentions of the parents positively, i.e. they have tried to repeat what was good or correct what they felt was bad about their own experiences. This often leads to a discussion of whether these attempts have been helpful or not, and possibly how they might be altered, strengthened or elaborated.

A systemic format for exploration of corrective and replicative scripts can include prompt questions such as: “What are your thoughts about how similar or different your relationship with each other and with your children is to your parents’ (grandparents’) relationships?” “What have you tried to make similar or different to either of these relationships?” “What do you value versus feel critical about in either of your parents’ relationships?” “Does what you have tried to repeat or change work?” “Is there anything that you want to alter, strengthen, abandon about what you have been trying to repeat or change?" and "What do you hope your children will learn from you for their future?" (Dallos and Vetere 2014). In this way, parents can be assisted in developing a more integrated and reflexive narrative of themselves as parents and of their parenting practises, for now, and for the future.

Trauma and Loss

Loss and danger can be seen as an inevitable part of life. Crittenden (2008) writes that "the function of resolution is to enable the individual to take forward into the future information that is relevant to future protection and comfort, and to keep in the past that which was unique to the specific event. 'Unresolved' individuals are unable to differentiate these two classes of information." The use of extreme attachment strategies of emotion regulation and self-protection can interfere with the resolution of trauma states of mind. For example, if we use a de-activating or dismissing strategy, we may dismiss too much information and thus leave ourselves unsafe and unaware of danger or cues to potential future danger. I sometimes see this with some women I work with therapeutically in our family violence intervention project, when they appear to continue to choose to live with different men partners who all behave with violence towards them. At the other extreme, an anxious or preoccupied strategy might mean we are overwhelmed by carrying too much information forward, leaving us anxious, hyper-vigilant and over-aroused so that nothing feels safe. I might see this with someone who fears to leave their home because of the constant danger in the outside world. Attachment theory meets trauma theory at this point because attachment figures can assist in the processing of dangerous and extreme events. They validate and acknowledge our experiences. They help us to integrate what information we carry forward and they help us to make connections between different representational memory systems. Thus resolution balance, or dual-processing, is the ability to carry forward relevant and to discard irrelevant information and to connect information from different representational systems. They assist in developing effective coping strategies for future safety and enable positive narratives of healing to emerge. The attachment figure can be a family member and it can be a therapist. For some people, the first person they learn to trust is a therapist. However the development of unresolved trauma states can also be shaped by the reactions of family and friends, for example, with secondary trauma responses, so that preferred coping strategies become one of avoidance and dismissal of disturbing thoughts and feelings or of being constantly emotionally overwhelmed and agitated by unprocessed experiences. Here we see how the systemic theories can be helpful with couples, family groups and communities by paying attention to feedback, patterns in interaction, relational and social contexts, meaning and personal relationships.

Attachment figures can also be a source of danger, for example, the only person who cares for and comforts you in childhood is also the person who frightens and sexually abuses you. This creates an unresolvable dilemma for the child. On the one hand they need to approach the parent for comfort and reassurance, but on the other hand they fear, avoid and cannot trust the parent. Early coping responses to such unresolvable dilemmas include dissociation, freezing, confusion of thought and self-harm (Van der Kolk et al. 1996). If the child does not have another adult who can help them talk about their dilemma, reflect on their dilemma in safety, even though the bind continues, there is a risk the child will bring forward these coping responses into their future relationships. Trans-generational traumas are complex by definition. The child is positioned and takes positions, for example, (a) victim of adult abuse; (b) abuser of parent in that the parents appears frightened of the child as their own trauma responses are triggered by interactions with the child; (c) carer of the parent; and (d) as a child who is cared for by the parent. Similarly parents are positioned and take up positions in the context of inter-generational trauma responses, for example, (a) abuser of the child; (b) victim, in that the child's behaviour re-evokes their own unresolved traumas and losses; (c) child, in that the child is caring for them; and (d) carer of the child (Liotti 2004). Bentovim's (1992) work with trauma organised family systems describes the complexity of trauma responding when abusive actions (physical, sexual and/or emotional) become part of the family dynamic, for example, fear that the perpetrator may commit suicide; fear that the family might break up and encounter shame and poverty, and a potential re-activation of the parents' own traumatic memories, leading to an inability to act. This creates the context for blaming the victim, minimising events, blame of the other parent for failure to protect, a failure to confront abusive behaviour and of course enabled by secrecy. Thus we see how an integration of attachment theory, trauma theory with intergenerational systemic theory and practice enables us to understand this complexity and find ways forward to help families and communities.

In Conclusion

Attachment theory has had a chequered relationship with family therapy, with some practitioners fearing that it is used to either blame parents, especially mothers, for their children's distress, or that it is misused to categorise, classify and thus pathologise people. In fact, attachment theory does not pathologise dependency in relationships. Rather, it affirms that autonomy and dependency are crucial aspects of a secure attachment relationship and form the secure base in our relationships, i.e. we are happier and more productive when we know we have the support of trusted persons should problems arise (Bowlby 1973).

As systemic therapists, we strive to help people in their relationships achieve more secure and satisfying bonding interactions. This aim is supported by recent empirical research. Mikulincer and Goodman (2006) have helpfully summarised a body of cross-sectional correlational research from the adult romantic attachment literature. They conclude that a self-reported sense of felt security in our close relationships is positively correlated with the following: (a) more balanced affect regulation, i.e. less reactivity, hyper-arousal and under-arousal; (b) with support seeking and the ability to see others as potentially helpful; (c) with enhanced information processing and relational problem solving, i.e. openness to new information, curiosity and the enhanced tolerance of uncertainty; (d) straightforward communication characterised by self-disclosure, assertiveness, empathy for self and other, collaborative responding and the capacity for meta-communication; and finally, (e) positively correlated with a more positive, elaborated and articulated "sense of self".

The ability to reflect on and integrate thought, feeling and action requires a secure base of trust, responsiveness and accessibility. In other words it needs to be emotionally safe in order for us to be able to think reflexively about what is happening in our relationships. Initially this is learnt in our interactions with our caregivers, characterised by a sensitive attunement and naming/acknowledging the child's needs and the parents' ability to both follow and lead their interactions with the child. This interaction does not primarily rely on over-responding (anxious and preoccupied responding) nor on under-responding (deactivated avoidant responding)—it is a balance that can be reflected upon. Such reflection involves an awareness of contradictions and inconsistency within and between our representational memory systems. We could argue that all psychotherapy models aim to promote integration of thought, feeling and action, perhaps with a different theoretical emphasis on each, and to create the emotional safety (or containment) that enables us all to risk thinking reflexively about our thinking, feeling and behaviour—in therapy and in supervision. Thus integration and reflection need to both involve and integrate across all the representational memory systems.Acknowledgements Professor Rudi Dallos has been my systemic theoretical integration companion for some 20 years. He too shares a passion for attachment theory, narrative theory and trauma theory as part of systemic theory and practice. Thank you Rudi. This work could not be possible without you.

Jan Cooper has been my systemic practice companion working with couples and families where violence is of concern. Attachment theory, trauma theory and narrative theory have helped us work relationally to understand why violence happens and how to helps stop it, and repair relationships, while holding people accountable for their behaviour that harms others. Thank you Jan. This work could not be possible without you.

References

Anderson, H., & Gerhart, D. (2006). *Collaborative therapy: Relationships and conversations that make a difference*. New York: Routledge.

Anderson, H., & Jensen, P. (2007). *Innovations in the reflecting process*. London: Karnac.

Bentovim, A. (1992). *Trauma organised systems: Physical and sexual abuse in families*. London: Karnac.

Bowlby, J. (1973). *Separation: Anxiety and anger*. New York: Basic Books.

Bowlby, J. (1982). *Attachment and loss*. New York: Basic Books.

Bowlby, J. (1988). *A secure base: Parent-child attachment and healthy human development*. New York: Basic Books.

Bruner, J. (1990). *Acts of meaning*. Cambridge, MA: Harvard University Press.

Byng-Hall, J. (1995). *Rewriting family scripts*. New York: Guilford.

Cooper, J., & Vetere, A. (2005). *Domestic violence and family safety: A systemic approach to working with violence in families*. Chichester: Wiley.

Crittenden, P. (1998). Truth, error, omission, distortion and deception: The application of attachment theory to the assessment and treatment of psychological disorder. In M. Dollinger & L. DiLalla (Eds.), *Assessment and intervention across the lifespan* (pp. 35–76). London: Lawrence Erlbaum.

Crittenden, P. (Ed.). (2008). *Raising parents: Attachment, parenting and child safety*. Portland, OR: Willan.

Crittenden, C., Dallos, R., Landini, A., & Kozlowska, K. (2014). *Attachment and family therapy*. Maidenhead: Open University Press.

Dallos, R., & Draper, R. (2010). *An introduction to family therapy* (3rd ed.). Maidenhead: Open University Press.

Dallos, R., & Vetere, A. (2009). *Systemic therapy and attachment narratives: Applications in clinical settings*. London: Routledge.

Dallos, R., & Vetere, A. (2014). Systemic therapy and attachment narratives: Attachment narrative therapy. *Clinical Child Psychology and Psychiatry, 19*(4), 494–502.

Fonagy, P., Gergely, G., Jurist, E., & Target, M. (2002). *Affect regulation, mentalization and the development of the self*. New York: Other Press.

Goldner, V. (2014). Romantic bonds, binds and ruptures: Couples on the brink. *Psychoanalytic Dialogues, 24*, 402–418.

Gottman, J. (2011). *The science of trust. Emotional attunement for couples*. New York: Norton.

Jensen, P. (2007). On learning from experience. *Child Clinical Psychology and Psychiatry, 12*(3), 375–384.

Johnson, S. (2002). *Emotionally focused couple therapy with trauma survivors*. New York: Guilford.

Liotti, G. (2004). Trauma, dissociation and disorganised attachments: Three strands of a single braid. *Psychotherapy: Theory, Research, Practice and Training, 41*, 472–486.

Mikulincer, M., & Goodman, G. (2006). *Dynamics of romantic love. Attachment, caregiving and sex*. New York: Guilford.

Schore, A. N. (2012). *The science of the art of psychotherapy*. New York: Norton.

Stratton, P. (2005). A model to coordinate understanding of active autonomous learning. *Journal of Family Therapy, 27*(3), 217–236.

Tulving, E. (1987). Multiple memory systems and consciousness. *Human Neurobiology, 6*, 67–80.

Van der Kolk, B., McFarlane, A., & Weisath, L. (1996). *Traumatic stress: The effects of overwhelming experience on mind, body and society*. New York: Guilford.

Vetere, A. (1993). Family therapy in services for people with learning difficulties. In J. Carpenter & A. Treacher (Eds.), *Using family therapy in the 90's* (pp. 111–130). Oxford: Blackwell.

Vetere, A. (2006). The role of formulation in psychotherapy practice. *Journal of Family Therapy, 28*, 388–391.

Vetere, A. (2014). Alcohol misuse, attachment dilemmas, and triangles of interaction: A systemic approach to practice. In R. Gill (Ed.), *Addictions from an attachment perspective: Do broken bonds and early trauma lead to addictive behaviours?* (pp. 57–68). London: Karnac.

Vetere, A., & Dallos, R. (2003). *Working systemically with families: Formulation, intervention and evaluation*. London: Karnac.

Vetere, A., & Stratton, P. (2016). *Systemic concepts and solutions for personal and professional development in counselling and psychotherapy*. London: Routledge.

Part III
Applications

Chapter 10
How to Give Voice to Children in Family Therapy

Maurizio Andolfi

Synopsis In this chapter, Maurizio Andolfi describes a very original model of multigenerational family therapy in which children are engaged in therapy as significant relational bridges in the dialogue/clash between generations. The goal is then to build a solid therapeutic alliance with the family through the active collaboration of the problem-child, who becomes a sort of co-therapist guiding the therapist in the exploration of still open wounds and broken emotional bonds. His symptoms can be reframed and transformed to relational indicators connected to the affective, behavioural characteristic of a family member or to the dramatic or painful events that marked the family development. The model of therapy described by the author is experiential, that is to say, a special personal-professional encounter shared by therapist and family in a safe and active context. Several clinical examples are described, showing a therapist keen to use himself and his affective resonances to make direct contact with each person, by attuning to the pain and desperation expressed by many families in therapy, as well to the implicit aspects of vitality and hope, in order to transform them into elements of strength and change.

The Stages of My Professional Journey

My interest in family therapy started because I was a child psychiatrist; therefore the child was the door to enter into the family. Unfortunately, at that time (late sixties), in Rome the concept of family therapy in child psychiatry was totally unknown and my early work was based on "play therapy" with the child alone. My discomfort in seeing the child as an island brought me to include the mother in the play and then to call in the siblings and to engage the fathers in the session. In this way, I started to experiment myself with the entire group. At that point, I was learning by myself how to do it, but very soon I was fired from the Department because I was a strange

M. Andolfi (✉)
Accademia di Psicoterapia della Famiglia, Rome, Italy
e-mail: andolfiinternational@accademiapsico.it

M. Borcsa, P. Stratton (eds.), *Origins and Originality in Family Therapy and Systemic Practice*, European Family Therapy Association Series,
DOI 10.1007/978-3-319-39061-1_10

psychiatrist. I decided to choose my master teachers, who I could find only in the USA. My first magic encounter was with Nathan Ackerman in 1970. His model of therapy was very provocative and direct. He engaged children in the triad with parents. He was the one that introduced the metaphor of the child as the family scapegoat in the field. Inspired by this powerful encounter, I left my Country 2 years later and I went overseas. I got a Fellowship in Social Community Psychiatry at the Albert Einstein College of Medicine in New York under the sponsorship of Israel Zwerling, who was an outstanding social psychiatrist. Therefore, the kind of family therapy I learnt was much broader that seeing families in a private office. It was community work, like home visiting in situations of family crisis, engaging pre-delinquent adolescents in the school system. Incidentally, Mony Elkaim was in the some programme in Social Community Psychiatry at the same time and together, before coming back to Europe, we organised in New York an outstanding conference on Family Therapy in the Urban Ghetto.

Then I was "chasing" my teachers everywhere in the East Coast of USA. At the Ackerman Family Therapy Institute I was trained with Kitty La Perriere and Peggy Papp.

I joined a clinical team at the Child Guidance Clinic in Philadelphia during the golden period of structural family therapy. The Clinic was a three storey old house in the centre of Philadelphia's urban ghetto. I saw dozens of family sessions of Sal Minuchin, and I got supervision from Jay Haley and Braulio Montalvo, who were very active and creative during the 70s. On the other side, I was profoundly influenced by the clinical work of Carl Whitaker with whom I have been associated for over 15 years. For him, enlarging the system was never enough; his idea of healing was based on building up in the session an intergenerational network of affective connections around a specific problem. But, his mastery was the description of the inner self and the self disclosure of the therapist as the main tools for change. Having been trained in Hornian psychoanalysis, I got inspired by the most outstanding psychodynamic intergenerational therapists, like Jim Framo, a dear friend and mentor of mine, who brought very innovative ideas in the area of intergenerational couple therapy.

I was very influenced by the seminal work of Murray Bowen, Ivan Boszormenyi-Nagy on the Differentiation of Self from family of origin and on the Invisible Loyalties—all concepts that I incorporated later into my multigenerational model of family therapy.

However they were mostly concerned about adults' development, connecting cut-offs and immaturity with the adults' process of differentiation from family of origin. But children were not present in their concept of intergenerational work. Therefore, they didn't invite them in the session. For example Bowen, after the exploration of a very elaborated family genogram, would send problematic adults back home to repair family ruptures, Framo would prepare couples very well, before special sessions with their own family of origin. The idea to go "downstairs in the children floor" and to explore family development with the child in the role of an expert and a guide into the previous generational conflict and life events is a very original contribution of the author. Once returned to Europe, I implemented this multigenerational approach, first at the Istituto di Terapia Familiare and in the latest 24 years at the Accademia di Psicoterapia della Famiglia in Rome.

Together with Mony Elkaim and other very enthusiastic therapists, living in different parts of Europe, we build up a very creative *European Family Therapy Network* in order to exchange ideas, clinical experience and training modalities. In the 80s family therapy in Europe became more differentiated and established than in the USA. Several International Conferences were organised in those years in Brussels, Rome, London, Zurich, Heidelberg, Rotterdam, showing how family therapy and systemic thinking were well developed in many European countries. Then, in 1990, EFTA was born and just 2 years later I was organising the first EFTA Conference in Sorrento on a much needed topic of *Feelings and Systems*. I kept very active in the Board of EFTA for 7 years and, when I was supposed to become President at the Barcelona Conference in 1997, I resigned, not for any fear or worry, just because I realised that I was not appropriate for the structure of this Association, which was becoming too complex and political. However, through the years, I participated as a speaker to many EFTA conferences and I kept long term friendships and professional exchanges with many colleagues from any part of Europe.

A Child Centred Multigenerational Family Therapy

This chapter draws on the roots of *Relational Psychology* (Andolfi 2003) a new and fascinating discipline that utilises the triad as a unit of measure of interpersonal relationships and that, in coming decades, will make a vital contribution to other better-known disciplines such as *Dynamic Psychology and Cognitive Psychology*, that are strongly anchored in individual therapy. Such contribution will encourage rethinking and stimulate new clinical research on the primary triangle, where the father is included too on all observational models of child development, enriching and transforming the core of *Attachment Theory*. Systemic Theories pioneered a new territory in the understanding of human relationships. However, without a study into the evolutionary dynamics of the family through generations, the observation of family interactions in the here and now only provides a static picture, without offering valuable insights from the past and from how this critically influences present perspectives and future expectations.

In the observation of the family spanning several generations, an important role is given by the author to the children, who are engaged in therapy as significant relational bridges in the dialogue/clash between generations. This active role of children and adolescents, especially when they are the bearers of symptomatic behaviours, is without doubt the most original aspect of the author's long-term clinical experience and of the *multigenerational therapy* model proposed in this chapter and described in several publications (Andolfi 2003, 2016; Andolfi et al. 1989; Andolfi and Mascellani 2013). By starting with their symptoms, we can initiate a search for those relational meanings and affective connections that facilitate a retrospective journey into the previous generations. Then it is possible to return to the present with a new and constructive perspective of the family. This empowers the family to move from the passive position of delegating to the expert the solution of children's problems, to assuming an active and dynamic role, within a therapy that helps it to discover its own resources rather than highlighting its failures.

We do not deny the need to assess children presenting problems, to give individual treatment and to prescribe medication to children with severe disabilities, especially inside Institutional contexts (Children Hospital, Mental Health or Child Protection Agencies etc.). What we consider damaging is to focus only on his symptoms, reducing the child to an object of investigation and for this reason depriving him of any personal-relational competence.

The limitations and often the harm caused by the widespread categorization of mental/psychological disorders according the DSM 5 and the overwhelming use of medication for children, reinforced our conviction that the family is the best medicine, to provide the very cure of many symptomatic behaviours.

In this chapter, we would like to illustrate our primary goal, to building a solid therapeutic alliance with the family through the active collaboration of the problem-child, who becomes a sort of *co-therapist*, a special bridge to enter into the family and to identify the nodal points in family development. The presenting problem becomes the doorway to the family's world and the child a privileged guide in the exploration of still open wounds and broken emotional bonds Even when the presenting problem is related to a couple's crisis, the physical or symbolic presence of their children in the session can help to establish a better alliance with the couple and to find a positive direction, if we are able to give a voice to children in therapy (Andolfi 1994).

The model of therapy described in this chapter is *experiential*, that is to say, a special personal/professional encounter shared by therapist and family in a safe and active context. For this to happen, it is necessary for the therapist to keep in mind a multigenerational map of the family—a kind of living genogram, where he can access active resources and open healing pathways, with the curiosity of an explorer who launches with enthusiasm into an unknown world.

The chapter also highlights the cognitive and affective qualities required by therapists to enter with passion and empathy into the most difficult and painful issues of the family without a judgmental or culturally stereotyped attitude. The therapist should be able to use herself, her affective resonances, approaching and establishing physical contact with this or that family member, facilitating new connections and mending the emotional disconnections of the past. Her physical and internal presence, besides the professional one, is the most effective therapeutic instrument to make direct and authentic contact with each person. This allows the therapist to attune to the pain and desperation expressed by many families in therapy, as well as to their implicit aspects of vitality and hope, in order to transform them into elements of strength and change.

The Triangle as a Basic Unit of Observation of Children' Problems

Within the field of family therapy many authors have proposed the triangle as the unit of measurement of evolving family relationships: Bowen (1978); Framo (1992); Whitaker (1989); Walsh (1982); Haley (1976); Hoffman (1981); Minuchin (1974); Andolfi et al. (1989); Andolfi and Mascellani (2013); Andolfi (2016). At the beginning of the 1960s, Bowen was the first to introduce the theoretical concept of triangles, regarding them as the basic structures of all relationships, including those that apparently involve only two people. The triangle is the way in which the emotional forces of every relational system are organised and the dual relationship is certainly a more restricted view of a wider relational system (Bowen 1978). Closely related to the concept of triangles is the notion of triangulation, which refers to the relational dynamics within emotional triads. Haley (1976) was one of the main authors to have studied pathological triangulation in families. He proposed the definition of the characteristics that need to be present to form a *perverse triad*. This pathological triangulation is produced where a child is brought into a coalition with one parent against the other, who is disqualified in his/her role of parent. But this coalition might remain latent and denied at the explicit level. Incidentally, the main elements of Haley's perverse triad are present in the newer Parental Alienation Syndrome, where the alienating parent takes the child away from the nurturing of the vilified parent, especially in situation of very hostile marital separation or when the vilified parent comes from another country and culture. Another version of a pathological triad is defined as *favouritism*. In this case, one parent favours one child at the expense of the other children. In this process, the other parent is cut-off, indirectly alienated from the normal and necessary even-handed nurturing of all the children. Minuchin (1974) advanced the study of triadic family structures. He was interested in triangulation especially in relation to the "detouring of marital conflicts" and from this premise he described *rigid triads*. Selvini Palazzoli et al. (1989), later proposed two further dysfunctional triadic dynamics, connected to the onset of serious psychotic symptomatology in the child, which they described as *instigation and relational deceit*.

Parentification better described as *role reversal* is a very common and potentially damaging affective family distortion (Andolfi et al. 1989; Minuchin 1974; Selvini Palazzoli et al. 1978). Here the child assumes the role of caretaker over one or both parents, who are unable to perform the expected nurturing roles and to carry out adult responsibilities. The "parental child" configuration is always the result of emotional abuse and, if persistent through time, can cause severe psychosomatic and relational problems in a child or adolescent. On the other hand, many parentified children might develop a great deal of resilience and in adulthood can become very competent professionals, and sometimes, sensitive psychotherapists! The process of triangulation can also have a positive connotation, when a third person can be the stimulus for discovering hidden personal or relational resources or for the evolution of the entire system. In triadic interactions, in fact, each of the participants can observe what happens between the other two or can mediate or inform the others. For example father and mother may argue because they have different opinions on a particular matter, the child can intervene in the discussion by adopting a less controversial attitude and defusing the tension when the interaction becomes too intense. A parent can do the same, when the other spouse argues with their child, making situations more tolerable and productive. Under this perspective the presence of a third party becomes important to increase knowledge and facilitate intimacy, providing emotional support, especially during family transitions, like the one brought about by the birth of a child, or after marital separation, a sudden loss or when children leave home.

Tri-generational networks are those relational triangles in which those who are involved are placed on three different generational levels. If we add a third dimension to our observation of family functioning, we can pull together more complex aspects of current relationships and individual presenting problems. For example, if a wife has a difficult relationship with her own mother or her husband, who fail to meet her emotional demands, these demands will probably get redirected towards the daughter. The daughter's relationship with the mother, therefore, is complicated by the presence of two super-imposed components. One, which involves her directly and another, in which she becomes the mediator of a demand initially directed to someone else, as her maternal grandmother or her father (Andolfi et al. 1989; Andolfi and Mascellani 2013). The introduction of the older generation in observing the parent-child relationship has therefore allowed us, not only to observe the actual interactions among several people, but also to better understand the individual, by using the resources that emerge, once we move in and out of the present issues. Understanding the individual means to include the context in which he lives and the unit of observation cannot be only a single person. It must include all the networks of triadic relationships in which the person is involved.

The Birth of a Child: A Major Transformation in Couple Relationship

The transition from being a couple to becoming a family is a very challenging stage, which requires a shift at the cognitive and emotional level. The passion and intimacy shared by two partners as exclusive, have to open up now, to include a newcomer, the child, who becomes a priority in terms of love and care. During this transition, the adults have to learn how to remain intimate and loyal to one another through the active presence of a third person and, in this new triad, rules, roles and interpersonal space have to be redefined and transformed.

Becoming parents also involves a shift in connection, responsibilities and roles within the extended family, where the grand-parents functions and love for the child will need to be given room.

We described different family configurations according the more or less balanced position of the couple as a unit in relation to the process of personal differentiation of each partner from parents and family of origin (Andolfi 1999, 2003; Andolfi et al. 2006, 2007; Andolfi and Mascellani 2013).

In *harmonious couples* the child does not represent a threat to the couple's intimacy and love. They learn easily how to include a new dimension in their relationship and the parenthood does not interfere with their couple alliance. On the contrary, it enriches their bond and the affection and care for the child is also shared and enjoyed by the family of origin, who respects boundaries without intruding in the couple's life. If they request a therapy because of any kind of children's problem, they know how to ask for help and how to join forces and collaborate for its solution.

High-conflict couples come for couple therapy because they are in deep crisis caused by competition, mutual misunderstanding, betrayal etc. Sometimes they come to therapy because of their suffering or the sense of failure in the marriage, together with the fear of a difficult separation. Often they are brought to therapy because of psychosomatic, behavioural or relational problems manifested by one of their children. We describe this situation as *camouflaged couple therapy* (Andolfi 1994; Andolfi et al. 2007; Andolfi and Mascellani 2013). The initial request is based on the children's symptoms while, in reality, the real problem is the couple's relationship, where complicity and alliance have been transformed in mutual mistrust and resentment, often reinforced by the intrusiveness of family of origin of one or both partners. It is rather common that one partner has been too dependent and submissive from parents while the other one might have suffered from a long term cut-off from his/her own family of origin and roots.

Therefore, the child's development might be at risk with high conflict couples, and we can expect a variety of child triangulations.

Unstable couples are made up of two very insecure and lonely people, who experienced similar condition of neglect or detachment from their own families. In this case, the attraction between the partners seems strongly centred on their mutual deprivation of care. This situation might be very painful, and sooner or later, an unstable couple will search for reassurance. If, it is not forthcoming from parents and extended family, and neither from their relationship and even less from each partner, because of lack of self-esteem, they will expect safety and security from the new born child. He runs a serious risk of becoming easily a parental child, who has to learn quickly how to care and support two vulnerable parents. The same expectation can guide implicitly a request of adoption. In this case too, the child might be thought as a solution to their immaturity.

The Assessment of the Sibling Relationship

Siblings grow up, mature and get often old together. The sibling bond covers all phases of the family life cycle. They are witnesses and active participants in all kinds of family events.

In this respect, Minuchin (1974) defined the sibling relationship as the "keeper of the family frontier". In fact, the relationship between siblings represents the first social laboratory where children can cement their relationships as peers. In this context, children support or isolate each other, accuse each other and learn from one another. In this world of peers, children learn to negotiate, to cooperate and to compete. Siblings are often neglected in therapy, especially when adopting a medical model, which focuses mostly on individual symptoms and very little on family development. Why to invite siblings if the issue is to fix up the problem of one specific child?

A relational assessment, on the other hand, can benefit from the presence of the sibling subsystem in joint family sessions. Their participation is an excellent opportunity to evaluate the permeability of family boundaries, the presence of positive or negative triangulations in the family's history, to explore sibling alliance, early parentification or emotional disconnections. Sometimes they are caused by family unfairness and coalition, related to child age, gender, physical feature, favouritism etc.

A very important element attesting to the quality of the relationship between siblings is what Bank and Kahn (1982) define as "level of access". Belonging to the same gender and age proximity determines high access. For example, when siblings play together, attend the same school, share the same friends and common life events, their relationship is characterised by reciprocity, and empathy, and by the sharing of emotional experiences. This might lead to an intimate and tight bond, qualified by a high degree of loyalty, which might be even deeper in situation of inadequate or dysfunctional parental presence.

At the other extreme, siblings with low access often belong to opposite genders or have an age gap which does not allow for the sharing of family events: sometimes they don't even live in the same house, and they might act as if they belong to different generations. Low access can also be caused by hostile marital separation. In this case, children can be split or have to take side with one of the parents against the other.

Moreover, nowadays the growing number of step-families has caused an increase in siblings with a low level of access, with a large age difference between the children of the first marriage and the children of the new couple and, sometimes, older siblings become envious of the newcomers.

In our clinical practice, we also found the opposite situation, with children who were close in age but totally incapable of collaborating and sharing life experiences, as well as siblings of widely different ages, where the eldest became a kind of hero for the youngest, a guide to follow in times of difficulties.

In short, the horizontal relationship between siblings, regardless of gender and age, depends greatly on how much the parents allow their children to become siblings, without triangulating them negatively and without involving them in their couple dynamics, which sometimes undermine the natural generational alliance between siblings.

When we observe siblings in the same room, during a family session, it is very easy to make a family assessment. By the way, in which young children can play freely together or create physical distance refusing to participate in common activities, we can make hypotheses on the family's functioning.

Once, during a session with a family with four children, I asked to the firstborn girl Zoe, 10 years old.

T.: “Where, would you like to stay? Playing with the other children on the floor or sitting between your parents”?
Zoe: “Playing with my siblings”.
T.: “Then, come down”.
Zoe: (almost crying) “I cannot!”

The Child as a Co-therapist

Unlike individual therapy, where the alliance needs to be formed by the dyad therapist-patient, things get more complex when we have to build an alliance with the family as a group.

When an individual client asks for help, she knows what she is looking for, has a personal motivation and an idea of what to get from therapy. When a couple asks for help, we first need to understand whether one partner brought the other one to therapy—sometimes pushing or forcing the second to join—or whether they have a shared motivation. Then, we need to understand the nature of the problem and their definition of it and, often, we should expect possible disagreements at many levels. To the simple question: “How long have you been experiencing this difficulty in your relationship”? one might answer: ”For the last six months” and the other might state: “For more than 15 years”.

The situation is even more complex when we have two generations in the room, like two parents and a child, who presents a psychological or psychosomatic problem. One parent might push for therapy, while the other is against it, or has come just to accompany the anxious partner. Or it might be, that one had in mind therapy to help the child and the other would, instead, like to fix the marriage through the child’s problem. Not to mention the possibility that the problematic child might totally disagree with the parents' idea of looking for help through psychotherapy, denying any need for personal help.

So, how do we build an alliance with the entire family, which will transform competition or disagreement into collaboration and commitment in therapy? And how, as therapists, do we avoid the risk of taking sides with one part of the family unit, as more or less happens with children when they get triangulated and split up?

We have been facing these crucial questions for a number of years in our clinical practice. In the early years, we experienced and described an attempt to protect the child from being the scapegoat in the family, by replacing him in the rigid family interactions. Becoming ourselves the temporary target of family projections, we took a very central position in the session (Andolfi et al. 1983).

Later on, through our own mistakes and our better use of a triadic model, we were able to build up quickly an alliance with each family member, together with a solid “meta-alliance” with the family as a group. Instead of positioning ourselves as the third side of the primary triangle, we were able to move in and out of the interactions and become a relational link, capable of activating different family triadic configurations on three-generational levels.

The therapeutic relationship creates a dynamic movement between each person and the family as a whole, between the past and the present. Therefore we need to understand and take into equal consideration the reality presented by each member of the family/couple. It is like being a "juggler" and playing with three/four balls concurrently with enough self-confidence, while being careful not to lose any of the balls!

By being aware that it is impossible to enter into earlier family and individual experiences and transform past history, it becomes possible to construct a new story with the family.

The greatest challenge in dealing with problematic children and adolescents has been how to free them from the label of being the patient. At the same time, we have been very careful to avoid giving ourselves the label of expert and, for that reason, we work towards empowering parents for the sake of their children as quickly as possible.

In several publications (Andolfi 1994, 2016; Andolfi et al. 1989, 2007; Andolfi and Mascellani 2013) we have described the problem child as co-therapist or consultant. The best and quickest way to de-label the child is to transform her into a subject of competence from the very beginning of family sessions. The first, almost obvious question routinely posed to the parents by the therapist: "What's the problem with your child or how can I help you with your child?" This can be changed by asking the child directly: "How can we (you and me) help your family today?"

The child might be surprised and reply: "I don't know. They (parents) brought me here!"

The therapist might continue: "Your problems brought your parents here, therefore we can explore how your problems can help your family."

The Art of Reframing Children' Problems

Reframing has been a well-used relational modality in the repertoire of the systemic therapist since the earliest experimentations of the group at the Mental Research Institute of Palo Alto (Watzlawick, Beavin and Jackson 1967). In its original formulation, reframing was understood as a predominantly, but not exclusively, verbal strategy that provided a new way to look and interpret symptoms and mis behaviours. Once "re-framed", they could change meaning.

The process of reframing has been greatly elaborated in family therapy up to recent times (Elkaim 1990; Cade 1992; Flaskas 1992; Fourie 2010; Sluzki 1992; Sprenkle et al. 2009). It profoundly inspired Milton Erikson's work on hypnosis (Erickson et al. 1976), the strategic work of Jay Haley (1976), the positive connotation of the Milan group (Selvini Palazzoli et al. 1978), the shift from problem to resource of Brief Focused Therapy (De Shazer 1985). It also influenced the Narrative Therapy of White and Epston (1989), with a shift of focus from the problem to the person, through the externalisation of symptoms.

In the redefinition of the child presenting problem, we have been inspired by Keeney's original method (1983) in its description of the therapeutic conversation as a "visit to the museum", moving from a gallery of presentation to one of therapy. For example, decomposing the sentence "exploration of the parents' history" into its three words, we could take the word "exploration" and move it: thus, we would no longer be exploring the parents' history but, perhaps, explore the animal world and, in so doing, we would change the entire meaning of the sentence and of the conversational content.

Re-framing the problem and shifting the context of the encounter to a family exploration (Andolfi 1979a, b) can have a number of advantages It elicits curiosity in the child towards the therapist, who is asking for his help. This might implicitly encourages a collaboration from parents, who see a therapist eager to look at their child's problem in a positive way.

Therefore, children's symptoms can be reframed and transformed from individual symptoms to relational indicators. They can be linked to the affective, behavioural characteristics of a family member or to the dramatic or painful events, that marked the developmental history of the family. A child's encopresis can be transformed into a special "glue" to keep the parents together. An anorectic behaviour can become an extreme request for the mother's love. A school phobia can become a protective device to defend a mother from the father's violence A very angry face can be a "scream" to get the parents' attention A depressed child through his eyes can convey the sadness of mum or dad.

Let us see an example.

John, 10 years old has been presenting encopresis for the past years. Therefore, John crapping in his pants was the first link between family and therapist. John's poo offered the opportunity to meet two divorced parents, who have never been able to fully separate as a couple, keeping the child in the middle of their unfinished business.

If John's poo was a big gift for his parents when he was a small child, maybe, it is another gift at a different developmental stage. Perhaps, now it is the glue that holds together two partners in a very dysfunctional way, because they keep accusing each other of being the cause of the psychosomatic symptoms of the child.

If the therapist is able to play with the image of the poo-glue, he might help parents to stop pushing John in their controversy and to separate. Then John can give up from his function as a bridge, which is not needed anymore and stop crapping in his pants!

The Genogram: The Map of the Family World

This research for family's main events can be carried out, by drawing together *the family genogram*. Children get very curious and active in making the genogram. They have the same interest in exploring the family history as they can have in exploring the map of the world, looking for a specific country, town or ocean. With the help of the therapist, they can outline very important nodal points in family life: painful losses or chronic diseases, couple splitting up as well as sadness related to emigration and cut-off from family and community. In the same time, the parents can be involved deeply in the session by remembering important family events.

We can also explore more in details the structure of the extended family. Often parents are overinvolved with one side of the family of origin, while distant from the other side and children internalise the distortion out of their sense of duty and loyalty. The genogram might reflect this unbalance; one part of the genogram might look obscure, unknown or distant, while the other one seems more relevant, or dominant or caring. In this way, we can learn how the nuclear family is emotionally linked with members of previous generations, or detached from them. Sometimes children tell us very quickly that they never had contact, affection or emotional bond with one set of grand-parents, while they visit frequently and love the other set of grand-parents, including uncles, aunts etc. From this information we can activate a process of emotional transformation, programing a special session, where the most involved family of origin will be invited. Then the distant side of the family can be invited to another session and it is very common to understand better about cut-offs and broken connections in the family development and the consequences of that on the younger generations.

Helping Your Father Is Your Mission?

Alì is an 11-year-old boy presenting problems of anxiety and school refusal. Parents emigrated from Algeria to France long time before his birth. Alì has an older sister with a very dark skin, but she refuses to belong to an Arabic family and denies completely her roots. She is proud to grow up as a French adolescent, while both parents consider Paris, where they live, as a "golden prison". They do not have friends and live with the sorrow and the pain of what they left behind. The consultation starts with family and myself, seating around a small table exploring the genogram and looking at the map of North Africa. Ali is very active in the drawing of the genogram, indicating on the map the town where family came from. Then, I asked the boy to help me to "enter in the Algerian grief" and the mother burst in tears because of the "loss of her parents", who live in Algiers and she could not see them for many years. Father too looks very sad because, just before Ali's birth, he lost his own father, the only person left from his family. In a few minutes, we moved from Ali's school issues to enter in very tough family dilemmas. Two parents in despair for long term losses and cut-offs an adolescent girl who cannot take the family grief and feel a stranger in her own family; a little boy who seems to be destined to carry on his shoulder a big weight.

This is a little segment of the dialogue between myself and the boy in the middle of the session, which illustrates well how parents who lost their secure base (Country, Parents, Community), can "program a child" to be over-responsible and over-caring. Fortunately, children can express with their body and their behaviour their deep discomfort for long-term "role reversal functions". It is up to therapists to join their symptoms in order to be guided by children in the complex family world.

Therapist: "Who is more in need: you of dad or dad of you?"
Alì: "Dad of me!"
Therapist: "The danger is that for an 11 years boy to carry on his shoulder other 60 years (the age of the father) could be too much!"
Alì: "From the moment in which I was born things function like that".
Therapist: "Then helping your father is your mission".
Alì: "Yes, yes".
Therapist: "Can you show me how do you embrace him? As a child or an old caring man?"
Alì: (before embracing him) "When I embrace dad, I almost suffocate him!!"

Children are witnesses to adult relationships from the moment they are born and even before, if we think that the formation of the primary triad begins during the pregnancy. Therefore, they have learnt a great deal about their parents and can inform the therapist about their vision of family life, if we are able to give them voice in therapy. But, the main goal of activating the child is to create a special emotional climate in the session, where parents can feel safe and reflect on the most significant events of their life, overcoming prejudices and blockages. Sometimes when parents are very depressed or feeling lonely, the therapist can ask the child to underline with a marker on the genogram the person/s who have been very important/caring for mum or dad in their growing older. We find useful to introduce the metaphor of the "lighthouse" to refer to the person who has been as a real guide for one or the other parent, to cope with life adversities. Looking for positive resources allow people in despair to get more connected with their resilience and to find the strength to go on with life.

Often children's voices get ignored when their parents are in turmoil. Unfortunately, many therapists and Child Protection Institutions collude with the parents in the idea that children are better off if they are not included in the family battlefield. Plus, too often children's symptoms are assessed as they would belong only to the child and treated in individual therapy, making children to believe that they are the problem. Through experience, we have found that this protective exclusion is, in fact, based on prejudices and in the professionals' inability to elicit children's genuine resources, to play with them and to learn from their simple and immediate language. If we are ready to listen to them and to respect their opinions, children will offer information, hope, sensitivity and a fervent desire to help the parents to be more harmonious.

Once, a therapist prepared a very detailed genogram: the identified patient, a young girl with a severe phobia, was represented by a circle, coloured in solid yellow, to underline that she was the problem in the family. In order to further highlight the difference from the other signs—white square signs for men and white circles for women—I started the consultation by playing with that yellow colour. Indicating the yellow circle in the genogram I said to the girl: "This is you, you are all yellow, because you are different from everybody else". Then, I encouraged her to take me inside her family story in order to find together other yellow signs. In 1 h, we discovered so many other problems and dramas in previous generations that

I could say to her: "Your yellow circle looks so relative and small at the end of the session, while at the beginning it seemed like the big problem of the family". She looked at me, feeling very reassured and supported and said: "You are right" and everybody understood.

Making Family Contracts in the Session

The therapeutic contract is a very productive and concrete task, which can be proposed by therapist, discussed by all family members until his final formulation, with a series of contents and rules that must be respected. The contract, once prepared has to be undersigned by everybody as a sign of commitment.

Contracts can be very useful with enmeshed families, where boundaries are confused or too permeable, where there is an open hostility in a couple's relationship or between parents and kids; in general, when triangulations and no respect for rules create confusion and suffering in family life.

Making a contract represents also a concrete way to test how everybody is engaged in therapy, committed to reaching a common goal and respectful of the therapist in his function of coach of the family team. Children love to be a relevant part of the family contract, because they like to be included in family projects where they can contribute with competence and creativity. Let's see an example, which outlines the main principles of the multigenerational approach, described in this chapter.

An Impossible Couple and Two Mature Boys

Jonathon and Joel are 11 and 9 years old. Therapeutic intervention is requested because the paediatrician checked Joel's headache and stomachaches and concluded that stress was causing child's symptoms.

In fact, stress and persistent tension among the two parents are the predominant moods in the family daily life and I could feel that myself during the two meetings with them: the first only with the parents, the second together with the children, when the contract was prepared and signed. The couple's relationship was very bad with escalating conflict on everything.

Anne and David met in Europe where they were studying and the mutual attraction was very strong. Anne's family was living in New Zealand while David' family lived in Belgium. For love David moved to a new continent, leaving behind him two caring parents, a younger and successful brother, his friends, his job at the University. Basically, he lost all his previous affective and working connections for a new land, he didn't like from the beginning, where he still feels a stranger twelve years later. David and Anne married and moved back to New Zealand while the wife was pregnant with Jonathon, because she wanted to deliver and grow up her child in her own

Country with the love and care of her parents, to which she is emotionally attached and over-dependent.

Love is gone from long time and both parents feel distant from each other; mistrust and arguing for everything are the main relational components in their daily life, plus they talk openly and very negatively of each other's family of origin in front of the children. They both love the children, for David they are the only precious thing left in his present life, for Anne a way to maintain a deep, emotional link with her parents, who are getting older and sick.

In the first, very difficult session, David and Anne tried to push me in their battlefield and I could imagine the painful position of the two young boys, constantly triangulated by insecure and angry parents. However, they accepted my proposal to invite the kids to the next session, reporting that the first session had been very good! (probably because "I survived" and I didn't accept to sit on the side of one or the other). I asked them to prepare well the session with them. I suggested them to talk together with the children with no animosity, explaining to them that I like to listen to children voice in order to help adults to become better parents. I also suggested parents to cancel individual counselling for Joel, because he was not responsible for the stress in the family, and it was not good for him to become a little patient.

Family arrived and I joined the children very easily: they are both soccer players and I was curious to know their position in the soccer field, their favourite players and team. Having an 11 years boy myself, it was easy for me to talk about x-box and children digital world. They were cute and very collaborative. I shared with the parents my positive thoughts about the children and complimented them for the good qualities of the kids, in spite of the fact they were constantly pushed in parents' battles for predominance.

Then, I suggested the family to make a therapeutic contract, asking the children to write down the contents of it after discussion with parents. Jonathon was acting as the family expert, understanding very well the idea of a plan to stop open conflicts and children triangulation at home. Joel was very active too, using his own creativity.

I introduced the soccer metaphor of the yellow and red cards to punish minor or major bad actions in the field and the boys identified three main areas of bad behaviour of both parents in front of the kids: arguing, swearing and talking negatively of the in-laws. David and Anne were both impressed by the children honesty and clarity and could easily agree on the points presented by their sons. Everybody, me included, signed the contract; parents could continue to disagree and argue, but they had to avoid any interaction which would include children in their marital conflict. Jonathon and Joel had to keep a diary, writing down the content and the circumstance of each "bad action", which has to be punished with a red or yellow card.

Beside this plan, I anticipated to Anne and David my second therapeutic request. Too encounter in the near future their own families to better understand and appreciate each partner's personal development, but without entering into marital issues. Anne's parents were old, but they lived at the end of the road and that would make easier to invite them to one session. For David was more complicated because of the distance, but he suggested the possibility of a skype session with his family in Belgium.

Therefore, the family contract was a concrete way to re-establishing boundaries and respect for Jonathan and Joel: The proposed meetings with family of origin had several goals. To learn about David's affective position in his own family constellation and his cut-offs from them and his country. While the session with Anne's parents would have explored her dependency and loyalty, as well as her fears to lose them, who seem to be the main security device in her life.

Building Metaphors with Children

We already described in previous publications (Andolfi et al. 1989, 2007) the usefulness of constructing metaphorical images and objects in therapy. In reality, constructing metaphors is one of the best ways to strengthen a therapeutic alliance with the family. Often is the family itself that brings metaphorical images to the session and the therapist can join them and suggest new relational meanings. At other times, the therapist might offer an image that represents the family's intricate relational bonds.

Whitaker called this way of working "metaphorization process" to highlight its characteristics of connection and sharing. We will limit ourselves to mentioning only some of the dozens of metaphors that exist in the language of families so that, we will be better able to understand the therapeutic meanings of metaphors and use these in a clinical setting.

"I feel like a caged bird"; "My children have been growing under a bell jar"; "I feel like a doormat, trampled on by all"; "He built a wall between us"; "I feel as empty as a squeezed lemon"; "He treats the house as a hotel, coming and going as he pleases", "I feel like a worm".

The language of images allows a special match between feelings, relational difficulties and concrete objects to take place: the cage, the s bell jar, the doormat, the wall, the lemon, the hotel, the worm can become important pieces of the therapeutic puzzle in our search for transformation in the quality of family relationships.

Let's see the use of metaphoric language in the following clinical dialogue (Andolfi 2016).

The Locked Door

A mother brings Vincent, her 16 year-old son, to therapy because he is always locking himself in his room to play on the computer. The parents have been divorced for some years and Vincent does not see his father "because he doesn't want to upset his mother".

T (therapist): "So, the reason you have brought your son to therapy is because his door is always locked?"

M (mother):" Yes, I don't think it's normal that when he's at home he locks himself in his room".

T: "What is it that's not normal?" "That he locks his room because he's sad or because he doesn't want to speak to you?"

M: "Because he plays on the computer all the time".

T: "When you were a child, did anyone in your family lock their door?"

M:" Yes, it was often my mother and I really hated that."

T: "So, you don't like people who lock their door."

M: "No, no".

T: "But in fact it is really YOU who locks the biggest door!" (relational statement)

M: "I don't understand. Could you please explain it to me?"

T: (addressing the son) "Would you like to explain it to mum?"

Vincent: "As I don't feel I can go to my father's, that is the door you have locked."

M: "Yes, that's true."

T: (addressing the son) "But what is it that stops you from opening the door of your house and going to see your father?"

Vincent: "Because she doesn't like him."

T: "I know many wives who don't like their husbands, but their children use their legs and go and see their fathers, spend time with them and enjoy their company. But, if you are locked in your room, how can you knock on his door?"

Vincent: "Yes, that's how it is."

T: "Was he really such a bad father?"

Vincent: "Not with me, but with my mother, yes!"

T: "So, if your mother tell you… I have no problem if you want to see him. Would you like to see him?"

Vincent: "Yes, I would like that very much!"

After this session, many doors will be opened!

Physical Contact to Creating Connections

Physical contact is one of the essential elements in human development, a profound way of communicating, a critical component in the health and development of the child and a powerful force in healing illness (Bowlby and Robertson 1952). Montagu (1971) asserted that a lack of tactile stimuli in infancy gave rise to an inability to establish relationships involving touch with others. Starting from these premises, studies on baby observation and Attachment Theory have led to extraordinary results in the understanding of child development.

In our clinical work, we always try to integrate language—the questions we ask this or that family member—with eye contact, bodily movements. Physical contact represents, without a doubt, a positive reinforcement of the therapeutic relationship and has the power to transmit warmth, closeness and connection better than any word. Certainly, working with children in therapy has helped us to unblock our creative, child-self from the excess of "adult" always present in every therapist, too often burdened by a sense of duty and responsibility.

There are many symbolic ways of greeting such as shaking hands, high-fiving young people or a pat on the shoulder, that may be viewed simply as ritual ways of taking leave. However, even these greetings can convey very meaningful messages.

For example, the warmth and strength of a father's handshake at the end of a session can communicate a feeling of gratitude towards the therapist; a satisfaction about what happened in the meeting or a gesture to confirm a desire to engage in therapy. The same applies to "giving a high-five" to an adolescent, or a pat on the shoulder, as if to say: "We did it!"

In previous publications (Andolfi 1979b; Andolfi et al. 2007; Andolfi and Mascellani 2013), we described the active use of the space and how to ask a child or adolescent to move chairs and come closer to the therapist in order to increase the therapeutic alliance. This movement can be followed by a complicit glance, a physical contact intended to transmit an affective connection or the understanding of a relational difficulty. At other times, it might represent a kind of challenge to confront the child with a specific situation, perhaps using plastic toys to mimic fighting, such as a hammer, an axe or a sword and so on.

Contact can be mediated through the exchange of objects, of parts of clothing such as a hat, a scarf or a shoe, that can be taken and passed to another family member, to facilitate connection with the other person. All this must have an objective, which is always that of conveying a message of empathy and an understanding of the relational problems.

From our clinical observations, we can confirm that many fears, hidden desires, emotional disconnections, myths and family secrets reappear during the course of family therapy and that this unfinished business of the past can find, through present difficulties, an opportunity for resolution. The reconstruction of interrupted bonds has significant repercussions in couple's relationships, in parenting, in the general wellbeing and health of children. For anyone who has not been able to satisfy the primary needs for care and love during their upbringing, therapy with the family can be a safe and welcoming context for repairing interrupted or damaged bonds. This mending operation represents the best treatment for resolving intergenerational conflicts and couple's crises. Touching has a fundamental place and value in healing old, but still open wounds, and the therapist can play the role of a relational bridge.

Yvonne and the Magic Wand

Yvonne is an 8-year-old girl that mother got out of wedlock in Zambia. Child's father disappeared and mother's parents sent daughter to study and work in Sydney. Mother had a poor relationship with her parents. She did not see Yvonne for 6 years, speaking with her on the phone from time to time and receiving a few photos of her growing up.

Grandfather brought the child for a visit in Australia when Yvonne was 6. After that visit, child became very angry and distant from mother. Two years later the child got a Visa and moved to live with her in Australia. But now, she is angry, distant and defiant to mum. Runs away in the playground, refuses to go home, wants to stay with friends, and does not listen to mum, who had to work full time.

Mother wants her, but she focusses only on Yvonne doing practical things like homework and bedtime, but she does not know how to bond and develop any emotional connection with the girl. Yvonne is missing her grand-pa and mum is not coping, thinking of sending the girl back to Zambia.

In the consultation I had with them, I could see from the beginning their difficulty to connect as mother and child. They have been strangers to each other for almost 8 years! I tried, first, to create a bond with the girl, asking her to show me where Zambia was on the map of the world, recollecting memories of my visit to the Victoria Falls on the Zambian side. Yvonne was very excited because she could remember too her visit with grand-pa to these gigantic falls, the second tallest in the world!

Then I tried to encourage Yvonne to check Australia on the map and to indicate where Sydney was located and to include the mother too in this search. Looking together to places in the map was the first step to get them closer and more relaxed. Toward the end of the session, I gave a "magic wand" to the child, to see if the wand would make possible to embrace mum, because this very concrete expression of love was missing in their new life together. Yvonne accepted the invitation and mother too, but the girl broke away from mum very quickly. I encouraged her to try again, saying that she has the "magic wand" to open mum's heart, but that they both needed more practice and time to do that, in order to feel their mutual love. Yvonne embraced mum again and mum responded with much more intensity, crying for the joy. This was the first healing moment to re-establishing a real bond.

I have been encouraging the expression of affection and love in therapy any time I felt that embracing, hugging, kissing, cuddling would be useful to repair broken connections in a safe and trusting context. A father can embrace a little toddler when he is not sure to be a good father and by doing so, can feel reassured A depressed mother can hug an angry preadolescent boy and relax him. A man can holds hands and embrace a mother after many years of disconnection and distance A brother and a sister can embrace tenderly after long-term competition and lack of complicity Two partners can share a kiss to move to a new chapter of their relationship etc. The therapy room is an extraordinary place to experience new forms of care and tenderness, which have been missing for too long in family relationships.

Being Direct with Children: Toward Authenticity

Being direct is a real antidote to protectiveness and political correctness, which both operate according to the relational scheme of hiding difficult realities or truths from persons—mostly children—considered fragile and vulnerable; a kind of defence, to avoid the "danger" of facing conflicts and losses in affective relationship. As we recently described (Andolfi and Mascellani 2013; Andolfi 2016) being direct implies the ability to be authentic and to go to the heart of the matter, without beating about the bush. It is a relational skill whose aim is to relate to everyone with true curiosity and openness. By being clear about our opinions and intuitions, we can get in touch with our clients' conflicts and suffering without hesitation or prejudice. Being direct could result in a kind of therapeutic provocation, but it is very different from being directive, which implies a certain level of authoritarianism and imposition on other people's opinions. In regard to children, I often say that for them *the worst truth is better than the best lie!* But how often, parents and therapists, do prefer to lie about difficult truths or to keep secrets in order to protect children?

Being direct is a very important therapeutic skill because it helps us to reassure and give people permission to open up on painful issues. But, family secrets cannot always be addressed easily because of the lack of mutual trust among family members and with the therapist. To force people to disclose secrets or reveal lies can be damaging and abusive. Therapists must learn about right timing and the quality of the therapeutic relationship must be safe to permit family transformations. They also need to feel very comfortable and serene within themselves in order to be authentic and direct.

I remember the incredible courage of a father, who, during a session, was finally able to inform their young boy affected by haemophilia how the parents had reacted to the news of his illness, when in the hospital. Very moved, with the child on his knees, the father revealed his incredible happiness at his birth, and how "the world seemed to fall down on him" the following day, when he was informed of the problem. At that point I encouraged the boy to acknowledge the father's courage and, even more, the respect he showed towards him by sharing his deepest feelings with him; the child then put his head on his father's chest and kissed him!

It is important to mention that, for a long time, both parents had denied even the fact that haemophilia was a serious medical condition, treating the child as if he had the flu. Being direct as a therapist and gaining the trust of parents and child gave the permission to the parents to shift from keeping an impossible lie to revealing their feelings and accepting a difficult reality, in a context of mutual love and respect.

Even more significant was the situation with a father and his two adolescent boys. The father brought the boys to consultation for a minor school issue with one of them, but as soon as I asked the kids the very simple question: "where is mum?" the father's face transformed and became pale and wordless. The children gave a very vague answer, saying that mother had died in hospital of some kind of illness 4 years earlier, but they had never asked the father for an explanation during the intervening years.

While the session was progressing I intuitively moved more directly to the mother's mystery, also motivated by the fact that during a previous phone conversation the father had informed me that his wife had died and, after a long pause, that: "she had committed suicide, but the children didn't know about it." Therefore, I encourage dad to speak with the children as with two mature kids, not as two little boys. He felt so reassured and safe that he was able to open up, describing in details the circumstances of her suicide, while the children held hands: they were finally hearing a very sad truth, which was much more acceptable then remaining suspended in a kind of limbo.

Playing and Playfulness in Child Centred Family Therapy

Playing and playfulness represent the most articulate and personal means of engaging the family and the therapist in the therapeutic encounter. It is, nonetheless, still little used by family therapists, who prefer by far an adult and serious model of communication. Perhaps the discomfort that the therapist encounters in playing is related to his difficulty in moving from understanding emotional situations to representing them in the session. While understanding is based on a cognitive analysis of verbal data, ludic representation has an element of make-believe that allows to dramatise desires, fears and painful experiences through words and actions.

In order to play, in contrast to observing play, it is necessary for the therapist to rediscover firstly the value of playing for herself and then to suggest it as a vehicle for interacting and searching for resources in therapy. This requires the therapist to learn to use herself and her own personal characteristics, such as gender, age, way of laughing or speaking, getting closer or moving away, modulating them according to the needs of the situation (Andolfi et al. 1989).

If the therapist knows how to take on different parts and roles in the session and, above all, if he knows how to move from one generational level to another—playing now the child, now the old sage—family members will be able to move out of the same stereotyped functions and become unblocked (Whitaker and Keith 1981).

Playing with Words

Playing with words helps to construct a metaphoric language that originates from images that paint, and sometimes camouflage or transform, deep moods, denied fears and conflicts, and dysfunctional relational patterns. Such a language, built on visual images, has a much longer and deeper period of permanence and of cognitive resonance than a language based on abstract concepts or on verbal statements in session.

The curiosity sparked by the language of images, kept purposely cryptic and incomplete, helps to tempt the individual and the whole family to participate in a therapeutic story belonging to all.

Playing with Objects

The use of metaphorical language and metaphorical objects are based on our ability to play with our clients through images, in order to create or discover relevant connections (Andolfi 1979a, b, 2016; Andolfi et al. 1983, 1989; Andolfi and Mascellani 2013).

We refer to tangible objects chosen by the therapist or by family members for their aptness to represent behaviours, relationships, interactive processes or rules of the family in treatment.

These objects allow the therapist to "play" with what he observes, meaning by play the creative fantasy that stimulates him to produce new associative links. He offers them to the family, urging them, in turn, to participate by playing with their own associations.

A little crown, a hat, a shoe, a pile of books, a ball, a tie, a little mask, a scarf, a doll, a plastic sword, a family drawing, a world map, an empty or high chair etc. are objects that can be used in the session and transformed into relational links. They can change shape and meaning, depending on their contextual frame and the intensity with which they are attached to different people's functions and to specific sets of interactions.

Several examples of metaphorical objects are described in my books because of their profound impact on people's conflicts and fears. The alternation between the concrete and the abstract, between reality and metaphor introduces uncertainty and probability into the therapeutic system, opening new doors for change. Plus, it produces a sense of lightness and playfulness because of the "as if" quality of the message in substitution of the yes/no logic of common language.

A very convincing proof of the usefulness of metaphors—through language and objects—came from long term research on the follow up of family therapy reported in the book *La Terapia narrata dalla Famiglia* (Andolfi et al. 2001).

To the question posed to several families after treatment—from 3 to 5 years later—about what they remembered most from the therapeutic process, a very frequent answer was around the reverberation and efficacy of specific metaphorical objects, like the ones described above, on their family life. They would mention the object as a familiar presence in the house, often laughing while responding to the question.

Playing with Toys and the Therapist's Own Small Objects

Of course, it is very easy to start playing with children and, apart from the toys in the therapy room, the therapist might offer his own toys to start a special conversation, which often allows the inclusion of siblings and parents in the picture. It is very good to play with children and adults in session, just in order to enjoy playing, especially when this is not a common experience in the house. Children might say: "They don't play with me: my dad is too busy at work or my mum is too busy in the house". Most of the time, playing becomes a relational language to reach family issues and worries about children's problems or marital conflict in a very powerful and relaxed way because, after all, "this is just playing", with the positive result of removing the adults' concerns and rigid thinking.

Personally, I always go to a session with a little object in my hands: it is generally something like a slinky or a flexible thing for my hands to play with. Sometimes I can hold it as a way of concentrating on my inner dialogue, by looking at it and manipulating it for a short time, moving out of the intensity of the session. In other situations, I like to pass it to a family member: a problem child, an overinvolved mother or a detached father, to transmit my presence or to send a specific message.

Toddlers and Pre-school Children in Family Therapy

I would like to conclude this chapter by describing briefly how to engage toddlers and small children in family therapy. When therapists have incorporated a triadic lens in looking at family interactions, it is possible to observe the triad even when child is still in mum's womb. It is amazing to see how emotions and love can be expressed and shared by touching wife's belly or by listening to the baby's kick from inside. It is also very illuminating to look to people faces and at the way in which a parent or a grandparent hold and pass the baby to another family member during a session. Through these small gestures and interactions, we can observe family's preferred patterns of communications and affective organisation.

When a couple is in love you see caring movements with the little child, who can be held, shared and passed freely. A totally different story is when the couple is splitting or is in a big crisis.

Let us see a short clinical dialogue:

Marianne, a 3 years old girl, was playing on the floor next to mum, who was totally absorbed by her play, while father was seating two chairs distant from mother and child, in silence as he did not belong there.

This was just a simple and clear picture of the family dynamics when I entered the therapy room to meet them. After a few minutes the family problem was on the table: Mario loves the daughter but he doesn't seem able to have any access to her who belongs to mum; Rosa is very sad for the marital crisis, and holds the girl as she is her property and her security system too. Rosa is lonely, her family lives far away in Puerto Rico and Mario is very dependent and enmeshed with his own Italian of origin family, even more recently, after the loss of his own mother, and all his attention and energy go to them.

I started playing on the floor with Marianne while giving words to family discomfort, saying "through the girl" that in the family there were two marriages, mum and Marianne on one side and dad and his own family on the other. Then I asked Marianne if she belonged to both parents and if she would like to go and sit on father knees, to see if dad could hold and cuddle her for a while. Marianne trotted a long way to reach Mario, but she could stay on dad's knees only a few seconds. Father did not do anything to make her comfortable. I asked Marianne to go back and kiss him too. She went back, kissed dad and Mario embraced her with tenderness. She remained there, while I sent a verbal message to both parents.

> Mario, now try to relax and feel your baby on your body; she loves you, but you are too busy with your family memories and sorrow. Your head is too crowded to take care of Marianne. Then, if you want your wife back, you have to divorce from your Italian family and Rosa has to divorce from this little girl. If you two are able to remarry, Marianne can share her love with both of you and feel safe.

Conclusion

This chapter describes my 45 years' journey in family therapy through several continents. In my search for family resources and family healing, I never travelled alone: the child accompanied me everywhere I went. His/her love and care for the parents and for the members of the extended family he belongs to, have been lighting up the road to get in touch with family issues.

Children are aware whether therapists really want to help their families in distress or if they perform a job or, even worse, if they become judgmental or rude because of the objective difficulties to find a solution. Children are by nature "systemic thinkers". They do not learn about triads through books or University degrees. They are part of the primary triad and they are witnesses of their parents' behaviour and emotional bonds from the period in which they were in mom's stomach (unconsciously) until their adult life. Too often therapists do not care to understand and recognise children's competence and knowledge about their own families. They believe more the adults' truths and explanations about family events, without giving space to children and listening to their voice.

I got relevant teachers and mentors during my professional development but, certainly, children have been the most profound source of understanding about family relationships and a great inspiration for expanding my creativity and humanity. I always played with their symptoms, looking for the best way to reframe them and bridging them to family events and conflict. I learnt that children like "deals" as I do. The implicit message in the deal is: "I know how to help your parents, but you have to help me by stopping your misbehaviour or psychosomatic disorder". Children are very skilful in transforming their own behaviour in order to seek peace and love in the family. Nevertheless, getting back harmony in the family is only a final step. First, therapist has to identify and work on family wounds and unfinished business of the past. Then parents can relax, overcome their conflicts and recreate positive connections. Let us see an example. A 12 years old girl had sleep problems from very young age and forced one of the parents to stay in her room all night in order to rest. This was an endless ritual, which created a great deal of stress in the family. Miraculously, she was "cured" after a dramatic family session, in which the father recreated the scenario of the domestic violence himself witnessed at age 12. With tears in his eyes, he sculpted her with open arms in the attempt to defend mother from the father's violent behaviour. Never before, had he been able to open up this issue of the past, which blocked him and froze the marital relationship for many years. In exchange, the daughter gave him a gift, by stopping her sleep problems. In the following sessions parents reported that, surprisingly, she did not ask them to stay in her room at night anymore. Taking children in high consideration is the best way for empowering parents often oversensitive to blame and guilt because of their family issues.

I hope this chapter will help family therapists to take risks that are more personal in working with families and encourage them to include children in their therapeutic endeavour. Then, they will discover that creativity and playfulness are magic tools to produce change.

References

Andolfi, M. (1979a). Redefinition in family therapy. *The American Journal of Family Therapy, 7*(1), 5–15.

Andolfi, M. (1979b). *Family therapy – An interactional approach*. New York, NY: Plenum Press.

Andolfi, M. (1994). The child as consultant. In M. Andolfi & R. Haber (Eds.), *Please help me with this family* (pp. 73–89). New York, NY: Brunner/Mazel.

Andolfi, M. (Ed.). (1999). *La crisi della coppia*. Milano: Cortina.

Andolfi, M. (2003). *Manuale di psicologia relazionale*. Roma: APF.

Andolfi, M. (2016). *Multigenerational family therapy*. London: Routledge.

Andolfi, M., Angelo, C., Menghi, P., & Nicolò-Corigliano, A. M. (1983). *Behind the family mask. Therapeutic change in rigid family systems*. New York, NY: Brunner/Mazel.

Andolfi, M., Angelo, C., & D'Atena, P. (2001). *La terapia narrata dalle famiglie*. Milan: Cortina.

Andolfi, M., Angelo, C., & Nichilo, D. (1989). *The myth of atlas: Families and the therapeutic story*. New York, NY: Brunner/Mazel.

Andolfi, M., Falcucci, M., Mascellani, A., Santona, A., & Sciamplicotti, F. (2006). *La terapia di coppia in una prospettiva trigenerazionale*. Rome: APF.

Andolfi, M., Falcucci, M., Mascellani, A., Santona, A., & Sciamplicotti, F. (2007). *Il bambino come risorsa nella terapia familiare*. Rome: APF.

Andolfi, M., & Mascellani, A. (2013). *Teen voices. Tales of family therapy*. San Diego, CA: Wisdom Moon Publishing.

Bank, S. P., & Kahn, M. D. (1982). *The sibling bond*. New York, NY: Basic Books.

Bowen, M. (1978). *Family therapy in clinical practice*. New York, NY: Jason Aronson.

Bowlby, J., & Robertson, J. (1952). A two-year-old goes to hospital. *Proceedings of the Royal Society of Medicine, 46*, 425–427.

Cade, B. (1992). A response by any other…. *Journal of Family Therapy, 14*, 163–169.

De Shazer, S. (1985). *Keys to solution in brief therapy*. New York, NY: Norton.

Elkaim, M. (1990). *If you love me, don't love me*. New York, NY: Basic Books.

Erickson, M. H., Rossi, E. L., & Rossi, S. I. (1976). *Hypnotic realities: The induction of clinical hypnosis and forms of indirect suggest*. New York, NY: Irvington.

Flaskas, C. (1992). A reframe by other name: On the process of refraining in strategic, Milan and analytic therapy. *Journal of Family Therapy, 14*, 145–161.

Fourie, D. P. (2010). Asking about ambivalence: A different kind of therapist neutrality. *American Journal of Family Therapy, 38*(5), 374–382.

Framo, J. L. (1992). *Family of origin. An intergenerational approach*. New York, NY: Routledge.

Haley, J. (1976). *Problem-solving therapy*. San Francisco, CA: Jossey-Bass.

Hoffman, L. (1981). *Foundations of family therapy*. New York, NY: Basic Books.

Keeney, B. P. (1983). *The aesthetics of change*. New York, NY: Guilford Press.

Minuchin, S. (1974). *Families and family therapy*. Cambridge, MA: Harvard University Press.

Montagu, A. (1971). *Touching: The human significance of the skin*. New York, NY: Harper & Row.

Selvini Palazzoli, M., Boscolo, L., Cecchin, G., & Prata, G. (1978). *Paradox and counterparadox: A new model in the therapy of the family in schizophrenic transaction*. New York, NY: Jason Aaronson.

Selvini Palazzoli, M., Cirillo, S., Selvini, M., & Sorrentino, A. M. (1989). *Family games: General models of psychotic processes in the family*. New York, NY: Norton.
Sluzki, C. (1992). Transformations: A blueprint for narrative changes in therapy. *Family Process, 31*(3), 217–230.
Sprenkle, D. H., Davis, S. D., & Lebow, J. (2009). *Common factors in couple and family therapy: The overlooked foundation for effective practice*. New York, NY: Guilford Press.
Walsh, F. (Ed.). (1982). *Normal family processes*. New York, NY: Guilford Press.
Watzlawick, P., Beavin, J. H., & Jackson, D. D. (1967). *Pragmatics of human communication. A study of interactional patterns, pathologies, and paradoxes*. New York, NY: Norton.
Whitaker, C. A. (1989). *Midnight musings of a family therapist*. New York, NY: Norton.
Whitaker, C., & Keith, D. (1981). Play therapy: A paradigm for work with families. *Journal of Marital and Family Therapy, 7*(3), 243–254.
White, M., & Epston, D. (1989). *Literate means to therapeutic ends*. Adelaide, AU: Dulwich Centre Publisher.

Chapter 11
Blind and Mute Family Sculpting in the Training of Family Therapists

Jorma Piha and Florence Schmitt

Synopsis Family sculpture has been defined as a dynamic, active, non-linear and non-verbal technique to portray family relationships. To emphasize the non-verbal character of the technique, we created a "Blind and Mute" modification.

The cornerstones of the "Blind and Mute" method are: (1) the sculptor doesn't tell anything about the situation to be sculpted (2) the leader of the process chooses the actors into the roles which are unknown to everyone, (3) during the actual creation of the sculpture no words are used.

In this arrangement the actors portraying the family members have to rely only on their inner feelings and sensations derived from the body and from the spatial configuration of the sculpture.

The method is used in the training of family therapists to increase their self-awareness of their family of origin issues. Additionally, it is used as a means of clinical supervision when trainees work with families. In this way the meaning and importance of non-verbal interaction within the family therapeutic system is highlighted.

Introduction

From the mid 1980s, the first author worked as Professor and Head of Child Psychiatry Clinic in the University and University Hospital of Turku, Finland, being responsible for research, teaching and clinical activities, and also for administration. An important sector within the teaching activities was the promotion of psychotherapy trainings, especially those trainings which were targeted to serve professionals working with children and families. The authors learned to know each other in the beginning of 1990s, and have been working together since then in research, teaching and clinical work.

J. Piha (✉) • F. Schmitt
Department of Child Psychiatry, University of Turku, Turku, Finland
e-mail: piha@utu.fi

M. Borcsa, P. Stratton (eds.), *Origins and Originality in Family Therapy and Systemic Practice*, European Family Therapy Association Series,
DOI 10.1007/978-3-319-39061-1_11

Within the field of child mental health and child psychiatry the family approach is the main treatment measure due to the fact that children do not seek psychiatric help and support themselves—there are always adults (parents or persons "in loco parentis") behind the help needing child. This simple, but elementary clinical notion lead us to start to develop and to advance child centred family therapy as a clinical mode of treatment. This also meant facilitation of family therapy trainings.

In family therapy trainings essential elements are the family background exploration and clinical supervision. We found family sculpture as a useful tool to help the trainees to get inner perspective and understanding on their family-of-origin issues. Family sculpture was also most suitable to use in family therapy supervision in training context to increase therapeutic insight of trainees. These were the motifs to remodel family sculpture technique, and emphasize the non-verbal dimension of it. This emphasis was also in congruence with our idea of child centred family therapy where the non-verbal elements play an important role. Our modification of the technique was given the name "Blind and Mute Family Sculpting" (BMFS).

As part of the university work we presented our Blind and Mute modification in workshops and training programmes, in conferences and congresses in various Nordic and European countries, and also in South-America and Africa. The first workshop presentation took place in the Congress "Family Therapy … and Beyond" in Amsterdam in 1993. We noticed the non-verbal sculpture was workable everywhere. It was interesting to find out how the method transcended the language barrier—in many events the English language was for us and for all the participants a strange language, and in this regard we all were on the same level. This refers how the body speaks a universal language.

In the beginning of the millennium a progress in the use of the non-verbal sculpting technique took place when it was applied into the trainings of psychotherapists working with early infant–parent interaction (pregnant women, infants and toddlers until 3 years). In these training programmes—of course—the attention to the non-verbal communication was strongly emphasized, and we found Blind and Mute Family Sculpture modification highly profitable in clinical supervision and in working with family background of trainees.

Literature Review

David Kantor, Fred Duhl and Benny Duhl published in the beginning of 1970s an article on an expressive family therapy technique they called family sculpting (Duhl et al. 1973). Jeffrey Gerrard, who was trained by Fred Duhl to use sculpting, has formulated the idea of family sculpting as follows. "Family sculpture is a method of physically and dynamically representing family relationships in space and time. It captures the meanings, metaphors and images of relationships in a way that is shared by participants and observers. Once the sculpture is enacted information is experienced through action and observation. Words are necessary only in the setting up and processing of the sculpture" (Gerrard 1981, p. 109). Peggy Papp and colleagues (Papp 1976; Papp et al. 1973), and Virginia Satir (1972) were working with similar ideas.

In the literature the technique is described as non-verbal, offering the possibility to portray perceptions of the family constellation in several dimensions such as relationships between family members, boundaries, relational balance (closeness-distance), hierarchy, power, conflicts and structures by using space, physical postures and gestures, and direction of glances. Hearn and Lawrence (1981) tried to grasp the theoretical backgrounds of the technique and came to the conclusion that several theoretical and technical frameworks are involved: psychoanalytic, communication theories, structural approaches, more broadly "family sculpting can be set in the theoretical context of psychology and sociology of personal spaces."

The Use of Family Sculpting Method

The literature concerning family sculpting is scarce. In the text book articles the main emphasis is on the clinical applications of the method (Barker 2007; Goldenberg and Goldenberg 1996; Nichols and Schwartz 2008; Stratton et al. 1990). It has been used in diagnostic evaluations, as clinical interventions and as a method to explore changes (evaluation) in family therapeutic processes (Andolfi 1979; Gerrard 1981; Hearn and Lawrence 1981, 1985; Jefferson 1978; Simon 1972). Andolfi (1979) states that with sculpting it is possible to highlight the family problem, an important intra-familial relationship, or the family history. Hearn and Lawrence (1985) suggest that sculpting could, for example, be used to reveal to the therapist areas of particular concern or sensitivity in the family, or to reveal a particularly vulnerable individual.

Family sculpting has been used as an intervention with psychosomatic patients (Onnis et al. 1994). Onnis and colleagues saw sculpture as a therapeutic language similar to the non-verbal language of psychosomatic symptoms. They found sculpture to be a useful therapeutic tool in family therapy with psychosomatic families, where the language is often rigid around the physical symptoms.

Papp, Scheinkman and Malpas (2013) focused on using family sculpture in couple therapy especially with couples in impasses. Through case examples they describe different ways of using sculpture including staging metaphors, and utilizing enactments. They discovered the powerful impact of sculpture to capture and change stalemates in couple relations.

Some authors point out its advantages as a tool to involve children in family therapy (Andolfi 1979; Hearn and Lawrence 1981, 1985; Papp et al. 1973).

Lawson (1988) describes the use of family sculpture as a kind of preventive measure in helping undergraduate students in their problems with emotional and psychological separation from their families of origin. Papp et al. (2013) used the sculpting method in preventive work with "well families", that is, families with everyday problems in situations before problems escalate into crisis. Their conclusion was that family sculpting was a valuable tool for psychoeducational work and enhancing behavioural change. Also Jefferson (1978) saw family sculpture as a way to reinforce change in therapy.

According to Papp et al. (1973) one of the major advantages of family sculpting in clinical work is the ability to cut through intellectualization, defensiveness, and projection of blame. Hearn and Lawrence (1981) pointed out that "one specific possibility of family sculpting, that is particularly noteworthy, is the portrayal of ambiguity in relationship and within individuals". They add that sculpting can also be used to enable the family to understand the complexity of its own relationships.

However, it remains slightly unclear what are the indications for using family sculpting in family therapy. Exceptions are Gerrard (1981) who gives indications for its use with families, and Papp et al. (2013) who are offering several indications how to use family sculpture in couple therapy.

Other uses of family sculpture include a group of overlapping themes linked with family therapy supervision, family background explorations (family-of-origin-work), training of mental health professionals, and administrative workgroup interventions or staff development. Boundaries between these entities are vague, and especially supervision and family background explorations are partly clinical work.

In articles dealing with family therapy supervision the main focus is on the role of the therapist in the therapeutic system (Simon 1972) or the interaction between therapist and family (Simmonds and Brummer 1980). The same authors emphasize also the exploration of counter-transference of the family therapist. The main objective is to increase the insight of the therapist into the therapeutic system, and/or the intra-familial dynamics.

Many articles describe how family-of-origin-work is included in family therapy training programmes (Baldo and Softas-Nall 1998; Costa 1991; Gerrard 1981; Hearn and Lawrence 1985; Marchetti-Mercer and Cleaver 2000; Simon 1972). This is logical due to the fact that family-of-origin-work is an elementary part in training family therapists.

The experiences of the authors are generally positive, and they have found family sculpture as a useful and fresh, and even dramatic method to explore family-of-origin issues of the trainees. Trainees reported they felt empowered as therapists, and more aware about their own handicaps linked with the difficulties with the client families (Baldo and Softas-Nall 1998). This kind of working also improved trainee's knowledge of the universal features of family systems (Marchetti-Mercer and Cleaver 2000).

Baldo and Softas-Nall (1998) and Marchetti-Mercer and Cleaver (2000) used in training of family therapists family-of-origin sculpture with the three generational family genogram (McGoldrick et al. 2007). The combined use of these methods was an enriching experience for the trainees.

Gerrard (1981) and Baldo and Softas-Nall (1998) combined in training programmes family-of-origin-work and clinical supervision both carried out using sculpting. Baldo and Softas-Nall (1998) state that in supervision family sculpting may provide insight and directions as well as indications to the problems the therapist is encountering. After the supervision sculpture they invite the trainee to continue by making a sculpture of his/her family of origin that reminds him/her of being stuck or frustrated with the client family. According to the authors the technique is powerful and seems to facilitate therapeutic progress with the families.

The Non-verbal Quality of the Technique

Nonverbal communication means wordless communication between people. The early interaction between the parent and infant occur on preverbal level, and the primary experiences of an infant are nonverbal (Stern 1985). As a consequence, the nonverbal communication is a constituent feature of human beings. Nonverbal communication includes body language, touch, eye contact (direction of glance), voice, and spacing (distance). Usually in family sculpting, body language, touch, eye contact, and distance are operating.

In the literature the non-verbal aspects of the technique has been strongly emphasized (Andolfi 1979; Duhl et al. 1973; Hearn and Lawrence 1985; Onnis et al. 1994; Papp et al. 2013; Simon 1972). However, when illustrating the sculpting with case examples, authors report long sequences of conversations between the participants involved in the sculpting. This was also our experience when participating in the sculpting demonstrations in seminars and conferences—words were usually used in the most sensitive parts of the process—before and during the actual sculpting.

Some examples from the literature follow

> She (Joan) … selected Bob, whose solemnity she felt reminded her of him (father), and Bob was instructed to ask questions of her as if he were the father.
>
> - "Am I a quiet man?"
> - "Yes, very depressed."
> - "Do I seem busy? How do I move?"
> - "You're quiet and speak to no one until they come to you."
>
> The monitor (the leader of the process) asked that Joan give Bob a typical gesture that summarized her father for her. She suggested he sit down and hold his head in his hands with his body turned away into the corner. (Duhl et al. 1973, p. 54)

In this piece, the appearance and depressiveness of the father, and also his body posture are verbally explained.

> While the sculpture is being created, words are used sparingly; in fact words are used only to describe the position that each family member is asked to assume (and to describe the inner states that the sculptor wants to express through his choice of positions and postures). (Andolfi 1979, p. 80)

In this example, even the inner states of the family members are verbally prescribed.

These kinds of verbal statements during the sculpting will interfere with the process. These statements reflect the assumptions of the sculptor, and their use in such a way will distort the experiences of the actors. The verbal prescriptions make it difficult for the participants to get freely in touch with the impressions and bodily sensations which will arouse during the sculpting process.

Objectives

The use of family sculpting is described in several papers but usually the entire protocol is not described in detail. The articles by Duhl et al. (1973) and by Andolfi (1979) are exceptions. These quite old (and consequently hard to reach) texts give good specifications about the practical sculpting procedure. Papp et al. (2013) explain clearly how to introduce the protocol to the client family, and in connection to the case presentations some practical hints are given. In the paper by Marchetti-Mercer and Cleaver (2000) only a general outline has been sketched. Other articles mostly lack information how to conduct the sculpting.

It seems that, in the field of family therapy an oral tradition of teaching the use of sculpting technique has been prevalent. This is understandable due to the nature of the technique and the way family therapy has been taught but it makes it difficult to compare and assess the similarities and differences of sculpting practices explained in various articles.

In our tasks as family therapy trainers we became dissatisfied with the abundance of the verbal aspects in the sculpting exercises, and started to develop the technique into the direction of non-verbality. The main aim and ambition was to avoid on the verbal level all preconceptions about the family situation to be sculpted, and of course, at the same time all mystifications and attributions of participants.

"Blind and Mute Family Sculpting" (BMFS) is a set of modifications we undertook in order to make family sculpture a truly nonverbal method. The construct BMFS refers to (1) that the participants do not know anything about the situation to be sculpted, and (2) that during the actual creation of the sculpture no words are used.

During the years our experiences as family therapy trainers and practising clinicians convinced us the Blind and Mute Family Sculpting is a most effective method to demonstrate for trainees the meaning and importance of non-verbal interaction within the family and therapeutic systems. We see the accentuation of non-verbal interaction to be significant in family therapy trainings which nowadays are prone to underline almost entirely the verbal aspects of communication. In the frame of this EFTA book, we share our way to use family sculpture as a family therapy training method. We also wanted to describe thoroughly the whole sculpting procedure as a guide because the adequate use of the technique needs training (Stratton et al. 1990).

The Stages and Main Features of Blind and Mute Family Sculpting

We use Blind and Mute Family Sculpting in training of family therapists for two purposes. Firstly, when doing the family-of-origin-work (FOOW) with the trainees, and secondly when providing clinical supervision (CS) for family therapies conducted by the trainees as a part of the training. The trainee-therapist is always included in the supervision sculpture. The main difference between doing the family-of-origin sculpt and the supervision sculpt is that the emotional involvement of the sculptor is much more intensive in the FOOW than in CS. In practice, the technical procedure of the sculpting is the same.

From here onward we refer to the use of BMFS in family therapy training context, assuming that everything will take place in a group of trainees lead by at least one trainer. Usually there is one trainer for a group of six to eight trainees. We are working in a large room, sparsely furnished, and well secluded. For the process we reserve 2 full hours.

The main objective of BMFS is to explore the condition of family of origin (in FOOW) or the state of the therapeutic system (in CS) to increase understanding about the situation. Increasing understanding may open new perspectives or a meta-level approach to the involvement of the sculptor as a family member (in FOOW) or as the therapist (in CS).

We wanted to emphasize the non-verbal dimension of communication which is many times disregarded in family therapy. This happens although family therapists are aware and accept that nonverbal or analogical language is in many cases more powerful than verbal or digital language. We found BMFS to be a powerful tool to demonstrate the significance of nonverbal, analogical communication to the trainees.

The Roles in Sculpting

According to Duhl et al. (1973) the roles in the making of the sculpture are the sculptor, the monitor, the actors and the audience.

1. The *sculptor* is the trainee who is presenting his/her family of origin or a clinical family in therapy. This trainee risks to reveal his private view.
2. The *monitor* is the trainer who guides the sculptor toward clarity and definition, and protects the process. The whole sculpting process is on the responsibility of the monitor.
3. The *actors* are those trainees who became chosen to enact the family members of the sculptor's family-of-origin or the members of the clinical family. The actors lend themselves to portray members of the sculptor's system only as the sculptor sees them.
4. The *audience* is composed of those trainees who are not otherwise involved. The audience observes and comments from its special vantage point as observer to

the whole process. Their task is to follow how the sculptor is working with actors portraying the family members, and how the actors are processing their experiences.

We have found this assignment and these roles useful and practical in the sculpting processes. Duhl et al. (1973) do emphasize the importance of the leadership of the monitor, and our experiences refer to the same.

Preparatory Stage

In the beginning of the process, the monitor gives the following instructions to the sculptor who is going to present his/her family-of-origin or a clinical family in therapy: "Please, go silently to your inner world, in your mind, think about a situation, or an event, or a key moment, or a turning point in your family life cycle (in FOOW) or in the therapy (in CS) you would like to explore, to understand or to ponder over. Who were involved? Don't say a word, don't ask questions and take your time." In family-of-origin-work we add "Think how old you were at that time? How old were the others involved? Just think and remember. Don't tell anything".

When the sculptor has decided what would be the event in the family life cycle or in the clinical therapeutic process he/she likes to sculpt, he/she has only to show with fingers to the monitor how many actors are needed. Specifications like "I will need a mother, a father, a grandmother, a big brother etc." are prone to build preconceptions on the situation and would verbally direct the process. To preserve the sculpture uncontaminated it is better the actors do not know there will be "a mother" or "a father" or "a big brother" etc.

If the number of actors needed is superior to the number of available trainees in the audience, it is possible to use a chair or a toy to represent a family member. We find it important that these first moments should be silent and calm, without any laughing or joking in the audience/training group. The seriousness of the monitor is of first importance in order to emphasize the whole group is working together.

Placing the Actors in Space

The process of choosing the actors to be involved in the sculpture seems to be an important part of the sculpting (Hearn and Lawrence 1985). Usually the sculptor is the person who is choosing the actors (Andolfi 1979; Baldo and Softas-Nall 1998; Duhl et al. 1973). Simmonds and Brummer (1980) describe in their model that the first actor is chosen by volunteering, and then this person will choose the second actor, and this one the next etc. In all these models the actors do know which roles they are portraying, and consequently they will be verbally directed by the sculptor, and they will more or less adopt the stereotype roles prevalent in the society and culture.

In BMFS the monitor asks the sculptor to think and decide in his/her mind the spatial arrangement of the planned sculpture. The sculptor has to define the approximate places of all actors/family members in the space available, and what are the distances between actors/family members. Then the monitor will ask the sculptor to show to which place to put the first actor/family member. The sculptor points out the spatial position of the first family member without knowing who of the actors is going to be placed there. The monitor chooses randomly the actor from the audience, and gives to the sculptor the first actor without knowing the role of the actor in the sculpture. The process is "blind".

The actors to be sculpted don't know who they will portray—"Do I enact a child or an adolescent or a grown up or a senior?"—"Do I enact a male or a female?" If the sculptor would choose the actors by him/herself, there would be some risk of "manipulation", for instance choosing from the audience a tall man the to portray a violent father, or the oldest woman to represent a grandmother.

The same procedure is repeated with all family members. When each actor is placed in the space in relation to each other, the monitor asks the sculptor to check the distances between actors, and that everyone is in the right place. Some corrections can be made, but without words. If an actor is not in a correct place, the sculptor can direct him/her physically to the new place (Fig. 11.1). The monitor has to check the sculptor is satisfied with the spatial arrangement. When the main frame of

Fig. 11.1 Placing the actors in space. The sculptor is by touching checking the actor is in the correct place. Reprinted with permission from Jorma Piha

the sculpture is created, no one, except the sculptor, knows who the actors are portraying. One of the actors is portraying the sculptor as a family member (FOOW) or as the therapist (CS).

Sculpting Stage

In the sculpting stage “the overall form of the body” of every actor will be modelled by the sculptor. Hearn and Lawrence (1985) consider with this term “not only the specific posture of the body, limbs and so on, but also the overall combination and pattern of elements within the context of the sculpt.” In the following text, we also use the term “overall form of the body” (or “body form”) to refer to the posture, gestures, facial expressions and direction of glance of the actor.

The monitor asks the sculptor to create—without words, only by touching—the actual sculpture. He/she has to give an expressive overall form of the body to each actor (Fig. 11.2). Usually it is wise to start with the actor who physically has the easiest form of body. When the modelling of the actor is finished, the monitor gives the actor the instruction: “Make a mental note of this body form, and then you can relax”. This is important because the sculpting process can take quite a long time, and it would be too hard to stay in the sculpted position all the time.

Fig. 11.2 Sculpting stage. The sculptor is creating—without words, only by touching—the actual sculpture. Reprinted with permission from Jorma Piha

The sculptor sculpts like an artist by physically touching the actors like they were clay. One may have the arm stretched or a fist clenched, one may have the legs as if running. One may sit with his head in the hands, one may have the arms around the shoulders of somebody, or one may lie on the floor. Facial expressions are modelled with the sculptor's fingers, and the direction of glance is indicated by showing the direction hoped for.

Touching physically is a key element in the creation of the sculpt because touching is an integral part of nonverbal communication. Through touching the sculptor is mediating his/her nonverbal attitude toward the family member he/she is currently sculpting. The touch of the sculptor becomes an important source of information to the actor (Sansone 2004).

Still and Steady Stage

In the beginning of this step, the monitor gives the actors the following instructions: "Now I will explain what will happen in a while. In a moment I'll ask you to take the original body form the sculptor gave you. Then I'll ask you to hold the position still and steady, and to try to get in touch as sensitively as possible with the inner feelings and all the physical sensations derived from your own body in this sculpture. You should also be aware of your fantasies and whatever comes to your mind as openly as possible. I'll tell when the time will start and when it will end." After this instruction the monitor is asking the actors to take the original form of the body. The sculptor has to quickly check that all the body forms are correct. Then the monitor asks the actors to stay still and steady, and says "The time starts now".

The actors have to keep the given body form for a sufficient time to enable the arousal of the inner feelings, bodily sensations, and fantasies in the sculpture (Fig. 11.3). Baldo and Softas-Nall (1998) suggest the time should be 60 s but we found that 90 s seems to be the reasonable minimum and 2 min the maximum time.

The length of the still and steady stage is modulated by the difficulty of the overall body forms. If one actor has a somehow uneasy or physically demanding body form, the monitor has to shorten the duration of the still and steady stage but keeping it at least in the minimum time. We have seen several sculptures where the still and steady time has been only some 10–15 s, and this is not enough to get properly in touch with the feelings and bodily sensations invoking in the sculpture.

The monitor has to take care of the time. When the time is over, the monitor tells the actors: "The time is over, and you can relax now but do not move from the place you are, and remain silent. Try to keep in your mind those feelings and sensations and fantasies aroused in the sculpture".

It is possible to stop the sculpting process at this stage, and to proceed into the feedback and disclosure stage. However, if the sculpting will continue into the dynamic stage, the sculptor is allowed at this point, to make some short questions to the actors but this is not necessary. If questions are presented, they must be formulated so that the roles are not disclosed.

Fig. 11.3 Still and steady stage. The actors are keeping the given body form for a sufficient time (in this case 120 s) to enable the arousal of the inner feelings, bodily sensations, and fantasies in the sculpture. Reprinted with permission from Jorma Piha

Dynamic Stage

In the literature a change after the first sculpt has been described. Usually the change is meant to describe "the ideal family" (Baldo and Softas-Nall 1998; Gerrard 1981; Marchetti-Mercer and Cleaver 2000; Papp 1976) or "the future family" (Onnis et al. 1994). However, in practice, "the ideal or future family" is very far from the present reality, because the creation of it is led by imagination, hopes or fears. Our experience is that, if an ideal or future family situation has been sculpted, it is hard to take advantage of the differences between these two sculpts, because the new imaginary sculpture is usually totally different compared to the first one.

These experiences were the background to our modification we call "minimal change". Minimal change means that the overall form of the body of one actor will be changed without moving from the original spatial place in the sculpture (Fig. 11.4). The posture, gesture, facial expression and direction of glance of this actor/family member are changed in order for the actor or the whole family (FOO or clinical family) to feel more comfortable, and/or simply to check the effects of this change. The experiences of the actors after the minimal change may be quite unexpected. This is very powerful and a fruitful way to demonstrate to trainees how

Fig. 11.4 Dynamic stage—minimal change. The overall form of the body of one actor has been changed without moving from the original spatial place in the sculpture. Reprinted with permission from Jorma Piha

a minimal modification of the overall body form of one actor/family member will affect the feeling or configuration of the system.

The actor whose body form will be changed can be chosen by (1) the sculptor, (2) an actor named by the sculptor, or (3) by the whole family after non-verbal negotiation (voting by pointing). The sculptor can decide how to manage with this but the monitor has to conduct the process. The monitor has to tell the sculptor the alternatives of how to choose the actor whose body form will be changed.

Each of these options is based on different rationales and perspectives. If the sculptor chooses the actor he/she can explore his/her own idea about how the change of this family member would affect the family. If the sculptor asks one actor/family member to make the choosing he/she can study another aspect of family dynamics. The third possibility—to let the family members to decide "what would be the opinion of the family"—will again open new perspectives to the family system and family dynamics.

There are two ways to create the new overall form of the body. The sculptor can sculpt him/herself the new body form of the chosen actor in the original place. In this case, when the sculptor has finished the new figure, the monitor asks all the other actors to take the original body forms. The sculptor has again to check all the forms are correct.

The other option is to give the selected actor/family member the freedom to choose him/herself the new body form. The convenient way to do that is that the monitor is asking all the actors to take the original body forms, and when the sculptor has checked these, the chosen actor can change his/her posture and gesture, facial expression and direction of glance without moving from the original place.

In both options a new still and steady stage will follow. For this second sculpture, the following instruction is given: "Additionally to what has been said previously, you should make observations on the differences between the sculptures."

Instead of the minimal change manoeuvre, or as a continuation to it, it is possible to create a new sculpture called "maximal change". Maximal change means a new sculpture describing another stage in the family life cycle (FOOW) or in the therapeutic process (CS) using the same actors in the same roles (which still are unknown to the monitor, the actors, and the audience). This stage can be, in regard to time a phase before or after the first one. In clinical supervision the new stage can be first session or present stage supposing that the sculpted situation was some time point between these.

Minimal change and maximal change both are independent ways to progress the sculpting but can also be subsequent stages of the process if there is time enough. The monitor has to explain the aims and meanings of these changes to the sculptor. Technically the sculpting procedures are the same described earlier.

Feedback and Disclosure Stage

Until this point only a few sentences have been said verbally. The feedback and disclosure stage has two parts. The first feedback part is the verbal description of feelings, experiences, and fantasies invoked in the sculpture. The second disclosure part is the discussion in the dual role of the actors—as a sculpted family member and as a family therapy trainee. During the first part all the actors are standing at the places they were in the sculpture (or alternatively they may sit on chairs put on the original places). At least for the second part all the actors are invited to sit.

In this feedback and disclosure stage the monitor is in a crucial role. His/her duty is to facilitate and protect the process. The monitor interviews each actor according to the order they were put in the sculpture. The monitor is asking about the distances between the actors (spatial arrangement), about which actors were visible (direction of glance), about the physical posture (light, heavy, hard, painful etc.). He/she should also ask the actors about their experiences and fantasies—"Did you feel like a child or an adolescent or an adult?"—"Did you feel like a male or female?" The monitor emphasizes also the differences between the first and the second sculpture–what was different and how it was different. Experiences of having been touched during the sculpting process are explored carefully.

After this interview, the sculptor has the possibility to pose specific questions to the actors. Still, the sculptor is the only participant who knows the roles of the actors, and he/she can put his/her questions from this point of view—the monitor is able to questioning only on a general and theoretical level.

Before the monitor is asking the sculptor to disclose who was portraying who in the family-of-origin or in the clinical family, the actors may like to try to guess the roles of themselves and others. For the sculptor this is usually a most exciting moment. Many times the actors are able to experience exactly the given role but sometimes the answers will open totally new perspectives to the family situation sculpted—for example if the actor in the role of father felt in the sculpture like a child or a female.

After the disclosure of the roles the sculptor is asked to describe and elaborate the structure and dynamics of the sculpted family situation and share the details of family history and intra-familial relations. The actor-trainees can continue the discussion from their role perspective using this broadened view. During this discussion the monitor will invite the audience to participate.

Exploring the Whole Experience

To close the discussion in the dual role, the monitor is asking the actors to get rid of their roles. This is an enormously important action to the actors because the non-verbal technique is so powerful–the roles continue very easily to stay alive. Every actor at a time must stand up and say in a loud voice: "I am not (specification—the role in the sculpt) but I am (full name—first name, family name)". Standing up and expressing the whole true name are means to restore one's physical and personal identity. After this the participants (no more monitor, sculptor, actors) have to change the chairs.

Usually it is useful to continue the discussion and explore experiences of all the trainees and the trainer.

Comments on BMFS Method

Becoming a family therapist demands familiarity with theoretical models, and knowledge of techniques. In addition, personal skills, which are linked with awareness of own life experience, are required. In the family therapy training programmes we have been involved in, increasing trainee's awareness of own life experience has been carried out, among others, with sculpting the family-of-origin, and performing family genogram.

The family background exploration in a new training programme will be started with family-of-origin sculpture. New trainees are not yet informed about each other's family backgrounds, and usually are without preconceptions concerning these. This allows free and fresh experiences in the sculpture. Starting the training with sculpture emphasizes the importance of non-verbal communication in family interaction and in family therapy. It also offers the possibility to avoid rationalizations and defensiveness linked with the verbal genogram exploration.

The most common feedback of trainees has been a profound astonishment of the powerfulness and authenticity of the experience in the sculpting process. Some trainees reported the actors in the feedback stage used almost the same words as the real family members had used. Baldo and Softas-Nall (1998) referred to the same, also pointing out that the sculpting process is an important emotional learning experience for the trainees.

Some trainees have been most excited about the new and unexpected ideas and insight into the family-of-origin, or into the therapeutic system of the family in therapy. This is based on the essential element of the BMFS that one of the actors is playing the role of the sculptor as a family member (in FOOW) or as the therapist (in CS) without being aware of that. The actors have to base their feelings, sensations and fantasies on the nonverbal stimuli derived from the body and from the spatial configuration of the sculpture. The process is mute. The experiences of the actor portraying the sculptor as a family member or as the therapist, might for the sculptor be the most challenging moment, and this is the main advantage of BMFS.

Family therapy trainers should know how to carry out a family sculpting procedure to be able to act as a monitor. The first prerequisite for learning the use of Blind and Mute Family Sculpting is to participate in several sculpture exercises, preferably four to six times in order to experience all the roles involved in the process. It is interesting to note that according to Duhl et al. (1973) a therapist has to participate in the sculpting exercises at least five times to be able to edit or improve it. Additionally, it is of great importance to be familiar with the subsequent stages of BMFS procedure, and to follow carefully the whole protocol.

Monitoring the family sculpting process is demanding. The monitor has to be sensitive and mature as a person as well as professionally. He/she has to combine rigour with creativity, meticulousness with flexibility and seriousness with imagination in directing the process. The monitor has to be able to manage strong feelings and various emotions or reactions, especially in the feedback and disclosure stage. The monitor needs a capacity to keep a balance between inviting participants to go deeper in the process, and at the same time avoiding intrusiveness. This is something similar to what has to be learned to become a psychotherapist—to acquire a capacity to keep the balance between containing and risk taking, between safety and provocation.

The technique of Blind and Mute Family Sculpting has been developed in the early nineties to explore family dynamics, structures and stories in order to increase self-awareness of trainees. At that time, we couldn't understand how research on infants, early interaction, prenatal and postnatal communication would totally revolutionize our knowledge of the ontogenesis of narratives. The works by Stern (1985), Siegel (1999), Damasio (1999) and others in the late nineties and at the beginning of the new millennium opened new doors to understand how stories start from bodily movements and sensations. Human interaction between the baby and the caregiver gives meaning and intentionality to all this flow of what happens between them. The infant is not a passive stimulus–response mechanism but an embodied creative and developing mind. Moreover, according to Trevarthen (2012) and Delafield and Trevarthen (2015) all human communication is mediated by motor signals of high complexity—of the head, the eyes, the face, the vocal system, the hands and the whole body. By rediscovering the body in family therapy (like in family sculpting), it was possible to move from a very cerebral intellectual vision of psychotherapy to a more embodied, concrete way of working. Suddenly, working with emotions, feelings, and stories was more linked to their physical expression in the body.

References

Andolfi, M. (1979). *Family therapy. An interactional approach.* New York: PlenumPress.

Baldo, T. D., & Softas-Nall, B. C. (1998). Family sculpting in supervision of family therapy. *The Family Journal: Counseling and Therapy for Couples and Families, 6*, 231–234.

Barker, P. (2007). *Basic family therapy* (5th ed.). Oxford: Blackwell Publishing.

Costa, L. (1991). Family sculpting in the training of marriage and family counselors. *Counselor Education and Supervision, 31*, 121–131.

Damasio, A. (1999). *The feeling of what happens: Body and emotion in the making of consciousness.* New York: Harcourt Brace.

Delafield-Butt, J. T., & Trevarthen, C. (2015). The ontogenesis of narrative: From moving to meaning. *Frontiers in Psychology, 6*, 1–16.

Duhl, F. J., Kantor, D., & Duhl, B. S. (1973). Learning, space and action in family therapy: A primer of sculpture. In D. Bloch (Ed.), *Techniques of family psychotherapy: A primer* (pp. 47–63). New York: Grune & Stratton.

Gerrard, J. M. (1981). Family sculpture. *Australian Journal of Family Therapy, 2*, 109–122.

Goldenberg, I., & Goldenberg, H. (1996). *Family therapy: An overview* (4th ed.). PacificGrove, CA: Brook/Cole.

Hearn, J., & Lawrence, M. (1981). Family sculpting: I. Some doubts and some possibilities. *Journal of Family Therapy, 3*, 341–352.

Hearn, J., & Lawrence, M. (1985). Family sculpting: II. Some practical examples. *Journalof Family Therapy, 7*, 113–131.

Jefferson, C. (1978). Some notes on the use of family sculpture in therapy. *Family Process, 17*, 69–76.

Lawson, D. M. (1988). Using family sculpting and choreography in a student growthgroup. *Journal of Counseling & Development, 66*, 246–247.

Marchetti-Mercer, M. C., & Cleaver, G. (2000). Genograms and family sculpting: An aidto cross-cultural understanding in the training of psychology students in South Africa. *The Counseling Psychologist, 28*, 61–80.

McGoldrick, M., Gerson, R., & Petry, S. (2007). *Genograms: Assessment andintervention* (3rd ed.). New York: Norton Professional Books.

Nichols, M. P., & Schwartz, R. C. (2008). *Family therapy. Concepts and methods* (Vol. 8). Boston-New York: Pearson.

Onnis, L., Di Gennaro, A., Cespa, G., Agostini, B., Chouhy, A., Dentale, R. C., et al. (1994). Sculpting present and future: A systemic intervention model applied to psychosomatic families. *Family Process, 33*, 341–355.

Papp, P. (1976). Family choreography. In P. J. Guerin Jr. (Ed.), *Family therapy: Theoryand practice* (pp. 465–479). New York: Gardner Press.

Papp, P., Scheinkman, M., & Malpas, J. (2013). Breaking the mold: Sculpting impasses in couple's therapy. *Family Process, 52*, 33–45.

Papp, P., Silverstein, O., & Carter, E. (1973). Family sculpting in preventive work with "well families". *Family Process, 12*, 197–212.

Sansone, A. (2004). *Mothers, babies and their body language* (p. 22). London-New York: Karnac.
Satir, V. (1972). *Peoplemaking*. Palo Alto, CA: Science & Behavior Books.
Siegel, D. J. (1999). *The developing mind: Toward a neurobiology of interpersonal experience*. New York: Guilford.
Simmonds, J., & Brummer, N. (1980). The family sculpt as an educational experience: An exploration of appropriate professional involvement. *Journal of Family Therapy, 2*, 389–399.
Simon, R. M. (1972). Sculpting the family. *Family Process, 11*, 49–57.
Stern, D. N. (1985). *The interpersonal world of the infant*. New York: Basic Books.
Stratton, P., Preston-Shoot, M., & Hanks, H. (1990). *Family therapy: Training and practice*. Birmingham: Venture Press.
Trevarthen, C. (2012). Embodied human intersubjectivity: Imaginative agency, to share meaning. *Journal of Cognitive Semiotics, 4*, 6–56.

Chapter 12
A Multi-level, Multi-focal, Multi-voiced Journey: Not Without Family Therapy—Not with Family Therapy Alone

Kyriaki Polychroni

Synopsis In this chapter the author shares a narrative of her scientific journey from its origins to its today's originality. Theoretical concepts developed at the Athenian Institute of Anthropos such as the "Multi-level, Multi-focal Model of Intervention", "Subjective Culture" and "Cultural Chronos and the Multiplicity of Inner Voices" are presented. Methods of application that include "Systemic Group Therapy" and Experiential Training in Family Dynamics/Therapy are described showing how the integration of other modalities into family therapy models can optimize our systemic practice. Weaved throughout the chapter are more personal experiences that illustrate the author's development. In closure, the author shares aspects of her current clinical practice where she has incorporated Attachment Theory in systemic therapy and Emotionally Focused Therapy (EFT) in working with couples and families.

Introduction

It seems like only yesterday when in 1972, I knocked on the door of the Athenian Institute of Anthropos.

Then studying towards my first degree in Psychology at the University of British Columbia (UBC) in Canada, I had returned the previous summer to the homeland—Greece—for a vacation and to reconnect with my extended family of origin. I was surprised by what I discovered. I had expected to find the mentality of the Greek immigrants that I had grown up among—a mentality extremely different to that of my fellow Canadians of the late 1960s with their focus on the individual and his/her freedom from social norms and restrictions.

K. Polychroni (✉)
The Athenian Institute of Anthropos, Epidavrou 9, Athens 152 32, Greece
e-mail: k_polychroni@otenet.gr

M. Borcsa, P. Stratton (eds.), *Origins and Originality in Family Therapy and Systemic Practice*, European Family Therapy Association Series,
DOI 10.1007/978-3-319-39061-1_12

I was not aware at that time that, in their attempt to survive and make meaning of the threatening waves of new experience, first generation immigrants tend to "freeze time" in the new country—to strongly hold on to the traditional roles, values, norms, behaviours and relational patterns characteristic of the period when they leave their original cultural context.

I thus found the Greek reality in Athens had moved on and was more open than I had initially predicted. And while the individual—particularly the woman—was now more free to engage in developing autonomy, there was still a very strong emphasis on the human need of belonging to family and the "ingroup". In traditional cultures such as Greece, the ingroup has been shown to be central in understanding the individual and the family (Vassiliou, 1970). The ingroup is not broadly or abstractly defined as "people like me" as is the case in more modern western milieu. For the Greek it means "people who show concern for me and with whom I can form interdependence". This group then is not primarily based on blood ties, but includes friends and friends of friends, and is open to change according to the criteria of an on-going, active show of concern.

The discovery of this new reality of my cultural origins was illuminating with respect to how I had perceived my family and the confusion I had experienced with its attempts for integration into the modern context of Canada. And so I decided to stay in Greece for what, at that time, I had planned a year.

One other aspect that drew me to prolong my visit was the broader political context of Greece at that time. The Greek nation was under the rule of a horrendous dictatorship where democratic social rights had been done away with and all individuals with visions of liberty and justice were severely punished. Young people my age, particularly students, were slowly joining together in a common struggle to change their destiny. I soon came to understand that I yearned both to connect more deeply with my origins and to learn how they had influenced my personal development and to also contribute to the joint effort of bringing change to our broader sociopolitical system. This is where I belonged.

I enrolled in the American University where I met Vasso Vassiliou, Professor of Social and Clinical Psychology and Chair of the Department. I did not know then that Vasso would become my "scientific mother" and would have a major influence on my professional and personal development. Vasso Vassiliou had recently completed years of research on the Greek Traditional Family as compared to families of other cultures, particularly those of the US. Her collaboration with Harry Triandis on this widespread cross-cultural research resulted in the publishing of an important book of that time, *"The Analysis of Subjective Culture"* (Triandis, Vassiliou, Vassiliou, Tanaka & Shanmugam, 1972). This book illustrated in depth the need of social scientists to grasp a clear understanding of the way one experiences their social environment, to have a grounded knowledge of individual and group dynamics in the specific culture so as to develop effective means of therapeutic intervention. Subjective culture can be considered forefront of what today is the social constructionist perspective (McNamee & Gergen, 1992) and its focus on uncovering the ways in which individuals and groups participate in the construction of their perceived social reality.

The new knowledge transformed, not only my understanding and appreciation of my traditional origins, but also challenged my view of self and important others. I immediately requested to begin training at Anthropos and there met George Vassiliou, my trainer in systemic epistemology and practice, my mentor, one of my most influential teachers in life.

This was an exciting time, a crucial evolutionary period. Through my connection with the Vassilious and my new learning of systems science and its application to family therapy, I felt I was contributing to changing the field. Through my systemic understanding of broader social systems and my active involvement in the student movement against the dictatorship, I felt I was contributing to changing Greece.

Throughout my subsequent journey, my major "lighthouse" principles have been: the essentiality of systemic therapy being embedded—both in its theories and practice—in knowledge and experience of the socio–cultural context in order to understand and honour the meaning of perceptions, emotions, behaviours and relational patterns and, so, to effectively intervene; and secondly, that family therapy is optimized through opening up its boundaries and integrating modalities that prove operative in intervening on the other interconnected systems levels (i.e. individual, group, community).

In this chapter I share with the readers a narrative of my scientific journey from its origins to its today's originality. Along the way I refer to professional "stations" in terms of theory and methods that I found significant and useful over the years. These include theoretical concepts such as the Multi-level, Multi-focal Model of Intervention, Subjective Culture and Cultural Chronos and the Multiplicity of Inner Voices.

The methods of application I refer to include Systemic Group Therapy and Experiential Training in Family Dynamics and Therapy.

Finally, I share aspects of the current state of my clinical practice through two illustrations where I have incorporated the attachment paradigm in systemic group therapy and the model of Emotionally Focused Therapy (EFT) to my work with couples.

I throughout weave into the above more personal "stations" and experiences so as to illustrate their meaning to my development.

The Athenian Institute of Anthropos[1]: Early Learnings

George and Vasso Vassiliou, a husband and wife, psychiatrist—psychologist team founded the Anthropos Institute in 1963 upon their return to Greece after studying/working in the United States for many years.

[1] *Author's Note*: My work over the years has developed largely within the context of on-going collaboration with colleagues at "Anthropos", Petros Polychronis (Director), Dionyssis Sakkas, Mina Todoulou and Georgos Gournas. Although this chapter is written from my personal perspective, I wish to honour our interdependent group process and thus will use "I", "We", "Our" interchangeably.

According to Mony Elkaim, (personal communication, 2002) Anthropos was the first centre for the practice and training of family therapy in Europe. Moreover, from the Don. D. Jackson Archive studied by Wendel Rey (2015), it was one of the pioneering four Institutes to practice and train in systems and family therapy in the world.

Violeta Kaftatzi (1996) reports that the epistemological and theoretical approach of the Anthropos Institute synthesizes a systemic perspective with a humanistic one entailed in the ancient Greek philosophy of Diogenes and his search for Anthropos (Greek—refers to a whole integral human being).

George and Vasso had lived in the US during the period when systemic thinking was just beginning to emerge and flower. Their connection to the systemic approach—from the beginning—did not concern only family therapy, but was an integral part of their involvement in the then fore-fronting Social Psychiatric movement.

The Systemic-Dialectic approach they developed with its Multi-level, Multi-focal model concerned intervening at the various systems levels: the individual, couple, family, group, community (Vassiliou & Vassiliou, 1968).

At that time the Systems epistemology among practitioners in the States was particularly applied to group therapy.

The Vassilious became close with pioneers both in family therapy—Nathan Ackerman, Paul Watzlawick, Virginia Satir, and others, and also systemic group therapy—William Grey, Jay Fidler, Helen Durkin, Adriane Beck and Yvonne Agazarian.

Yet, when trying to apply the learning and experience of their work in the US to Greek families of that period, the Vassilious confronted difficulties.

The dynamics of the Greek family were very different to that of the American and, consequently, many of the therapeutic techniques they had acquired proved ineffective. Through this initial disappointment, the Vassilious realized that research on the family in the context of our specific Greek culture was necessary so as to understand the milieu—our specific perceptions and attributes of roles, behaviours, emotional expression, communication and relational patterns.

During this early developmental stage of family therapy, practitioners were not sensitive to the cultural context of families and so did not appreciate in actual practice the influence it had on members and their patterns of relating. This is supported in Britt Krause's study of Gregory Bateson and his ideas of schismogenesis, feedback and other cybernetic concepts developed in his book *Naven*. In her article, *Reading Naven: Towards the Integration of Culture in Systemic Psychotherapy* (2007), Kraus attempts to answer why Naven, the text that puts forth Bateson's more cultural understandings, was left out by systemic psychotherapy. She explains that the exclusion of culture in systemic psychotherapy, was due to the fact that, by the time Bateson published *Steps to an Ecology of Mind* which was to become most famous in systemic psychotherapy (Bateson, 1972), the importance of complexity and cultural variation in the meaning aspect of communication, had *already* been left behind through the earlier unexpected publishing of *Pragmatics of Human Communication* by Watzlawick et al. (1967). And that this sudden publication, which took Bateson by dejecting surprise, led him to critically note (Bateson, 1972) how Pragmatics discussed communication in isolation from culture without any regard for its influence in communication. Krause concludes that the splitting of culture and emotions from other aspects of systemic thinking emerged very early in the life of the systemic psychotherapy discipline.

From this elucidating perpective, the Vassilious' insightful comprehension of the crucial importance of cultural patterns and their implications for therapy as described in their chapter *Milieu Specificity in Family Therapy*, published in Nathen Ackerman's early book *Family Therapy in Transition* (1970) can be appreciated today as pioneering work. This appreciation is also evident in the acknowledgement of Don Jackson that "Dr. Vassiliou's remarks are penetrating and his admonitions are well taken. In fact, I can find nothing to disagree with ... and am glad, for this reason, that I hope to study at his institute next year" (Jackson, 1967, p. 151).

Utilizing their acquired knowledge of the Greek milieu and family dynamics, the Vassilious integrated into their approach to family therapy the more psychodynamic work of Nathan Ackerman, Watzlawick's communication patterns, Minuchin's boundary structuring, extended family relations as described by Boszormenyi-Nagy, and Murray Bowen's work on differentiation. The conceptualization of family therapy as education for change developed by Virginia Satir also formed a fundamental basis for their work.

The Multi-level/Multi-focal model of intervention so emerged. Intervening strategically to enhance effective family relations is here seen as an outcome of shifting the focus of intervention from one member of the family to another and shifting the level of intervention from one subsystem to the other and to the family system as a whole, so achieving the required restructuring of family patterns most effectively (Vassiliou & Vassiliou, 1982).

From the very early years this model included all modalities of therapeutic intervention. "It does not dichotomize them in either/or categories—for instance, individual therapy or family therapy or group therapy or psychodrama or community therapy. On the contrary, it actualizes all modalities, alternating or combining them in a Systemic/Dialectic way" (Vassiliou & Vassiliou, 1981, p. 216–217).

Intervention in the family system starts with a diagnostic exploratory family session. One or more members may then be invited to join a group therapy process so as to be provided with opportunities for individual differentiation and growth.

In other family cases, troubled couples and parents are invited to workshops which offer an understanding of the transition of family living from more traditional patterns of interaction, roles, values and ideologies to the ones needed for adjustment in the changing milieu. At the same time, children or adolescents of distressed families may enter peer groups aimed at their sensitization to family dynamics.

In the family sessions that follow, the new learnings and skills acquired through the participation of different family members in their groups is seen as corrective *anotropic* feedback for the family system and its evolutionary restructuring. (Anotropy is the term proposed by G. Vassiliou as more suitable for what has been known in the field as negentropy, 1981).

Theoretical Influences

One of the earlier theoretical frameworks relevant to our approach was that of Alvin Toffler. In his 1980 book, *The Third Wave*, Toffler conceives civilization as divided into three major phases, three societal waves—each wave developing its own ideology with which it explains reality, so pushing previous sociocultural realities aside. "Every civilization has a hidden code—a set of rules or principles that run through all its activities—that impacts change on all spheres of human life: social patterns, information patterns, power patterns, technology" (Toffler, 1980, p. 46).

The First wave—the agricultural time in society—a period with limited resources where survival was at stake. Life was organized around the extended family in small close knit and stable communities where one interacted with a small number of people.

The Second wave—the revolution of industrialization with its need for social mobility required individuation and brought an end to the large multigenerational, extended family—the nuclear family emerged. The individual became the basic social unit and through mass media, man's image/values changed and independence became the basic goal. "Industrial capitalism needed a rationale for individualism… a free, independent individual. Each individual had rights…according to his or her own active efforts" (Toffler, 1980, p. 111).

Interpersonal relationships now entailed a set of transactions between individuals so changing behaviours based on friendship, kinship, or group allegiance. Husbands and wives began to speak of marital contracts.

The Third wave, the post-industrial society or the onset of the age of information particularly through the internet, brought possibilities for a vast number of relationships and abundant alternatives for satisfying personal needs. The decline of the nuclear family and the emergence in its place of a diversity of family forms followed thus changing families more in these years than in any previous century.

Other theorists later referred to this second and third period of societal development as "modernity". Foucault describes modernity as an era of questioning and rejection of tradition; with prioritization of individualism, freedom and formal equality—a movement from agrarianism toward capitalism and the market economy; industrialization, urbanization and secularization.

In his definition of modernity, German sociologist, Ulrich Beck (1992) includes much more the change of societal characteristics and normal biographies, changes in lifestyle and forms of love, change in the structures of power and influence, in the forms of political repression and participation, in views of reality and in the norms of knowledge—a much deeper process, which comprises and reshapes the entire social structure.

Still other theorists such as Lyotard understand modernity as a cultural condition characterized by constant change in the pursuit of progress, and goes on to argue that contemporary society moved into a literally *post-modern* phase distinct from modernity. Rapid on-going change culminated, becoming the status quo, *an end in itself* where the notion of certainty/truth became obsolete.

Others analyze the present as a development into a second, distinct phase that is though still "modernity": this has been conceptualized as "risk society" by Ulrich Beck (1992) and "liquid modernity" by Zygmunt Bauman (2000).

In the face of what he identifies as the human-made dangers of today's risk society, Beck introduces the idea of "reflexive modernization". He draws heavily on the concept of reflexivity as a new type of solidarity that offers a reconstructive counter balance to the postmodern paradigm and the loss of all previous sources of support with the rise of deconstructionism and individualization. Beck proposes the idea that, as a society examines itself, it in turn changes itself in the process.

Importantly relevant to our work is Beck's perception of individualism as an important consequence of social changes in late modernity and his stress on the reality that individuals are today increasingly required to construct their own lives and personal meaning.

Zygmunt Bauman (Bauman, Bertrando & Hanks, 2009) explains that the characteristics of today's 'liquid modernity' are the individuals' increasing feelings of uncertainty and ambivalence. It is a kind of chaotic continuation of modernity, where a person can shift from one social position to another in a fluid manner. Nomadism becomes a general trait of the 'liquid modern man' as he flows through his own life like a tourist, changing places, jobs, spouses, values and sometimes more—such as political or sexual orientation—excluding himself from traditional networks of support.

The result is a normative mindset with emphasis on shifting rather than on staying—on provisional in lieu of permanent (or 'solid') commitment—a shifting style that can lead a person astray towards a prison of their own existential creation.

Bauman goes on to stress the consequent new burden of responsibility that fluid modernism places on the individual—namely that "traditional patterns need to be replaced by self-chosen ones" (Bauman, 2000, p. 8).

Extrapolating from the above ideas of both 'modernist' and 'post-modernist' thinkers we clearly understand that the period we are currently undergoing, characterized by exploding social change and ever-increasing complexity, has deepened the disruption and fragmentation of cultural unity and meaning in the lives of individuals, families and their support systems.

Not only has that which we knew to be true yesterday changed, but tomorrow is now unpredictable.

This unpredictability is made even more complex through cultural globalization and the process of international integration arising from the transmission of ideas, meanings and values highly diffused around the world by the internet and popular social media and international travel.

And although cultural globalization has increased the individual's ability to partake in extended social relations and cross-cultural contacts, it is accompanied by a decrease in the once face-to-face more traditional communities, and the recognition of their unique and meaningful patterns of relating. Yet, Fritjof Capra (1997, 2002) reports that, through their close contact with nature and their place in it, traditional cultures had what Gregory Batson called, "systemic wisdom" in terms of relationships, connectedness and context.

Furthermore, we can appreciate a term coined by Ronald Robertson (1995)—"glocalization"—which combines the idea of globalization with that of local considerations. It presents a potential response meant to offer protection against the more negative effects of globalization. Robertson focuses on a more psychosocial approach that stresses the importance of a clearly identified local cultural identity of the past with conscious personal choice of aspects, values and patterns to embody, while being open to permeation through global interactions.

In order to gather the necessary collective mental resources to tackle 'thinking globally and acting locally', Jeremy Rifkin (2010) elaborates that our existing modes of consciousness are structured for earlier eras of development that have faded away. In his book, *The Empathic Civilization*, Rifkin focuses on empathy and its ever-increasing role in our emotional and intellectual development, connecting empathy with the biological function of mirror neurons and the social value of altruism. He argues in favour of relationalism and describes the meaning of human existence as being *to enter into relationships*. Rifkin proposes empathic relationalism as the functional pattern in the race for global consciousness in a world in crises.

We see the above theoretical understandings of the broader social context very relevant to that of Greece—a society that went through a relatively short period of industrialization and has been, and is still battling today, with a period of transition from traditional realities to modern and post modern ones. This context gives solid validation to how our approach views the needs of today's Anthropos (Greek—meaning the human being as a whole, whether female or male) and the psychosocial skills he/she is required to develop for a personally meaningful life—a life based on self-leading, self-regulating processes and personal choice, alongside skills of actualizing difference and cooperation with others—the necessary metaskills for '*Autonomy through and for Interdependence*' (Vassiliou, 1982).

This liberating but painful transforming process of designing the life of one's own entails the discovery of diverse inner voices, perceptions and emotions, many of which originate in previous sociocultural realities connected to and transmitted by intergenerational patterns.

A view of self as 'relational' (Gergen, 1991) is consequently essential and the crucial importance of reflexivity and inner dialogue becomes obvious.

Here, we are reminded of Bakhtin's inspiring study (1973) of Dostoyevsky's polyphonic characters and its influence on perceiving self as being a dialogue of multiple inner voices. Hermans (2001) refers to this multiplicity as the *dialogical self* and later, with Dimaggio (2004) goes on to elaborate on this concept as a synthesis of numerous and different 'subselves'.

In the wider area of systemic and family therapy, modern dialogical approaches such as those of Harlene Anderson, Tom Andersen, Jaakko Seikkula and Karl Tomm (Hoffman, 2002; McNamee & Gergen, 1992) emphasize the significance both of dialogue that opens up space for the emergence of the yet untold, and the internalization of external dialogue which allows new inner voices to be incorporated (Androutsopoulou, 2014). Karl Tomm (Hoyt & Madigan, 2001) regards self as constituted by an internalized community and the patterns of interactions among the members of that community.

In summary, it becomes evident that the creative processing and managing of today's cyclonic change and complexity imposes the inclusion of multiple perspectives which requires but also supports the *interactive–relational self*. Essentially, this favours a more differentiated Anthropos, an internally richer—cognitively and emotionally—human being, more open to relationships and ongoing self-development.

The fostering of these skills in personal differentiation and relating is considered an integral part of therapy.

"Cultural Chronos" and Relational Change

The concept of *cultural chronos*, initially developed by Vasso Vassiliou (Vassiliou, L.G., 1986) refers to patterns of relating within the context of sociocultural change and the subsequent multiple, diverse inner voices that contribute to relational difficultie. Within this perspective, the couple relationship can be conceptualized in "5 Chronos"— 5 periods of time.

In Fig. 12.1, the realities of the agrarian traditional milieu are represented in Time 1 (T1) where the basic goal was survival. The couple existed through the roles of mother and father within an extended family with open boundaries to the community. Spouses had a clear understanding of their division of roles—father the good provider and mother the raising of children and functioning of the home. Partners had "a back to back relationship" and although the exchange of more personal thoughts and emotions did not characterize their relationship, they supported each other through behaviours of their respective roles. The woman would seek emotional support in her difficulties in the next door female neighbor while men would exchange with other men of the community at the village coffee shop—the only then source of input regarding economy, etc. Through the son, the woman would gain social status since he would be the continuation of the family. The daughter was seen as belonging to the family of her future husband and would prepare herself by modeling after her mother (in traditional Greece there is a common saying of "I have one child and one daughter").

These traditional patterns of relating can be understood and honoured as functional only when placed in the broader social context of that period where the basic goal was survival.

Time 2 (T2) refers to the period of industrialization characterized by urbanization and social mobility. The closing of boundaries resulting in the evolution of the nuclear family deprived its members of past social support systems. The invasion of foreign values through mass media brings tensions to the couple and disrupts past views of partners' traditional roles. In this phase, the coalition of mother–child, particularly mother–son, becomes very durable, and is prioritized in family relations, a dynamic often leading to individual and family problems.

Time 3 (T3) sketches the furthering of industrialization - modernity - with its accentuated prominence on the individual and the goal of independence and self-

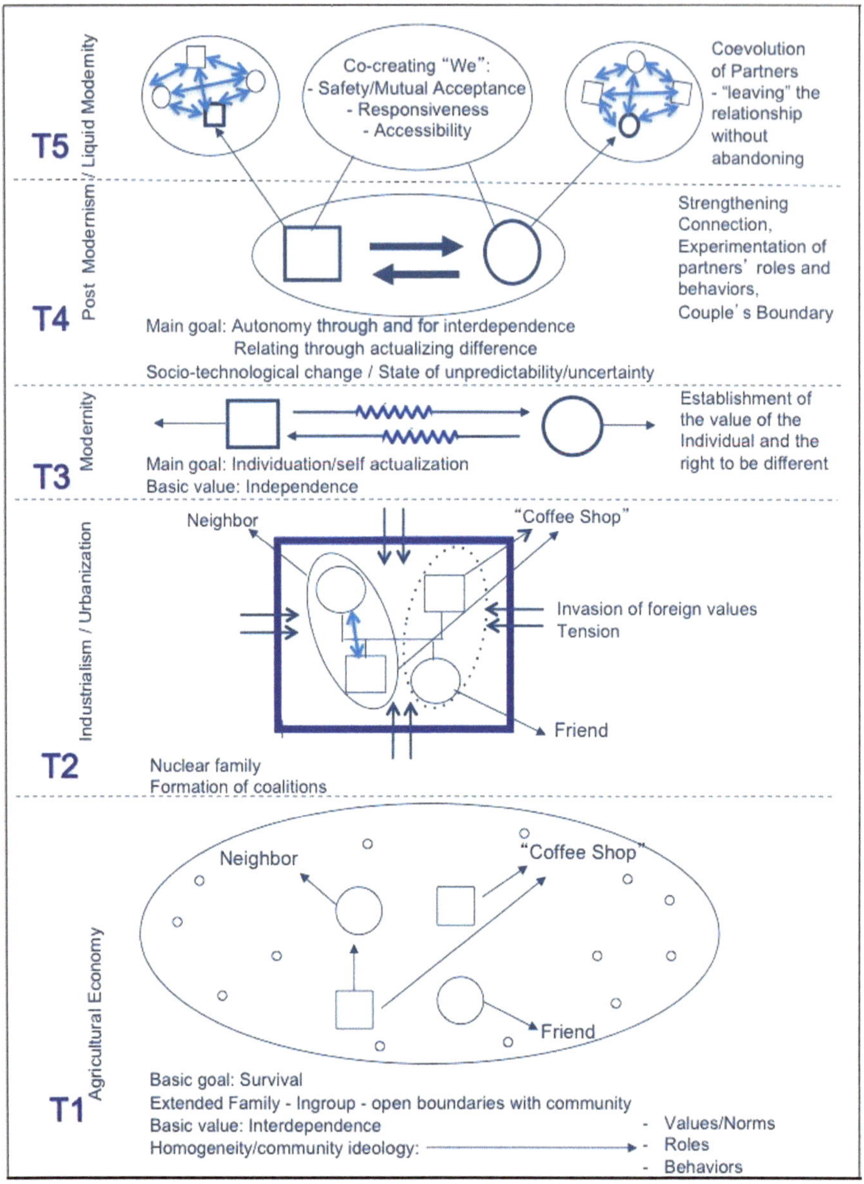

Fig. 12.1 Cultural chronos and relational change

actualization. Here, the manners of relating that couples had deployed so far become, in the most part, no longer effective and the volatile manners of partners' emotional expression often result in conflict and/or distance. On the social level, civil/political rights emerge and the care of others is now undertaken by welfare and social services.

Time 4 (T4) and Time 5 (T5) refer to the period of post-modernism or liquid modernity - the period characterized by an on-going tsunami of socio-technological change and permanent unpredictability. Thrown into previously untravelled relational waters without guidance, parnters' anxiety and uncertainty around relating intimately with each other increases. And, although they attempt to engage using their own personal wits, skill and dedication, in a time of constant distability, none of these bonds are guaranteed to last. Moreover, bonds today often tend to be tied loosly so they can be untied again, quickly and as emotionally effortless as possible, when circumstances change - as they surely will in our liquid modern society, over and over again. The uncanny frailty of human bonds, the feeling of insecurity that frailty inspires, and the conflicting human desire to connect and tighten bonds yet keeping them loose, are the principle predicaments that couples face in this contemporary period.

So, as to grapple with the inherent fears of this predicament, partners need to develop skills in fostering their personal development while, at the same time, strengthening their connection. Serving *autonomy through and for interdependence* becomes even more prominent and is achieved through openess to experimentation of new roles, behaviors and emotional risk-taking.

As shown in time 5, developing these new relational skills nurtures the couple's need to co-create a "We" which is characterized by safety, mutual acceptance, accessibility and responsiveness. At this stage, partners are engaged in the co-evolutionary process which allows safe space for "leaving the relationship" to serve one's autonomy without abandoning the other.

A most important dimension of Cultural Chronos is that today's partners, even those younger in age, have unconsciously internalized diverse inner voices and relevant emotional experiences from each and all of the five time periods.

These prompt confusion in partners' inner dialogue and, in turn, their perceptions of the other and their patterns of relating. Thus, when interacting with each other, particularly in moments of tension, partners fluctuate among the different chronos and "an inner conversation cultural chitter-chatter" is experienced (Stephen Madigan, Yaletown Family Therapy Center, Vancouver, B.C., Canada—personal communication). Chitter-chatter intensifies couples' problems and contributes to escalating their distress and conflict. This collision of cultural voices can be seen as similar to what Gergen (1991) refers to as '*multiphrenia*', a condition whereby one is simultaneously drawn to multiple and conflicting directions.

When using cultural chronos in therapy and in relational enhancement workshops, partners discover that this dynamic is common to most couples in our current transitional sociocultural context. They resonate with a cacophony of inner emotional voices which often results in negative interaction patterns and they feel relieved by the validating acceptance that this is a norm today.

Through the cultural chronos concept, the therapist moves away from labeling the relating of a couple as pathological and understands their interaction cycle in the context of transition from traditional to modern and post-modern patterns of relating. The ground is then laid to assist each partner to develop skills in recognizing his/her multiple culturally defined inner voices and in accessing their underlying related emotions; skills in reflexivity, emotional regulation and inner dialogue—a process which facilitates emotional expression and the restructuring of their negative interaction patterns as a couple.

Systemic Group Therapy

As previously described, the process of clients discovering multiple inner voices and emotions and developing their skills in inner dialogue is optimized through integrating family therapy and client's participation in didactic Systemic Group Therapy.

The value of the group has been documented by many theorists and practitioners over the years. Today, with the advances in neuroscience, participation in small group processes can be viewed as affecting the neuroplasticity of the brain, i.e. our ability to change our brain's structure and function (Cosolino, 2006).

As Daniel Siegel (1999) describes, the factors necessary for the promotion of neuroplasticity are: (a) strong emotional bonds, (b) an environment rich in stimuli, (c) learning through experience, (d) a state of safety which is characterized by cooperation, nurturance, positive reinforcement and a feeling of fairness. All these factors highlight the profound social nature of the human brain (Gournas, 2013).

The group's effectiveness can also be inferred from the writings of the narrative approach, which proposes 'story and re-story telling' of personal experiences so as to co-create new liberating narratives that foster a new meaning of life (White & Epston, 1990). Through the group members as *witnesses* of the alternative stories, the group process can be utilized in enhancing the development of new novel narratives and different personal identities.

I will illustrate this function of the group through a recent narrative shared by a member of a mixed-sex group comprised of eight members, aged 32–42 years, all initially referred to me for family or couple problems. The analogic tool used in this group was the Synallactic Collective Image Technique-SCIT (Vassiliou, 1981). This is essentially a cognitive-emotional tool that uses images in activating analogic processes, which facilitate the expression of personal stories. This is done in the three dimensions of time: in the past—through memories/stories; in the present—through narrating/sharing stories and related emotions while interacting in the here and now; and in the future—through members' reflections on the sequence and connection of the diverse shared narratives and the emerging new understanding of the group as a whole (Polychroni, Gournas & Sakkas, 2008).

Lella is a single 37 year old successful lawyer, living on her own in Athens and involved in a relationship with Dimitri. Her only brother to whom she was closely attached, committed suicide 10 years ago at the age of 24. From that time her family closed itself in and never openly expressed their emotions. Lella has been struggling to open up her emotions from her traumatic loss and make meaning out of its impact on her current partner relationship. She shared the following story.

"Last Sunday I was sitting in the airport waiting to return to Athens. I had spent the Christmas holidays with my parents at home in Thessaloniki where I had the time to relax and enjoy seeing my friends. I feel fulfilled from these holidays—I felt much lighter in my family's home. My outings with my friends, although many and intense, did not make me feel the urge to withdraw or drink too much. I still didn't express my feelings to Dimitris but I shared this difficulty with him and that I would like to be able to. At the airport I reflected on these days and how really different they were and I discovered that this was very much due to the group. When I felt less angry towards my parents, it was like I could hear Maria (fellow group member) trying to understand and connect with her mother. And I really felt that my parents are doing everything they think is best and so I didn't get so angry like I did all the previous years when I felt they didn't understand how I felt. When my anger faded, at times a sadness arose inside me and I thought about Eleni (fellow group member) and how she gets angry so that she doesn't feel her pain—so it's human.

When I was trying to open-up to Dimitris, Katerina (fellow group member) came to my mind and her joy when she succeeded in telling Niko how she felt. Also, Kostas (fellow group member) who is now able to clearly say what he wants and needs. I then got frightened that perhaps my change won't last for long but then I thought of Thanasi (past fellow group member), his joy and confidence during his last days before his closure in the group, and so I felt optimistic. I still feel optimistic along with a little fear. The title I give to my story is *"Along with the others you can succeed"*.

Through Lella's narrative, we can see that incorporating group therapy in our systemic practice, fosters the discovery of one's multiple inner voices and develops skills in inner dialogue and emotional expresssion.

Experiential Training in Family Dynamics and Therapy

In reading the above, one may understand that according to our approach, training and therapy are viewed as different aspects of the same process and based on similar systemic principles. An example of our use of multiple inner voices and dialogue in the context of family therapy training is described below. A more detailed description of this training process is given by Polychroni and Gournas (2004).

With the goal of learning family dynamics, the trainees' group is asked to simulate a specific family incident, the scenario of which is selected by the trainer according to the specific systemic principle that is to be experienced (e.g. triangulation and boundering). The family may be one of various forms, i.e. single parent, multi-generational, homosexual couple etc.

Figure 12.2 illustrates the family as a system with permeable boundaries in interaction with voices from cultural chronos processes. Each member, with multiple inner voices, is seen as interacting with others at times through one prevailing voice and at other times through a synthesis of diverse voices attained by inner dialogue.

Thus, in training, each member/role in the simulated family is formed, *not by one*, but by 4–5 trainees. Each trainee represents an inner sub-self of the role with its own voice and emotional experience. So as to grasp the influence of cultural processes on the family, we often ask a small group of trainees to bring in the voices

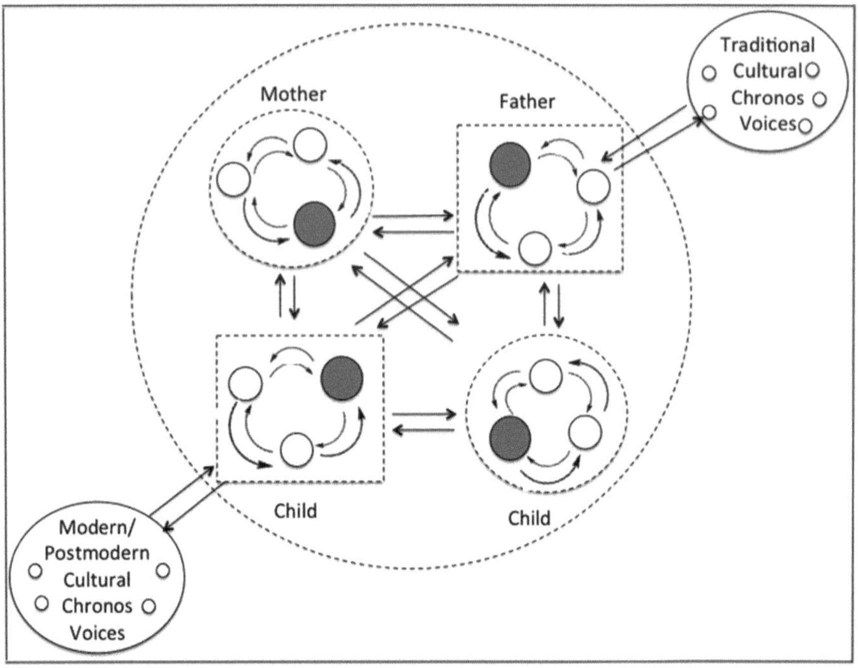

Fig. 12.2 Family simulation in experiential training: multiple inner voices and family relations in the context of cultural transition

of the more traditional cultural chronos and another group to voice those from the modern and postmodern perspective.

Each sub-self is then invited to come in contact with the emotions/thoughts/perceptions/voices catalyzed by the incident and to share these with the other sub-selves of his/her role—throughout speaking in the first person I-position of that particular role. An inner dialogue of each role emerges. The trainer actualizes this inner dialogue to facilitate interpersonal and intergenerational family interaction so that the dynamics of the family as a whole emerge and are experienced by the trainees' group.

Trainees then de-role and form new small groups of four. The goal here is for the trainees to process the experience through their personal resonance (Elkaim, 2008), their own emotions/reflections and to share their learnings that emerged. As the level of safety evolves over the process of training, trainees open-up and more fully disclose their relevant personal experiences and their understanding about their own selves/roles/families.

The training group is in the end brought together in full circle. Small group reports are shared and are actualized as the inner voices at a higher level of the system, i.e. the group as a whole. A collective narrative emerges which the trainer reflects back to the group, relating the overall training experience to principles of Anthropos and the family as a living system in continuous interaction with an ever-changing broader environment and to the implications/applications for therapy.

The feedback from a group of trainees illustrates the manner in which this method of training is experienced 'from the inside out': "Our experience was unique and at the same time enlightening. What impressed us immensely was the revelation of multiple voices. Particularly those that we have internalized without being aware of it. We could feel the different emotions inside each family role. We resonate with many of them. This complexity was illuminating but also frightening. But the fact that the different narratives in the exercise exposed common underlying emotional needs was relieving for all of us. And the common narrative we co-created together in the large plenary group revealed connections among all members of our group that before were hidden. This was like an embodying experience which at the beginning was surprising. Later we realized that indeed we are all members of one connected process and that what connects us as members of the whole and as human beings is much more than what separates us" (Systemic Institute of Cyprus, Training group, 2015).

Current Clinical Practice

Approximately 8 years ago, I was personally engrossed in a specific stage of our family life cycle—that of launching our adult children and moving on (Carter & McGoldrick, 1989). The stress I experienced by the inherent transition of this phase and the emotional upheaval it brought to my relationship with my spouse was unexpectedly intense.

I sincerely attempted to practice what I had been successfully preaching to so many couples for so many years, but was not fully content—something was missing. The need to make sense out of my experience brought me to searching for new developments in the field of couple therapy and in the process I discovered the enlightening framework of attachment.

In the development of the systemic field, we seem to have forgotten John Bowlby. We classically placed him in the category of psychoanalyst and viewed the application of his attachment theory as limited to the relationship between parent and young child. Yet, in his report to the International Society for the Systems Sciences, G. Metcalf (2010) proclaims that we need to rediscover Bowlby as a systems scientist. Metcalf describes in detail Bowlby's use of aspects of cybernetics control theory as part of his attachment theory and his systemic focus on making sense of the patterns of organization he perceived in relationships.

Attachment theory is easily integrated in to our systemic approach since it focuses both on self and system and views individuals' construction of self in the context of their closest relationships.

Yet, according to the more traditional systemic perspective, emotion, the primary signaling system that organizes interactions of attachment, was generally viewed as an individual phenomenon that does not need to be primed in order to modify interactions. "...emotion, if discussed at all, was seen mostly in terms of ventilation and catharsis and was generally avoided in couple therapy sessions" (Mahoney, 1991,

p. 186). Emotion was thus often perceived as part of the problem of distress, rather than as part of the solution. This led our field to an artificial dichotomy of the '*within*' emotional experience of partners and their '*between*' processes of relating. And even though clinicians such as Virginia Satir (Satir & Baldwin, 1984) had early formulated a number of relevent interventions, until recently there was no articulated model of couple therapy that combines a focus on inner realities and outer systemic interaction patterns.

Neuroscience research has today come to support attachment and primary emotional experiences by showing us that human's innate wiring to connect with others is primarily influenced by our early environment and that right hemisphere functioning from birth—responsible for much of our emotional experience—is most impacted by parental attunement or lack thereof (Fishbane, 2013). It is now evident that, in contrast to explicit memory, preverbal implicit memories register our early life experiences. These experiences are unconsciously carried into our current interpersonal interactions and are particularly potent in our most intimate relationships.

Their experimental and observational studies on the effect of attachment on perceptions of social support brought Collins and Feeney (2004) to conclude that adults' desire for comfort and support should not be regarded as childish or immature dependence; instead, it should be respected as being an intrinsic part of human nature that contributes to personal health and well-being. John Bowlby had earlier advised that "all of us, *from cradle to grave,* are happiest when life is organized as a series of excursions, long or short, from the secure base provided by our attachment figure(s). Dependency is an innate healthy part of your being, not something that we overcome growing up" (Bowlby, 1988, p. 62).

Focusing specifically on distressed interactions between adult partners, it now seems that the core elements of such interactions are 'absorbing states of negative emotions' which lead to rigid negative interaction patterns repeated over time. "The picture that seems to emerge…is that the power of rigid negative interaction patterns, with which all systemic therapists are familiar, is not simply about interpersonal homeostasis or systemic coherence. It is primed and maintained by powerful, attachment-related affect that reflects our basic sense of security in the world, and whether we can get others to respond to our needs. In distressed systems, negative patterns of interaction, and patterns of processing and/or regulating negative affect, become "stuck"—reciprocally determining and self-reinforcing" (Johnson, 1998, p.3).

It becomes clear that if we are to fully actualize our systemic principles that focus on context and wholeness, we need to integrate intrapsychic realities (i.e. emotional experience and how it is constructed and processed) and utilize them as feedback loops into couples' patterns of relating. In this way, we gain a whole picture and are able to comprehend distressed interactions and more effectively restructure them.

I was grateful for this new enriching knowledge—it offered me novel insight into my emotions and personal needs from my partner relationship during the launching of our children. It also opened up a new dimension for my clinical practice with couples. I thus went on to study and specialize in Emotionally Focused Therapy (EFT) and have since incorporated this approach in my work with couples and families and in training.

The EFT model was first presented and tested in the early 1980s (Johnson & Greenberg, 1985). Developed primarily by Susan Johnson (2004), EFT is a brief integrative approach to couples that focuses on helping partners in close relationships co-create secure attachment bonds. EFT's substantial body of research, both in terms of outcome and process, has illustrated its effectiveness (Johnson & Brubacher, 2016). The model has been applied and validated for different psychological problems and cultural contexts of couples (Furrow, Johnson & Bradley, 2011) and has now also been shown to be effective in family therapy (Stavrianopoulos, Faller & Furrow, 2014).

In practice EFT integrates—within a systemic approach to reciprocally reinforcing patterns of interaction—an attachment orientation to intimate adult relationships and an experiential humanistic perspective that values emotions.

In trying to connect, distressed couples get caught in negative repetitive sequences of interaction where partners express secondary emotions—the more reactive emotions such as anger, jealousy, resentment, and frustration—rather than primary emotions—the deeper, more vulnerable emotions of sadness, hurt, fear and loneliness.

The EFT therapist focuses, and works very deeply on the emotional responses underlying the interactional patterns and uses each of these—the emotion and interaction—to influence and recreate the other in the 'here-and-now' of the therapy session. The therapist helps partners access, explore and reprocess the more vulnerable emotions, which they usually avoid or disregard and so fosters the restructuring of new interactional patterns.

According to Lebow et al. (2012), the EFT therapist is a process consultant, helping partners expand constricted and constricting inner emotional realities and interactional responses, thereby shifting rigid interactions into responses that foster resilience and secure connection.

Over the years, along with the fundamental attachment base, what never ceases to intrigue and move me with the EFT model is the potency of its therapeutic moves. The therapist engages on an emotional level with the couple through validating each partner's position and emotions in their interactive "dance". Through simple - slow - soft interventions, honoring and repeating the clients' own words and images, a unique therapeutic attunement with each partner is attained. Behaviors, perceptions/attributions and reactive secondary emotions are validated and reframed in terms of unmet attachment needs. This process fosters a felt sense of safety and is extremely powerful in partners accessing their underlying primary or more vulnerable emotions which, through the span of therapy, they are assisted to share with each other. In my experience, we as therapists are permitted in this way to enter and in depth touch upon an essential aspect of human nature, that of our inherent need and yearning for emotional connection and the integral difficulties and fears this entails.

As a brief illustration of the EFT model in my work, I will describe a couple I saw in a live consultation to a couple therapist[2] who is currently in the process of learning the model. Anna (39) and Georgos (39) have been together for 1 year. They had not planned to marry but recently did so due to Anna's unexpected pregnancy.

---

[2] I thank Ioanna Koukkou and the couple for giving me permission to use the consultation session in this illustration. All names and relevant details have been changed.

They requested couple therapy since they were fighting quite often and Anna was worried about bringing a child into their relationship. The couple therapist shared that she was having difficulty in forming an alliance with Georgos and asked for my consultation. As she described, "Georgos talks on and on about how helpful and reliable he is and that Anna has no reason to worry."

Very quickly in the process of the session cultural chronos confusion was quite evident. This was particularly manifested in Georgos, a young man raised in a small city in northern Greece. As a more traditional man, Georgos focused on the task of being a good provider and trying to 'fix the problem'. He would withdraw from discussing Anna's worries with her, characterizing them as exaggeration; any emotions such as sadness that would arise from not having the acceptance and appreciation he needed from his partner were avoided and, as he expressed, "I delete and try again." He manifested extreme anxiety from not succeeding, in spite of all his many efforts to convince his wife of his value and reliability, so as to help her not be afraid of the new-coming realities their child would bring. Anna, on the other hand, felt insecure from Georgos dismissing her worries, she felt she was not seen and feared that Georgos was in the relationship because of the pregnancy. She experienced an underlying fear of abandonment (prompted by her attachment history with her primary attachment figure). Rather than express these vulnerable primary emotions, Anna would complain, criticize, become angry and push Georgos away. Although Georgos would then feel sadness and despair of being rejected by his spouse (emotions he accessed as the session progressed) he would not express them, but rather "delete" and either leave the conversation so that things would not become worse or defend himself and try to convince Anna of his reliability and worth.

Figure 12.3 portrays the inner emotional realities and interactional cycle of Anna and Georgos in the format first introduced by fellow EFT trainer, Scott Woolley (2011). The 'infinity loop' concept illustrates the layers embedded in the interactions of distressed couples. As can be seen, the couple's negative pattern of 'criticize/demand' responded to by 'defend/distance' is generated by inner attachment related affect. In this case, the use of slow, soft, repetitive validation of each partner's perceptions and positions in the relationship was particularly crucial in accessing their underlying emotions and attachment needs—particularly with Georgos who in the session acquired a felt sense of his more primary emotions and experienced in vivo - through enactments - how their expression softened his wife's response into one of more appreciation and acceptance.

Through this experience, their therapist now had a map of the territory of this couple's negative pattern, primary emotions and underlying attachment yearnings and could go on to use her EFT knowledge and interventions in her further work with them.

The incorporation of attachment and the EFT model has also affected the manner in which I conduct Multiple Couple Therapy Groups.

A number of therapists today have referred to the use of the attachment framework in group therapy (Flores, 2010). As individuals interact in the group, "they rely on their previous attachment experiences to manage group processes, meet internal needs and cope with their emotions. Their internal representation of self

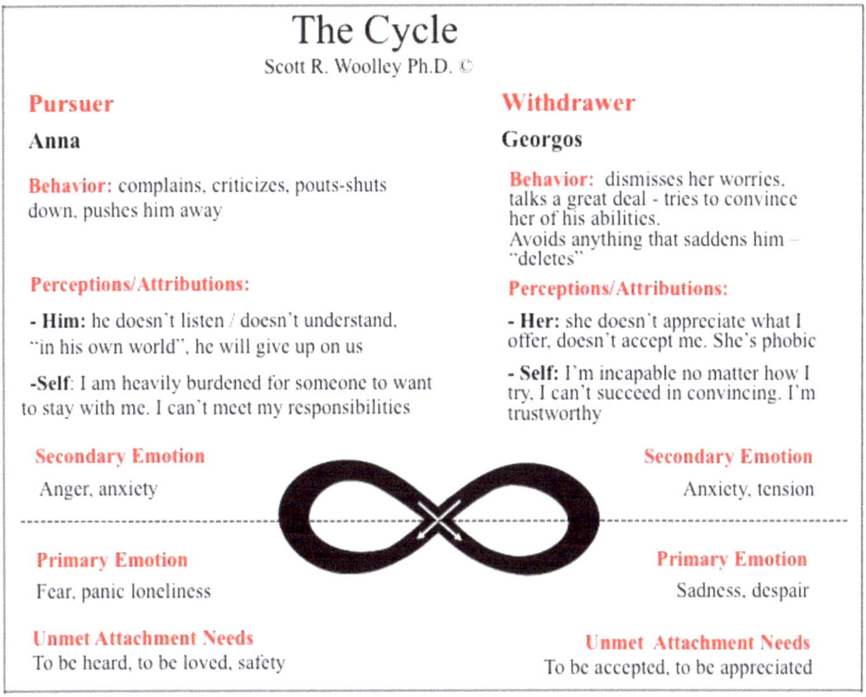

Fig. 12.3 Couple's Negative Interaction Cycle

and others and emotion-regulating strategies are automatically triggered in the group. The therapist must create a safe environment where individuals can explore these implicit attachment-based processes as they are activated in the group sessions. Through feedback from the group and the therapist, members explore their current emotional and relational difficulties in the here-and-now of the group process, allowing for corrective emotional experiences that contradict attachment failures and ultimately facilitate more attachment security" (Marmarosh, Markin & Spiegel, 2013, p. 4).

This process is particularly potent in couples' group therapy, where partners have the opportunity to experience each others' efforts in self exploration and attachment based emotions triggered by their relationship.

Along with the use of the Synallactic Collective Image Technique (SCIT), I have devised specific inner dialogue exercises used to foster partners' accessing of primary emotions and attachment needs and other experiential tasks that guide couples in restructuring their relational patterns. Four to five couples embark on a group journey where they are guided in discovering the underlying emotional realities of their relationships while at the same time being engaged in the group process. Through the group experience partners gain an understanding of the nature of adult love and realize that the disconnection and distress they experience is common to all couples and can be transformed.

Each couple is asked to individually draw an image symbolizing an emotion he/she is experiencing when entering in the group. The group votes on which couple's drawings they wish to focus on in that session. Each partner is then invited to allow the selected images to guide him/her in recalling a memory/story in the life of their relationship. Each couple then goes on to share their stories with the group. Interaction among the couples follows with mutual sharing of resonant experiences and expression of emotions that emerge in the process.

The chosen couple's images of a specific group session can be seen in Fig. 12.4.

I will here only refer to the collective narrative and title of the group experience that emerged through the process of interaction at the end of the session. The stories/memories of each couple, important for understanding the basis on which this collective narrative emerged, can be found in the sequence they were presented in the group in Appendix 1.

Title: "Searching for connection through forces in conflict"

Collective narrative: "When we get into conflict with our spouse we have difficulty in expressing our more vulnerable feelings. If though we take the risk and

Fig. 12.4 Drawings from Couples' Group Therapy

share our difficulties and fears openly, we feel relieved and come closer to our partner, united together in an upward direction. And then, in spite of previous obstacles, we feel intimacy and love. Yet, there are many other times when relating with each other becomes overwhelming, frustrating and sad. It's at those times that we experience a great deal of uncertainty and question in which direction to turn—perhaps just cut off the relationship. But then, when we open up space to hear ourselves more deeply like we hear the others in the group, we realize how a renaissance of our relationship emerges—when we allow ourselves to reach the sadness, pain and loneliness from having lost our connection and express these feelings to our partner without criticism. So, although we still have times of collision and upheaval and experience fear and tension in our relationship, we are also optimistic of our life's path together. We feel relief, hope, love and less worry in this upward development".

Personal Closing Reflections

I hope in this chapter to have succeeded in transporting to the readers, the importance for us as therapists to have a grounded understanding of the sociocultural context of the couples and families we offer our services to. This becomes more prominently crucial in an age where social mobility, immigration and refugee families are rapidly increasing.

As family therapists, we need to open our boundaries as a discipline to include other modalities that have proven useful in intervening on the different levels of systems. We will in this way '*go back to the future*' and emerge again as systemic practitioners.

Furthermore, understanding attachment and working more deeply on inner emotional realities underlying interaction patterns, can transform our clinical practice with couples and families and empower us as therapists.

Today, the attachment perspective is slowly being integrated in systemic couple and family therapy in the field in Europe. Important contributions being made include those from colleagues of the EFTA "family". My fellow EFTA Board Member from Italy, Rodolfo de Bernart, the new president of the International Association for the Study of Attachment (Dilorenzo, 2015), is currently attempting to utilize knowledge of attachment strategies in family assessment and treatment. Arlene Vetere, former president of EFTA from the UK and co-author in the present book (Chapter 9), has focused on narratives of attachment in relation to families and violence. Emotionally Focused Therapy is thriving in the various European countries through the work of many systemic family therapists. Among them, Barbara Kohnstamm, past EFTA Board member and cherished friend from the Netherlands who first introduced me to EFT, is conducting novel applications of the model with her passion for therapy and experiential supervision (Vetere & Stratton, 2016).

On a personal level, as I enter my later years, I am now involved in applying the principles I have elaborated in this chapter, in an area which comes 'full circle' in my life—perhaps this is a common process for all of us, a living process.

I started out as an immigrant returning to the homeland in search of personal and professional meaning through my training. And now, within the new reality of my homeland, with its overwhelming incoming wave of despaired individuals and families searching for new horizons, I am involved in training immigrants and refugees to become cultural mediators to offer their supportive services to the families of their people.

Using the knowledge and experience I have acquired over the years—subjective culture, cultural chronos and multiplicity of inner voices, the supporting process of groups in developing reflexivity and inner dialogue with their power to foster resilience, and the fundamental human need to feel emotionally connected, safe and loved—I hope to offer a small pebble in us co-creating an empathic civilization where, as Gregory Bateson has taught us, '*difference makes the difference.*'

Acknowledgement Petros Polychronis has been my partner in life and work for over 35 years. So much of this chapter is an outcome of my learnings from his unquenchable thirst for new knowledge, his clarity of values and our inspiring conversations. Petros has supported me throughout my personal and scientific journey. This work could not have emerged without him. Σε ευχαριστώ, Πέτρο.

Appendix 1

Partners' Recollections/Stories: Couples' Group (May 2015)

Couple A: Ioanna

A few days ago, I was very sad because my communication with Mihalis wasn't good at all. We had come against one another because I asked him to help me with our son in order for me to be able to go to some seminars and he only saw his own needs. That evening we discussed it and I told him that I can't tolerate one aspect of his character (I have to say here that I had great difficulty and fear to tell him that) and immediately after that I told him about my difficulty of saying this and my fear that he would not understand what I told him. I immediately felt relieved, freer and I saw that Mihalis was close to me.

At the beginning I felt fear and desperation. Now I feel freedom.

Title: "Connected in upward motion"

Couple A: Mihalis

On the images I see powers that are connected and have common traits—but uncommon ones as well—powers that wobble. There is though a centre core.

I remember when Ioanna and I were together on a trip in Egypt and we were climbing down the Sinai mountain. I felt love then and now hope when I remember.

Title: "Despite the obstacles"

Couple B: Anastasia

I remember an incident a few days ago, when we were on holidays. The atmosphere between us hadn't been good for a while now but both of us were making an effort, or at least that's what I thought. One afternoon I started a conversation and Nikos said that he hasn't seen any change in me, no effort on my part and that all the years we have been together, we have never been well.

I felt all the effort that I thought I was making was ruined and this burdened me. We said many things to each other, which made my confusion even bigger.

I felt very frustrated and now I feel sadness.

Title: "Which will be the direction of the ball?"

Couple B: Nikos

I see two forces colliding and finally following an upward direction. It reminds me of last week when we were away on holidays. Following consecutive "battles" and difficult times, Anastasia asked me when we return to Athens to find a place of my own to stay and that she takes the responsibility to put an end to this relationship that isn't going anywhere anymore.

The previous day and while we were both in a good mood, she had gone for a walk and while I was waiting for her, I was reading my book. When she returned I was happy to see her and I felt that there was potential for us. But when she looked at our son and again noted that he had gained weight lately, she told me that I must agree with her and start telling him that he has to stop eating so many sweets. We disagreed and we didn't talk any further ...

The next day she asked me to separate. I stayed alone on the beach for a long time trying to think how our lives will be. I felt anxious, stress and sadness. I cried very carefully because I didn't want her to see me.

After quite some time, I went to her and, with difficulty, I told her that we should wait one more week in order to come back to the group and decide after that.

She accepted and so here we are with that deadline hanging in the air...

I'm anxious about what is going to happen but without stress now because I think that she may be right and that only by breaking something can we fix it from the beginning.

Title: "Renaissance"

Couple C: Eleni

I see a sun rising and it's getting bigger and more luminous.

It reminds me of my relationship with my husband and our journey up to now. Yesterday morning, specifically, I said at breakfast: I can only imagine how much you may be suffering and how troubled you are lately, since you are at home but you don't seem to be here. When you return from work you are either on the phone, the couch, the TV or on the computer.

I told him that I say this with sadness and pain, without any criticizing mood. I feel like I have an angel next to me and I can't even enjoy him. He told me that he does many things in order not to think. I asked him if it crosses his mind that I might be feeling lonely. And then he told me that I don't support him as well. And we started to talk and feel each other.

At the beginning I felt lonely.

Now I feel some optimism because we talked.

Title: "Life's Path"

Couple C: Yiannis

I see a collision and then calmness, restoration and development of upward direction.

It reminds me of the upheaval we had in our house this morning when our son was leaving for camp. We talked about this with Eleni.

Then I felt little bit of fear, tension and worry, but now I feel relief, hope and love.

Title: "The development upwards"

References

Ackerman, N. (Ed.). (1970). *Family therapy in transition*. Boston: Little Brown & Co.

Androutsopoulou, A. (2014). Multiple inner writers: Understanding the "Polyphonic Self" in psychotherapy training. *Systems thinking and psychotherapy, 5, Journal of the Hellenic Systemic Thinking and Family Therapy Association* (Greek). Retrieved from www.hestafta.org.

Bakhtin, M. (1973). *Problems of Dostoyevsky's poetics* (2nd ed.). Ann Arbor, MI: Ardis.

Bateson, G. (1972). *Collected essays in anthropology, psychiatry, evolution and epistemology. Steps to an ecology of mind*. London: Jason Aronson Inc.

Bauman, Z. (2000). *Liquid modernity*. Cambridge: Polity.

Bauman, Z., Bertrando, P., & Hanks, H. (2009). Liquid ethics – Psychotherapy in a time of uncertainty. *Human Systems: The Journal of Therapy, Consultation and Training, 20*(2), 42–56.

Beck, U. (1992). *Risk society: Towards a new modernity*. London: Sage.

Bowen, M. (1978). *Family therapy in clinical practice*. New York: Jason Aronson.

Bowlby, J. (1988). *A secure base*. New York: Basic Books.

Capra, F. (1997). *The web of life: A new scientific understanding of living systems*. New York: Anchor Books, A division of Random House, Inc.

Capra, F. (2002). *Hidden connections*. New York: Doubleday.

Carter, B., & McGoldrick, M. (1989). *The changing family life cycle: A framework for family therapy*. Boston: Allyn & Bacon.

Collins, N. L., & Feeney, B. C. (2004). Working models of attachment shape perceptions of social support: Evidence from experimental and observational studies. *Journal of Personality and Social Psychology, 87*(3), 363–383.

Cosolino, L. (2006). *The neuroscience of human relationships: Attachment and the developing social brain*. New York: Norton.

Dilorenzo, M. (2015). The application of the DMM model to relational family therapy: An interview with Rodolfo de Bernart. In: *Electronic newsletter of the international association for the study of attachment, no. 20*. Retrieved from www.iasa-dmm.org.
Elkaim, M. (2008). Resonance in supervision and training. *Human Systems: The Journal of Systemic Consultation & Management, 19*(1), 26–43.
Fishbane, M. (2013). *Loving with the brain in mind: Neurobiology and couple therapy*. New York: Norton.
Flores, P. (2010). Group psychotherapy and neuro-plasticity: An attachment theory perspective. *International Journal of Group Psychotherapy, 60*(4), 547–570.
Furrow, J., Johnson, S., & Bradley, B. (2011). *The emotionally focused casebook. New directions in treating couples*. New York: Routledge.
Gergen, K. (1991). *The saturated self. Dilemmas of identity in contemporary life*. New York: Basic Books.
Gournas, G. (2013). Dealing with the crisis: Actualizing the power of the group. *Systems thinking and psychotherapy, 2. Journal of the Hellenic Systemic Thinking and Family Therapy Association* (Greek). Retrieved from www.hestafta.org.
Hermans, H. J. M. (2001). The dialogical self: Towards a theory of personal and cultural positioning. *Culture and Psychology, 7*(3), 243–281.
Hermans, H. J. M., & Dimaggio, G. (2004). The dialogical self in psychotherapy: Introduction. In H. J. M. Hermans & G. Dimaggio (Eds.), *The dialogical self in psychotherapy* (pp. 1–10). New York, NY: Brunner-Routledge.
Hoffman, L. (2002). *Family therapy: An intimate history*. New York: Norton & Co.
Hoyt, M. F., & Madigan, S. (2001). Honoring our internalized others and the ethics of caring: A conversation with Karl Tomm. In M. Hoyt (Ed.), *Interviews with brief therapy experts* (p. 245.264). Philadelphia: Brunner-Rutledge.
Jackson, D. D. (1967). The individual and the larger contexts. *Family Process, 6*(2), 139–154.
Johnson, S. M. (1998). Listening to the music: Emotion as a natural part of systems theory. *The Journal of Systemic Therapies, 17*, 1–17.
Johnson, S. M. (2004). *The practice of emotionally focused marital therapy: creating connection*. New York: Bruner/Routledge.
Johnson, S., & Brubacher, L. (2016). Emotionally focused couples therapy: Empiricism and art. In T. Sexton & J. Lebow (Eds.), *Handbook of family therapy* (pp. 326–348). New York: Routledge.
Johnson, S. M., & Greenberg, L. S. (1985). The differential effects of experiential and problem solving intervention in resolving marital conflicts. *Journal of Consulting and Clinical Psychology, 53*, 175–184.
Kaftatzi, V. (1996). From family to systemic therapy. In Systemic Associaton of Northern Greece (Ed.), *Systemic thinking* (pp. 21–38). Thessaloniki: Psychiatric Hospital
Kohnstamm, B., & Vetere, A. (2016). A supervisors progression: From personal and professional development training in group settings to the inclusion of the self of the therapist in supervision. In A. Vetere & P. Stratton (Eds.), *Interacting selves: Systemic solutions for personal and professional development in counseling and psychotherapy* (pp. 85–97). London: Routledge.
Krause, B. (2002). *Culture and system in family therapy*. London: Karnac Books.
Krause, B. (2007). Reading Naven: Towards the integration of culture in systemic psychotherapy. *Human Systems: The Journal of Systemic Consultation & Management, 18*, 112–125.
Lebow, J. L., Chambers, A. L., Christensen, A., & Johnson, S. M. (2012). Research on the treatment of couple distress. *Journal of Marital and Family Therapy, 38*, 145–168.
Mahoney, M. J. (1991). *Human change processes*. New York: Basic Books.
Marmarosh, C., Markin, R. D., & Spiegel, E. B. (2013). *Attachment in group psychotherapy*. Washington: American Psychological Association.
McNamee, S., & Gergen, K. J. (1992). *Therapy as social construction*. London: Sage.
Metcalf, G. S. (2010). *International society for the systems sciences: Report on the work of john bowlby*. Retrieved from www.isss.org.
Minuchin, S. (1974). *Families and family therapy*. Cambridge: Harvard University Press.

Polychroni, K., Gournas, G., & Sakkas, D. (2008). Actualizing inner voices and the group process: Experiential systemic training in personal development. *Human Systems: The Journal of Therapy, Consultation and Training, 19*(1-3), 26–43.
Polychroni-Protopsalti, K., & Gournas, G. (2004). Inner voices and dialogue in family therapy and systemic training: Actualizing sequence and diversity. *Context: The Magazine for Family Therapy and Systemic Practice, 73*, 11–12.
Rey, W. (2016 in press). Point of view matters. *Human Systems: The Journal of Therapy, Consultation and Training,* Special Issue on Embracing New Knowledge – Training for Integrative and Innovative Systemic Practice.
Rifkin, J. (2010). *The empathic civilization: The race to global consciousness in a world in crisis.* New York: Jeremy P. Tarcher/Penguin.
Robertson, R. (1995). Glocalization: Time-space & homogeneity-heterogeneity. In M. Featherson, S. Lash, & R. Robertson (Eds.), *Global modernities* (pp. 25–44). London: Sage.
Satir, V., & Baldwin, M. (1984). *Satir step by step: A guide to creating change in families peoplemaking*. Palo Alto, CA: Science and Behavior Books.
Siegel, J. D. (1999). *The developing mind: How relationships and the brain interact to shape who we are*. New York: Guilford Press.
Stavrianopoulos, K., Faller, G., & Furrow, J. (2014). Emotionally focused family therapy: Facilitating change within a family system. *Journal of Couple & Relationship Therapy: Innovations in Clinical and Educational Interventions, 13*(1), 25–43.
Toffler, A. (1980). *The third wave*. USA: Bantam Books.
Triandis, H., Vassiliou, V., Vassiliou, G. A., Tanaka, Y., & Shanmugam, A. V. (1972). *The analysis of subjective culture*. USA: Wiley-Interscience.
Vassiliou, G. (1970). Milieu specificity in family therapy. In N. Ackerman (Ed.), *Family therapy in transition* (pp. 81–98). Boston: Little Brown & Co.
Vassiliou, L. G. (1986). *The form of the important relationship in the Greek family. Technical report XXIX (Greek)*. Athens: Athenian Institute of Anthropos.
Vassiliou, G., & Vassiliou, V. (1968). A transactional approach to mental health: An experiment in Greece. In B. F. Riess (Ed.), *New directions in mental health* (pp. 280–300). New York: Grune & Stratton.
Vassiliou, G., & Vassiliou, V. (1981). Outlining the synallactic collective image technique as used within a systemic, dialectic approach. In J.-E. Durkin (Ed.), *Living groups* (pp. 216–228). New York: Brunner/Mazel.
Vassiliou, G., & Vassiliou, V. (1982). Outlining a systemic-dialectic approach to family functioning and malfunctioning. In M. Pines (Ed.), *The individual and the group: Boundaries and interrelations* (pp. 151–155). New York: Plenum Press.
Watzlawick, P., Beavin, J. H., & Jackson, D. D. (1967). *Pragmatics of human communication*. New York: Norton.
White, M., & Epston, D. (1990). *Narrative means to therapeutic ends*. New York: Norton.

Part IV
Outlooks

Chapter 13
Virtual Relations and Globalized Families: The Genogram 4.0 Interview

Maria Borcsa and Julia Hille

IT engineer, male, 43, works in Toronto, Canada:

"This evening I have to baby-sit. When my wife is home alone (in Bucharest) and she has to go downstairs, for example to prepare dinner, she focuses the webcam on the babies. I keep an eye on them and if one of them starts to cry, I let her know by SMS" *(Nedelcu 2012, p. 1351)*

Synopsis This chapter brings together two global developments: the increasing number of transnational families and the expansion of information and communication technologies (ICTs). It is assumed that we as family/systemic therapists and trainers have to react to these changes by providing new concepts as well as new methods. "World families" make visible how globalization becomes embodied in marital and family relations; this model criticizes explicitly the "methodological nationalism" (Beck and Beck Gernsheim 2010) usually applied in family studies.

We propose the Genogram 4.0 Interview for therapy, training and research. This tool scrutinizes unquestioned certainties like the concept of "home" and focuses on the use of digital technology in everyday communication processes. It shall help us to understand how one-national or transnational families are "doing family" (Morgan 1996) in the world today.

M. Borcsa, Ph.D. (✉) • J. Hille, B.A., M.A.
University of Applied Sciences Nordhausen, Nordhausen, Germany
e-mail: borcsa@hs-nordhausen.de

M. Borcsa, P. Stratton (eds.), *Origins and Originality in Family Therapy and Systemic Practice*, European Family Therapy Association Series,
DOI 10.1007/978-3-319-39061-1_13

Introduction

We, Maria and Julia, belong to two different generations: both finishing their degrees in Germany (which in the interim re-changed from being *two* nations into, again, *one* nation), Maria acquired a Diploma, while Julia's degrees were already called Bachelor and Master, following a change in European education policies named after a city in Italy. Both of us, we finished a systemic training in Germany; Maria participated in the very first curriculum in "multicultural systems" at a private training institute in the 90s, while Julia studied Systemic Social Work, M.A. in the new millennium. Maria was born behind the iron curtain, for Julia the unified Europe has been "normality". Maria witnessed the very early forms of mobile phones coming onto the market (big and heavy like bricks), while Julia cannot recall a world without Internet (but she points out that she knows what a "modem" is).

These are only few facets showing our similarities but also our differences and some socio-historical changes in the country we are living in, in Europe and the world.

During the joint work on this chapter Europe has been facing a flux of human mobility to the continent from war areas outside of the European borders. This phenomenon has created a situation which is perceived as a crisis in many European countries and has been challenging their citizens. We took this development on to consider some aspects of it which affect our profession on a theoretical, methodological and ethical level.

Mobility, Migration and Globalization: The Emergence of World Families

Not only since the refugee emergency reached Europe, mobility and migration have been the phenomena which have structured increasingly more lives in the past decades. Interestingly enough—and even the phenomenon in itself is similar—*mobility* is often described as a movement of the highly skilled, *migration* is connotated with that of the lower skilled and the poor (Castles 2010). This reflects how the division between "the poor(er)" and "the rich(er)" is a guiding distinction in observing and classifying human beings moving around the world—education is hereby categorized as symbolic capital (Bourdieu 1986). This distinction, which does create a difference, can be witnessed in the current discourse about refugees as well—immediately after the discussion transcends the issue of humanitarian aid. The richer are afraid that poverty is contagious.

In the last decades we have been experiencing major changes in political, economical, social and technological areas. In our globalized world we can identify an erosion of the definitive frontiers that once separated markets, states, civilizations, cultures, lifeworlds and even human beings (e.g. surrogacy, Beck and Beck-Gernsheim 2014). We arrived at a state of interdependence among individuals, groups and countries that is not just economic and political but also—and more and more—ethical. Technological change plays an important role in these developments, as it seems to increase mobility as well as helps to overcome social difficulties caused by the latter. "Whereas non-migrant families throughout the world commonly have discussions across the kitchen table, now many families whose members are relocated through migration conduct the same everyday discussions in real time across oceans" (Vertovec 2004, p. 222); social relations can be "kept alive" through information and communication technologies (ICTs) in a way our grandparents could only dream of.

The transcending of national, ethnic, religious and political boundaries and power relations due to these processes have to be highlighted and discussed with more attention. With regard to the history of ideas, social sciences are still connected to a tradition of thinking which goes back to the nineteenth and twentieth centuries with its grand narratives. One aspect of this dominant story is that people "belong" to a nation. Social sciences, including their empirical studies, (implicitly) refer to this paradigmatic framework. As the term "migration" stands in the same tradition (Castles 2010)—and this becomes evident when the discussion is directed toward national social care systems providing support to migrants and refugees—some analysts have suggested abandoning it.

> Nationalism has been identified as an early 19th century invention (...), resulting from the rapid replacement of existing absolute monarchies in Europe by units called nation-states and the subsequent establishment of such polities in other parts of the world. While the unifying content of nationalism varied from country to country, it was based on an ideology of the commonness of origins, purposes, and goals that allowed those in power to legitimate rule over large and diverse populations. Nationalism gave heterogeneous groups a sense of a shared common interest, and carried a vision of a nation-state as a "people," each nation making up a separate, equal, and natural unit. (Glick Schiller, Basch, and Blanc-Szanton 1992, p.14f).

Even before the right-wing political movements turned towards a revival of this concept in Europe and beyond, some intellectuals had begun to reflect on this issue more critically, highlighting its construction. "Nationalism" is done through shared symbolism referring to (often imaginary) common interests—allowing authorities to control their national populations most effectively (ibid p. 15). With regard to sciences a *methodological nationalism* of the social sciences can be found in all subsystems of social inquiry, also in family research (Beck and Beck-Gernsheim 2009, 2010, 2014). Here we discover an unquestioned implicit connection between the individual, the family and the (one) state which can be diagnosed as a blind spot of the methodological nationalism in family studies. In the discourse of nation-state the core of family seems a "secular version of the Holy Trinity: one household, one nationality and one identity" (Beck and Beck-Gernsheim 2014, p. 65). The link of this pattern to patriarchal structures (Coward 1983, cited in Bryceson and Vuorela 2002) is evident as "family loyalty and loyalty to the state mainly went hand in hand, mediated by patriotism and national identity" (Beck and Beck-Gernsheim 2014 p. 140). This way of thinking follows the rule that people *belong* to one place/nation on the earth (and can be exploited there, e.g. as soldiers).

The theory of cosmopolitanism (Beck 2006) makes a different offer. This model is based on the assumption that "the days of autonomy, of national self-sufficiency, of splendid isolation are gone for ever" (Beck and Beck-Gernsheim 2014, p. 68). We are in the process of creating "global generations", where various—formerly separated—elements are interlinked, even if people do not move at all: ICTs bring these components to our "homes". This globalized patchwork consists of mosaic pieces which are usually not fitted together to make a unified picture of one lifestyle, one religion, one national identity. However, in these globalized times we (are obliged to) physically or symbolically coexist with humans of different nationalities, religions etc.—even if we regard them as enemies. Actually we can observe how "people" hardly manage to cope with the challenges of adapting to these factual realities in many European countries and beyond. Anyway, the "global other" has become a part of our existence "acting from below and from within, in everyday life, often involuntary and unnoticed" (Beck and Beck-Gernsheim 2014, p. 75)—and, since the so-called "refugee crises", very much noticed, too. Through these ongoing human and data movement processes the "excluded other" becomes visible in our lives. Whether we like it or not, we are confronted with the world in the interior of our countries: global inequities—differences in capital, in power, in freedom—acquire names and faces.

Transnationalism and Transmigration

The concept of transmigration is one model which challenges the dominant narrative of describing migration as a one-way direction of mobility, being spatio-temporally limited to changing place from one country of origin to a country of destination (Apitzsch 2014). Mobility in this framework is not necessarily a one-way stream but is seen more as oscillating movement(s) between places. This new social field creates and maintains new forms of belongings and identities which develop against rigid forms of national affiliation. It implies at least imaginary ties to two countries or even two continents, and subjective projections of their future onto these places (Geisen 2014).

> We have defined transnationalism as the processes by which immigrants build social fields that link together their country of origin and their country of settlement. Immigrants who build such social fields are designated "transmigrants." Transmigrants develop and maintain multiple relations—familial, economic, social, organizational, religious, and political that span borders. Transmigrants take actions, make decisions, and feel concerns, and develop identities within social networks that connect them to two or more societies simultaneously. (Glick Schiller et al. 1992, p.1f)

We can speak of *multilocations*, which are multiple, overlapping spaces of belonging, multipolar systems of references, loyalties and identifications (Nedelcu 2012, p. 1343). This is a paradigmatic shift that requires, both in theory and practice, going beyond a binary framework, which used to be: leaving a country = emigration; going to another country = immigration. We can find many examples in Europe and worldwide: an estimation with regard to Italy (Lamura 2009, cited in

Beck and Beck-Gernsheim 2014) says that we have to consider around 774,000 home helpers, 90 % of whom are foreign nationals (many coming from the poorer European countries like Romania or Moldova), most of them employed privately as carers for the elderly. Most are female, having children in their respective country of origin and going back and forth to see their families, where other family members, like the father or other relatives, are taking care of the children (Parreñas 2001, 2005). Facing these "global care chains", globalized work in families (family services like child-rearing or elderly care) constitute the "gold of the poor", a "resource" that can be exploited by the richer; love and care become "commodities" which can be exported and imported. Furthermore, by taking care of background work in the family, transmigrant women stabilize the precarious state of peace in relations between the sexes in the richer countries (Beck and Beck-Gernsheim 2014).

This example shows clearly how mobility leads to social changes, both in the countries which are left as well as in the receiving countries. With regard to family relations, it has been empirically proved that, with mobility, changes in family positions and gender roles are taking place (e.g. Geisen 2014; Lutz 2008; Spitzer et al. 2003); for instance, men are taking care of children while women are working in another country. These processes challenge traditional self-concepts and gender roles in the outgoing countries as well as in the receiving ones by providing services which free women of the receiving countries from traditional family duties done now, e.g. by a foreign helper.

An important role in maintaining this transnational social fields is played—as already mentioned—by technological development. Social technologies are becoming core protagonists and "new family members" (Bacigalupe and Lambe 2011) in the lives of families in general and in those of transnational families in particular (e.g. Madianou 2012; Şenyürekli and Detzner 2009; Stern and Messer 2009). The mechanisms are interlinked and circular: on the one hand, globalisation changes institutions like families; on the other hand, the digital revolution changes socialization.

Family Relations and ICTs

Everyday communication practices are fundamental ways of "doing family" (Morgan 1996): family relations are actively constructed by small everyday performances, wherein the use of information and communication technologies become integrated. The use of mobile or smartphones, e-mails or text messages, apps etc. have become part of contemporary family life in more and more places of the world. Carvalho et al. (2015) focus in their literature review (of 45 papers written in English, Portuguese or Spanish between 1998 and 2013) on the relationship of ICTs and family functioning. The results—even if sometimes inconsistent and contradictory—show that ICTs have introduced qualitative changes in family functioning, creating new interaction scenarios and rearranging current family relational patterns. Even if in general we can say, "the more time individuals spend in activities involving ICTs, the lower the amount of time devoted to other activities (e.g. outdoor activities)"

(Carvalho et al. 2015 p. 104), the same ICTs seem to have different impact and effects on the family functioning of different family forms. Some studies show that ICTs seem to strengthen family bonds, are effective in improving family communication and increasing intimacy among members (see, with regard to couples: Duran et al. 2011; Jin and Pena 2010; Miller-Ott et al. 2012; Parker et al. 2013). Family communication can be improved through shared online activities between children and parents and daily management activities using ICTs. Other empirical studies point to mixed effects or even those going into the opposite direction, especially when the technology equipment and high frequency of use seem to reduce family time and intimacy and increase isolation of members living in the same household. Further, the so-called "digital natives" (Prensky 2001) may acquire a certain power through their edge in ICT skills, which has to be balanced out in the familial hierarchy by establishing rules of usage, thereby increasing the likelihood of conflicts between generations. ICTs have the capacity to change family patterns of interaction due to the redefining of family roles with regard to the respective levels of expertise in handling them (Carvalho et al. 2015, p. 105). Family boundaries might also be challenged: "ICTs have the potential to modify the permeability of family boundaries due to the change of the flow of information. If on the one hand, the family gets unrestricted access to a diversity of information unprecedented in our history, on the other hand they become more exposed, blending external world with family environments. (…) Thus, boundaries between the family environment and the external world are relevant and necessary, but are being blurred by the domestic use of ICTs." (ibid., p. 105). New media have to be viewed as an environment of affordances (Madianou 2014), especially smartphones, which are the result of convergence of mobile telephony and personal computing. The affordance of these "polymedia" (Madianou 2014)—feeling invited to post, e.g. family pictures in social networks—has to be balanced out by the structural aspect of privacy and intimacy families have been defined by up to now. It is obvious that through the emergence of these affordances media education becomes crucial—inside and outside the family.

A new level of being "permanently online, permanently connected" (Vorderer 2015) is reached with polymediatic smartphones. The management of relationships through this technology goes hand in hand with the perception of being able to (re-) create a contact anytime, even if other activities are in the forefront. These exchanges may lack coherence and completeness but can also generate a feeling of connectedness and permanent unity (Vorderer 2015). Polymedia create a dialectics produced through the *overlap of social settings*—being on the one hand virtually connected via the ICT and on the other hand physically available for face-to-face communication. This spatio-temporal texture creates co-presence, but also divided presence (Greschke 2013). The challenge is to be able to act appropriately "here and there" simultaneously, with your face-to-face interactional partner(s) as well as with the virtual one(s).

In terms of mediated circumstances, presence and absence are not conceptualized as distinct categories but more as a continuum. Co-presence does not necessarily mean a physical but more a *communicative availability in a social space* (Greschke 2013). The virtual co-presence can be described as a social space in which people have an ongoing awareness of others. ICTs "provide new opportunities for constructing a 'co-presence' in spite of distance" (Bacigalupe and Cámara 2012).

It is transnational everyday communication practices that are especially made possible through the digital revolution. We can observe the emergence of a new "transnational social habitus" and "deterritorialised identities" (Nedelcu 2012).

> On the one hand, ICTs allow migrants to form multiple belongings, to capture cosmopolitan values, to develop deterritorialised identities and biographies and to act at a distance in real time; on the other hand, while accelerating integration and incorporation paths in host societies, ICTs also enable migrants to defend particularistic values and to claim a particular belonging while living as global citizens. (Nedelcu 2012, p. 1340–1341)

To conclude at this point of research expertise, we may say that ICTs seem to have different impact on families' adoption of these technologies and on family functioning with respect to the developmental stage the family is in, the specific stage of their life cycle, and their degree of mobility.

> In families living geographically separated, in empty nest stage of the family life cycle (…) or in a transnational situation (…), seem that ICTs are an important key in maintain preexisting relationships and strength family bonds. In sum, families seem to experience different levels of cohesion associated with the same ICTs and activity, according to the stage of the family life cycle they are at. (Carvalho et al. 2015, p. 104)

As an illustration of these changes we will now turn to a single case.

Roulan Derke: A Family on the Move

The contact with this family—or, more precisely, with one member of the family—did not take place in a clinical setting. At the time of writing this chapter refugees were living in many German cities in gymnasiums of schools and universities for a couple of weeks, from where they were dispersed to other places. Volunteers helped where needed, being confronted with sorrow, courage and hopefulness at the same time. "It's not so much for us, but for our children" was a sentence we often heard, reflecting what we knew from research literature: refugee parents tend to rely on their children as vitally necessary resources for their own—physical and psychological—survival (Weine et al. 2004).

In this context we made the acquaintance of Roulan Derke[1] (we spoke English), 30 years old. He grew up in Damascus/Syria, where he studied Fine Arts (M.A.). In order to avoid being recruited and actively in the war, he left Syria in December 2011 for Turkey, working several months there for his way to Europe. His first attempt on the land route failed, he was picked up by the military and sent back to Turkey. After having earned enough money to pay traffickers, he left Turkey on a boat for Greece. On his way he passed FYROM, Serbia, Hungary and Austria and arrived in Germany in January 2015; now he is living in a bigger city in the east of Germany (Halle). Roulan's family is Kurdish; they are assigned to the Sunnitic Islamic group (Fig. 13.1).

[1] All information (names, places etc.) is anonymized and authorized.

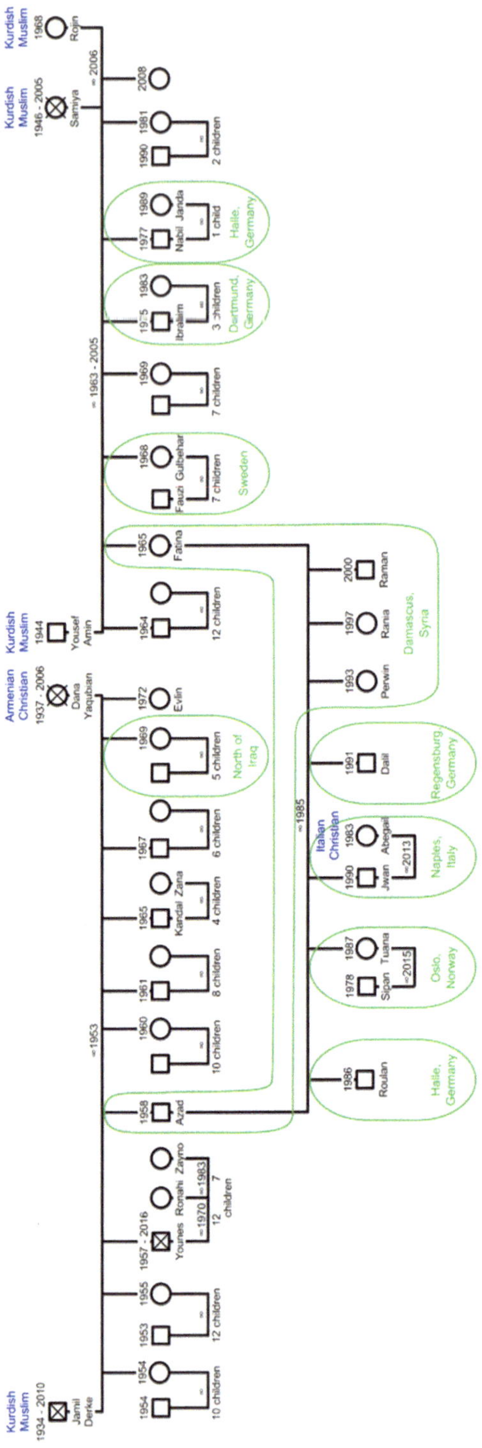

Fig. 13.1 Genogram of Roulan's family

Roulan's father *Azad*, 58 years old, is working as a medical doctor in a hospital in Damascus. Azad's family of origin is living in a smaller city in the north of Syria (Derek). Most of the family members from this part live a "traditional life" according to Roulan. Azad's father *Jamil Derke* (1934–2010) was a Kurdish Muslim. He worked as a businessman. Azad's mother *Dana Yaqubian* (1937–2006) was a Christian woman from Armenia. She converted to Islam to marry Jamil (resulting in the rupture of contact with her parents and the rest of the family). Azad has nine siblings. Three are his senior. The two eldest sisters left home to live with their husbands' families. The eldest son, *Younes* (1957–2016), lived in the childhood house with his parents, his two wives and his sister Evlin. With *Ronahi* he has 12 children. With *Zayno* (they got married in 2004) he has seven children. He became the head of the family after the death of Jamil. Azad's youngest sister *Evlin* (44 years old) has a mental disorder and a physical handicap. She never went to school and needs special care. She lives at Younes's house and the two widows are taking care of her. Azad's brother *Kandal* is, according to Roulan, the most educated in the family. His wife *Zana* completed her studies at the university. All siblings are living in Derek except one brother and his family; they are living in the north of Iraq.

Roulan's mother *Fatina* is 51 years old, a housewife, left school after 9 years of education. Fatina's family of origin is also living in the countryside of Derek, in the north of Syria. *Yousef Amin*, her father (72 years old), is "a farmer who can read and write" (which was an exception several years ago, according to Roulan). His first wife *Samiya* (1946–2005, died of diabetes), was a housewife and also a Kurdish Muslim. Yousef and Samiya have seven children. Fatina is the second oldest. After his first wife died, he married *Rojin* (48); they have one child (8). One sister of Fatina, *Gulbehar*, migrated with her husband Fauzi and their children to Sweden in 2013. This happened as the oldest daughter married a Kurdish-Syrian man in 2011 who had been living in Sweden for many years. With his help the parents and younger siblings could be brought to Sweden. One brother of Fatina, named *Ibrahim*, has been living with his wife and three children in Dortmund (Germany) since September 2015. During the escape the wife was pregnant with the youngest child. Another brother of Fatina, *Nabil* (39 years old), has been living together with his wife *Janda* (27) and their son Nour (7) in Halle since November 2015, arriving in Germany along the same route as Roulan. Before that, they had lived in Damascus, too, while the other family members lived and still live in Derek.

The Digital Native Generation

Roulan, 30 years old (see above). *Tuana*, 29 years old; in September 2015 she got her degree in engineering. She got married in Istanbul in October 2015. Sipan, her husband, is 38 years old. He is of Kurdish ethnicity, was born in the north of Syria in a smaller city (Sere Kaniye) and has been living in Norway since 2012. Now the couple are living together in Oslo, Norway. *Jwan*, 26 years old, left Syria in May 2012. In Istanbul he met his wife Abegail (33 years old). She was born in Naples,

Italy and has a Roman Catholic familial background. They got married in 2013 and are living and working in Naples now. *Dalil*, 25 years old, studied medicine in Damascus for 2 years; he left Syria in December 2013. He has been living in Regensburg/Germany since August 2015. *Perwin* (23) is living with her parents and Rania and Raman in Damascus. She is studying to become a teacher. *Rania* (19) started her studies in the nursery. She is also living in her parents' flat. *Raman* is 16 years old and goes to school. According to Roulan "he is the next one who has to leave Syria because he is old enough for fighting".

Roulan expressed that despite repeated requests his parents don't want to leave Syria. We asked him about his contact to his parents and the extended family. As he hasn't seen his parents and siblings for 3 years now, they have been communicating by smartphone applications (WhatsApp, Viber etc.) and calling each other at least 2–3 times per week. When they phone each other, he asks his sister Perwin for recipes and they talk about daily life—the different customs and traditions in the Eastern and Western societies .... He shared the following story:

A Wedding Story

Tuana, Roulan's sister, had a lot of admirers who wished to marry her. But her father, Azad, didn't give permission to the marriage of his daughter until she finished studying; he was concerned that marriage may interfere with her studies and she may never obtain her degree.

During her master's studies in Damascus Tuana met a fellow student named Samar. Her brother Sipan had been living (for 3 years) in Oslo wishing to marry a woman from Syria. Samar thought of Tuana as being a good match for him: she told her family how kind, friendly and beautiful Tuana is. Samar introduced Tuana and Sipan to each other via Skype. For a half year they continued their communication through Internet and finally decided to get married. Following the tradition, Sipan contacted Tuana's father by phone and formally asked permission to marry his daughter.

Now it was Azad's responsibility to gather information about Sipan, his background and family. Since Sipan was living in Norway, Azad could only meet with Sipan's relatives, living in Sere Kaniye (in the north of Syria). But driving to the other part of the country was not safe during the war and so Azad called his brothers and cousins from Derek and asked them to drive to Sere Kaniye. They accepted his request and travelled there to get more information.

After the visit to the village, they had a good impression about Sipan's family and Sipan. Sipan was described as friendly, hard-working and coming from a wealthy family. Now Azad asked his sons' opinion about the marriage. For Roulan, Tuana's judgement was very important as they have a very close relationship. Since Tuana sincerely claimed that Sipan was a "good guy", Roulan gave his consent. As for the other brothers, they followed the opinion of Roulan because he was the oldest. Finally, Azad had to make a decision. Considering all the information, he agreed to the wedding on one condition: Tuana had to finish her studies.

Half a year later Tuana had her Master's degree. Then, for the first time, Sipan and Tuana met each other face to face in Istanbul, in the flat of Sipan's relatives. Traditionally it is important that during the first meeting family members from both families are present. But most relatives couldn't travel due to the war or ongoing asylum procedures; only Jywan had the possibility to visit from Italy. After the official first meeting, Sipan and Tuana saw each other the next day in Jywan's hotel room and in his presence.

The wedding was one week later in Istanbul. The ceremony was modest and "didn't feel real" for Tuana, as her family was not present. The way they shared the special moments was by sending photos via social networks and apps to Tuana's and Sipan's family members who couldn't join the wedding ceremony.

Having finished the story, Roulan smiled in a melancholic way: when they phone, his parents often ask him to get married and have children ....

We do not know how Roulan's story continued.

Doing World Family

This case well the interlinking of traditional and transcontextual family patterns: using communication technology is here an instrument in the process of generating and maintaining close contact and creating (pre-)marriage rituals. These rituals are a hybrid of face to face (travelling to the community) and mediated communication (phoning, skyping, posting pictures). The ICT serves its role in the life cycle stage (Falicov 2011), not only in that of Tuana's but of the broader family system which is involved throughout. The communication tools are incorporated in shared—or at least respected—cultural values and family practices, which are both conveyed and understood by all participants. Through these practices—in this way of "doing family"—family cohesion and family roles are kept up, transcending several national and continental borders.

Family performances are fundamentally social in nature, where the meaning of one's actions has to be witnessed by relevant others if those actions are to be effective as constituting family practices (Finch 2007). Through the absence of familial witnesses during the ceremony, the pre-marriage rituals seemed to be more "real" to Tuana than the marriage itself—a phenomenon which was given tribute ex post by posting pictures in social media.

Following Beck and Beck-Gernsheim (2014), we can regard Roulan's family as a "world family". These kind of families are love relationships and kinship between people living in (multilocal) or coming from (multinational or multicontinental) different countries or continents. "World families are formed when the connection between family solidarity and loyalty to the state becomes attenuated" (ibid. p. 141), in the best-case scenario they are substituted by trust, tolerance and flexibility in family relations (Weine et al. 2004). Roulan's family show a high extent of resilience strategies in continuing family life across countries and continents, even if, because of the war, they might feel "scattered in the diaspora" (Weine et al. 2004,

p. 155). The challenge will be to form a patchwork of different life and family styles and to bear the contradictions between traditionalist and (post-)modern life models concerning family, including religion, gender roles etc. (Beck and Beck-Gernsheim 2014; Papadopoulos and Hildebrand 1997).

Concept of Acculturation: An Ideology?

Newer literature on working with migrants and refugees points to the insufficiency clinicians face by sticking to a linear model of migration and assimilation (Borcsa 2010; Falicov 2008; Voulgaridou et al. 2006; Weine et al. 2004). Observing and studying families today which live "across great geographic, state, and cultural differences brings forth a very different set of difficulties and calls for a very different set of strategies than those captured by the term "acculturation"" (Weine et al. 2004 p. 158), which has guided cross-cultural mental health work with transnational families for the past several decades. This is supported by health care research, pointing in the direction that trans-cultural familial practices and a hybrid self-conception are associated with higher familial and individual resilience (Falicov 2011, 2012).

Many of us work with transnational families and/or their children, and this number will increase. "The protagonists in the migration saga include those who leave, those who stay, and those who come and go for generations to come" (Falicov 2005, p. 400). In the work with globalized families, the focus cannot only be the "immigrant(s)" in the receiving country but the family as a whole interacting across national and continental borders with the help of ICTs. We agree with Bacigalupe and Cámara (2012) that clinicians working with world families, therefore, are situated in new communicational circumstances that have implications for how individuals, couples and families behave, think and feel. We as clinicians have to assume that family members abroad might play a significant role in decision-making processes, even in everyday life (Baldassar, Baldock, and Wilding 2007; Horst 2006; Hunter 2015; Schier 2009; Wilding 2006). We have to take into consideration intergenerational bonds, legacies and delegations which do not stop at the national or continental borders and are integrated into daily practices through communication. "A clinician working with the transnational family without the constraints of geography or time accepts the fluid nature of the virtual and real" (Bacigalupe and Cámara 2012, p. 1434). This is especially true for the "global generation" who never knew a world without ICTs—be it on the side of the client or on that of the therapist.

As shown, we as systemic therapists and trainers have to face new realities—most trainers may be "digital immigrants" (Prensky 2001), while the new generation of family/systemic therapists are more and more "digital natives". Even if the last years have been clearly marked by cultural sensitivity in systemic therapy and training, up to now there has been—compared to the mundane influence we can observe every day—not that much knowledge of how information and communication technologies might be a resource for families and their therapists.

The Genogram 4.0 Interview

Since the early days of using the family genogram there have been numerous developments and enrichments to this method. Especially cultural aspects have been reflected and implemented in the last decades—in therapy as well as in training (e.g. Hardy and Laszloffy 1995; Schellenberger et al. 2007; Watts-Jones 1997; Yznaga 2008). Inspired by the study of Roulan's family and based on the assumption that through global and technological changes we have to conceptualize families progressively as world families (even if they do not move), we want to question *the meaning of* the relational space(s) of belonging. Furthermore, by integrating ICTs as a "new family member" we wish to consider its impact on the one-national or transnational family life. For this purpose we have constructed an interview (see Table 13.1) which can be used (1) in therapeutic work with families, (2) in family therapy training for increasing self-reflexivity (a) in the influences of values and beliefs related to dominant stories of one-nation families, (b) in the impact of ICTs on relationships; and (3) in research, e.g. in family studies linked to these topics. It consists of four parts:

Part I: Structural Genogram

This part of the genogram graphically presents demographic information about the family. Questions asked and drawn in a genogram interview include information on education status, profession, relationship (marriage, divorce), medical histories; further who lives in the household and where other family members live (McGoldrick and Gerson 1985; McGoldrick et al. 1999).

Part II: Uniqueness Variables

Through the methodological nationalism, migrants or asylum seekers are often confined by their environment (and especially by the media) to one aspect of their identity, be it their status or ethnicity. Refugees might be pathologized after having experienced war, which is an "epistemological confusion between morality and pathology" (Papadopoulos 2001, p. 416) and therefore looked at through a certain lens. Asking questions about their "normal" and divers family relations can easily get out of sight.

Table 13.1 The Genogram 4.0 Interview

Part I. Structural genogram
1. Name, age, gender, date of birth (and death), number of siblings and place of birth in birth order, education and occupation, date of marriage (separation, divorce and remarriages) of three generations (McGoldrick and Gerson 1985)
2. Position and function of relevant others (Watts-Jones 1997)
Part II. Uniqueness variables
1. Does your name mean something (in your 'mother tongue')? Who gave this name to you? What stories were told about it? Do you have other names (you like/you do not)? Who gave them to you?
2. Do you like to be part of/the head of/the youngest etc. in your family? What makes your family/your role in the family special? Do you think your younger brother/older sister etc. likes to have the position s/he has? Why (not)? If you could exchange your position with someone of your family who would this be? Why?
3. What does it mean to you to be born as a woman/a man? Imagine you were born as the opposite sex—what do you think what would your life have been like up to now? What would be better, what worse?
4. What is the last event you spent with your family which you like to remember?
Part III. Relational spaces of belonging
1. What does your country of origin mean to you? What do you think what the people listed on the genogram would say to this question if I asked them?
2. What does the country of residence mean to you? Are there other countries where you or other family members have lived? How would you describe the impact of these places on your life/the life of your family members listed on the genogram? If you were to move to another country, which country would this be? Why? If you do not want to move, why not?
3. What does your ethnicity mean to you and your family members? What is its impact on your/their everyday life? What do you think where this impact comes from? What practices in your every-day life show the commitment to your/their ethnical belonging? If your ethnicity is/was (temporarily or permanently) in the minority, what does/did this mean to you/to your family members listed on the genogram?
4. Which language(s) do you use in your everyday life? Are there situations when you switch from one language to another? Do you use a different language with some family members from the one you use with others? Which language(s) do you like more/most? Why? Which less? Why?
5. What does "home" mean to you? What does it mean to your sister, father etc.? Are there differences between the generations from your point of view? If so, what do they look like? What impact does this have on your relationships?
6. How important is the continent, the country, the region you are living in for you? Why?
7. Does religion and faith mean something to you? If so, in what way? Imagine you were born into another religion how would this have impacted your life?
8. What does privacy mean to you?
Part IV. Use of information and communication technologies (ICT)
1. How do you use ICTs?
2. What do ICTs mean for your everyday life? Do you have a metaphor describing it?
3. Do you have rules/rituals when using communication technologies? What do they look like? Who came up with the idea of having them? What do you think, how come?
4. Which persons/social groups are of special interest for you in using ICTs? Why?
5. How do you use ICTs for sharing private information in your family and with friends?

(continued)

Table 13.1 (continued)

6. What kind of differences in using ICTs do you realize in your family and your relevant others? What kind of differences do you observe between generations? What impact do these differences have on your relationship? How do you deal with these differences?
Upgrade—questions for professionals with regard to ICTs
1. How do you use ICTs in your private life?
2. Do you use them in your professional life? If so, how?
3. What impact does (not) using ICTs in therapy have on your therapeutic relationship(s)?
4. Does using ICTs in therapy change the way you deal with closeness and distance in your professional relationship(s)?

Part III: Relational Spaces of Belonging

In this section the attention is drawn to geographical and symbolic spaces of belonging, like the country, the region, the language and "home" (Dutta 2010). How are these features constructed?

Part IV: Use of Information and Communication Technologies

In this part we focus on the use of information and communication technologies. Specificities among family members or subsystems in using ICTs as well as certain rituals are discussed.

Upgrade

This segment deals with the impact ICTs have on the life of the therapist, especially with regard to the relationship with the clients (Table 13.1).

Use in Therapy

The genogram interview can be applied in multiple ways, adjusted to the setting, the problem constellation or the mandate. The interview combines linear, circular and hypothesizing questions which make it an intervention and consequently have to be adapted to the concrete circumstances. They should be understood as inspiration and guidelines for the therapist, not to "know" before asking the concrete member(s) of the family about their subjective worldview. This goes hand in hand with a second order approach, where the therapist takes a self-in-system stance and shifts more into a collaborative role with the clients (Turner 1991), searching together for resources in the system.

The four parts can be applied with regard to how they fit into the given situation, e.g. using the circumstance that one child is texting during the session.

Use in Training and Supervision

Much has been written about the need of cultural competence or a self-reflexive stance of the therapist in working with families from other cultures (see for a critical review Rober and De Haene 2014). But what if we challenge "home" with all the positive connotations as a dominant narrative of our cultural heritage, including methodological nationalism? Could we imagine a life as nomads? Without possessions except what we can carry?

The part on ICTs should foster self-reflexivity as regards routine patterns in our everyday life. We respond in one way or in another to the "environment of affordances" which we face, e.g. through smartphones. The poles are "excluding the machine from our life" to "not being able to live one day without being permanently online". This attitude will obviously create a bias on how we look at the family members we work with and their use of/ their relationship to ICTs. It might happen that we are not open to investigating communication technology as a potential resource for a family system and to using it as an instrument in therapy or that we overestimate its potential.

Use in Research

The dominance of quantitative research playing its role in this development, over years an obvious gap has developed between psychotherapy research and practice (Lambert 2013). This is unfortunate and can be resolved especially by integrating research methods into training family and systemic therapists which better suit their everyday practice (Borcsa and Rober 2016).

"Few studies or practices have linked findings from existent ethnographic research and family therapy, when in fact there is a natural marriage between the two" (Tubbs and Burton 2005, p. 139; see also Simon 2012). Ethnographic research and the stance of respectful curiosity in systemic therapy have much in common. Both go along with the exposure of our selves to unknown realms while creating cooperation. When Falicov suggests that trainees should interview also non-clinical families, she refers to the different roles in the respective processes: "the trainee can explore culture more fully and with less pressure" (1995, p. 8), i.e. without the need to be helpful at the same time. The switch between the two positions can be enlightening and should be much more practised in training (not only in academic context but also in private institutes) from our point of view.

Conclusion

ICTs and mobility are the two expressions of our globalized world. It seems as if there is "no way back" with regard to these developments. "Globalisation has brought about a fundamental shift in the way families live their lives" (Mills 2014, p. 259). We have to consider a higher complexity in working with them, they being one-national or transnational. Real and virtual communication is used in an integrative manner in the lives of most families, those becoming globalized through technology. We as therapists and systemic practitioners have to face this interlinking, too. We have to acknowledge that ICTs can play a key role in keeping up family resilience in families living in different places and that they can be used as a resource in therapy (e.g. by inviting family members to attend a session virtually). There are technical, methodical and ethical questions and challenges to be resolved (data protection, higher risk of self-exposure in mediated communications, see Eichenberg and Stetina 2015), a process which is already very much on its way in individual therapy. Interestingly, individual therapy research shows that there is no general negative influence on the therapist–client relationship in doing therapy online (Cook and Doyle 2004; Sucala et al. 2012). Systemic research in this field is a desideratum.

References

Apitzsch, U. (2014). Transnationale Familienkooperation. In T. Geisen, T. Studer, & E. Yildiz (Eds.), *Migration, Familie und Gesellschaft: Beiträge zu Theorie, Kultur und Politik* (pp. 13–26). Wiesbaden: Springer VS.

Bacigalupe, G., & Cámara, M. (2012). Transnational families and social technologies: Reassessing immigration psychology. *Journal of Ethnic and Migration Studies, 38*(9), 1425–1438.

Bacigalupe, G., & Lambe, S. (2011). Virtualizing intimacy: Information communication technologies and transnational families in therapy. *Family Process, 50*(1), 12–26.

Baldassar, L., Baldock, C. V., & Wilding, R. (2007). *Families caring across borders. Migration, ageing and transnational caregiving*. Houndmills: Palgrave Macmillan.

Beck, U. (2006). *The cosmopolitan vision*. Cambridge: Polity Press.

Beck, U., & Beck-Gernsheim, E. (2009). Global generations and the trap of methodological nationalism. For a cosmopolitan turn in the sociology of youth and generation. *European Sociological Review, 25*(1), 25–36.

Beck, U., & Beck-Gernsheim, E. (2010). Passage to hope: Marriage, migration, and the need for a cosmopolitan turn in family research. *Journal of Family Theory & Review, 2*(4), 401–414.

Beck, U., & Beck-Gernsheim, E. (2014). *Distant love. Personal life in the global age*. Cambridge: Polity Press.

Borcsa, M. (2010). Kultur, Selbst und psychische Gesundheit. *Psychotherapie im Dialog, 11*(4), 290–293.

Borcsa, M., & Rober, P. (Eds.). (2016). *Research perspectives in couple therapy. Discursive qualitative methods*. Heidelberg, New York, Dordrecht, London: Springer International.

Bourdieu, P. (1986). The forms of capital. In J. Richardson (Ed.), *Handbook of theory and research for the sociology of education* (pp. 241–258). New York: Greenwood.

Bryceson, D. F., & Vuorela, U. (2002). Transnational families in the twenty-first century. In D. F. Bryceson & U. Vuorela (Eds.), *The transnational family. New European frontiers and global networks* (pp. 3–30). Oxford, New York: Berg.
Carvalho, J., Francisco, R., & Relvas, A. P. (2015). Family functioning and information and communication technologies: How do they relate? A literature review. *Computers in Human Behavior, 45*, 99–108.
Castles, S. (2010). Understanding global migration: A social transformation perspective. *Journal of Ethnic and Migration Studies, 36*(10), 1565–1586.
Cook, J. E., & Doyle, C. (2004). Working alliance in online therapy as compared to face-to-face therapy: Preliminary results. *CyberPsychology & Behavior, 5*(2), 95–105.
Duran, R. L., Kelly, L., & Rotaru, T. (2011). Mobile phones in romantic relationships and the dialectic of autonomy versus connection. *Communication Quarterly, 59*(1), 19–36.
Dutta, S. (2010). Working with refugee and asylum seeking families. In S. Dutta & R. Singh (Eds.), *Race and culture: tools, techniques and trainings: A manual for professionals* (pp. 55–82). London: Karnac Books.
Eichenberg, C., & Stetina, B. U. (2015). Risiken und Nebenwirkungen in der Online-Therapie. Misserfolgsforschung muss auf das Internet-Setting erweitert werden. *Psychotherapie im Dialog, 16*(4), 56–60.
Falicov, C. J. (1995). Training to think culturally: A multidimensional comparative framework. *Family Process, 34*(4), 373–388.
Falicov, C. J. (2005). Emotional transnationalism and family identities. *Family Process, 44*(4), 399–406.
Falicov, C. J. (2008). Transnational journeys. In M. McGoldrick & K. Hardy (Eds.), *Re-visioning culture, race and class in family therapy* (pp. 25–38). New York, NY: Guilford Press.
Falicov, C. J. (2011). Migration and the family life cycle. In M. McGoldrick, N. Garcia-Preto, & B. Carter (Eds.), *The expanded family life cycle: Individual, family and social perspectives* (4th ed., pp. 336–347). Boston, MA: Allyn & Bacon.
Falicov, C. J. (2012). Immigrant family processes. A multidimensional framework. In F. Walsh (Ed.), *Normal family processes: Growing diversity and complexity* (pp. 297–323). New York, NY: Guilford Press.
Finch, J. (2007). Displaying families. *Sociology, 41*(1), 65–81.
Geisen, T. (2014). Multilokale Existenzweisen von Familien im Kontext von Migration, Herausforderungen für Forschung und Theorieentwicklung. In T. Geisen, T. Studer, & E. Yildiz (Eds.), *Migration, Familie und Gesellschaft. Beiträge zu Theorie, Kultur und Politik* (pp. 27–57). Wiesbaden: Springer VS.
Glick Schiller, N., Basch, L., & Blanc-Szanton, C. (1992). Transnationalism: A new analytic framework for understanding migration. In N. Glick Schiller, L. Basch, & C. Blanc-Szanton (Eds.), *Towards a transnational perspective on migration: Race, class, ethnicity and nationalism reconsidered* (pp. 1–24). New York, NY: New York Academy of Sciences.
Greschke, H. M. (2013). Wie ist globales Zusammenleben möglich? Die Transnationalisierung der unmittelbaren sozialen Beziehungen und ihre methodologische Reflexion. In H.-G. Soeffner (Ed.), *Transnationale Vergesellschaftungen* (pp. 371–383). Wiesbaden: Springer Fachmedien.
Hardy, K. V., & Laszloffy, T. A. (1995). The cultural genogram: Key to training culturally competent family therapists. *Journal of Marital and Family Therapy, 21*(3), 227–237.
Horst, H. A. (2006). The blessings and burdens of communication: Cell phones in Jamaican transnational social fields. *Global Networks, 6*(2), 143–159.
Hunter, A. (2015). Empowering or impeding return migration? ICT, mobile phones, and older migrants' communications with home. *Global Networks, 15*(4), 485–502.
Jin, B., & Pena, J. F. (2010). Mobile communication in romantic relationships: Mobile phone use, relational uncertainty, love, commitment, and attachment styles. *Communication Reports, 23*(1), 39–51.
Lambert, M. J. (2013). Introduction and historical overview. In M. J. Lambert (Ed.), *Bergin & Garfield's handbook of psychotherapy and behavior change* (pp. 3–20). New York, NY: Wiley.

Lutz, H. (2008). *Vom Weltmarkt in den Privathaushalt. Die neuen Dienstmädchen im Zeitalter der Globalisierung*. Leverkusen: Barbara Budrich.

Madianou, M. (2012). Migration and the accentuated ambivalence of motherhood: The role of ICTs in Filipino transnational families. *Global Networks, 12*(3), 277–295.

Madianou, M. (2014). Smartphones as polymedia. *Journal of Computer-Mediated Communication, 19*(3), 667–680.

McGoldrick, M., & Gerson, R. (1985). *Genograms in family assessment*. New York, NY: Norton.

McGoldrick, M., Gerson, R., & Shellenberger, S. (1999). *Genograms: Assessment and intervention*. New York, NY: Norton.

Miller-Ott, A. E., Kelly, L., & Duran, R. L. (2012). The effects of cell phone usage rules on satisfaction in romantic relationships. *Communication Quarterly, 60*(1), 17–34.

Mills, M. (2014). Globalisation and family life. In A. Abela & J. Walker (Eds.), *Contemporary issues in family studies: Global perspectives on partnerships, parenting and support in a changing world* (pp. 249–261). Oxford: John Wiley & Sons.

Morgan, D. H. J. (1996). *Family connections*. Cambridge: Polity Press.

Nedelcu, M. (2012). Migrants' new transnational habitus: Rethinking migration through a cosmopolitan lens in the digital age. *Journal of Ethnic and Migration Studies, 38*(9), 1339–1356.

Papadopoulos, R. K. (2001). Refugee families: Issues of systemic supervision. *Journal of Family Therapy, 23*(4), 405–422.

Papadopoulos, R. K., & Hildebrand, J. (1997). Is home where the heart is? Narratives of oppositional discourses in refugee families. In R. K. Papadopoulos & J. Byng-Hall (Eds.), *Multiple voices: Narrative in systemic family psychotherapy* (pp. 206–236). London: Duckworth.

Parker, T. S., Blackburn, K. M., Perry, M. S., & Hawks, J. M. (2013). Sexting as an intervention: Relationship satisfaction and motivation considerations. *The American Journal of Family Therapy, 41*(1), 1–12.

Parreñas, R. (2001). *Servants of globalization: Women, migration and domestic work*. Stanford: Stanford University Press.

Parreñas, R. (2005). Long distance intimacy: Class, gender and intergenerational relations between mothers and children in Filipino transnational families. *Global Networks, 5*(4), 317–336.

Prensky, M. (2001). Digital natives, digital immigrants. Part 1. *On the Horizon, 9*(5), 1–6.

Rober, P., & De Haene, L. (2014). Intercultural therapy and the limitations of a cultural competency framework: About cultural differences, universalities and the unresolvable tensions between them. *Journal of Family Therapy, 36*(1), 3–20.

Schellenberger, S., Dent, M., Davis-Smith, M., Seale, J. P., Weintraut, R., & Wright, T. (2007). Cultural genogram: A tool for teaching and practice. *Families, Systems & Health, 25*(4), 367–381.

Schier, M. (2009). Räumliche Entgrenzung von Arbeit und Familie. Die Herstellung von Familie unter Bedingungen von Multilokalität. *IzR -Informationen zur Raumentwicklung, 1*(2), 55–66.

Şenyürekli, A. R., & Detzner, D. F. (2009). Communication dynamics of the transnational family. *Marriage & Family Review, 45*(6), 807–824.

Simon, G. (2012). Praction research: A model of systemic inquiry. *Human Systems: The Journal of Therapy, Consultation & Training, 23*(1), 103–124.

Spitzer, D., Neufeld, A., Harrison, M., Hughes, K., & Stewart, M. (2003). Care giving in transnational context: "My wings have been cut, where can I fly?". *Gender & Society, 17*(2), 267–286.

Stern, M. J., & Messer, C. (2009). How family members stay in touch: A quantitative investigation of core family networks. *Marriage & Family Review, 45*(6-8), 654–676.

Sucala, M., Schnur, J. B., Constantino, M. J., Miller, S. J., Brackman, E. H., & Montgomery, G. H. (2012). The therapeutic relationship in e-therapy for mental health: A systematic review. *Journal of Medical Internet Research, 14*(4), e110.

Tubbs, C. Y., & Burton, L. M. (2005). Bridging research: Using ethnography to inform clinical practice. In D. H. Sprenkle & F. P. Piercy (Eds.), *Research methods in family therapy* (pp. 136–154). New York, NY: The Guilford Press.

Turner, J. E. (1991). Migrants and their therapists: A trans-context approach. *Family Process, 30*(4), 407–419.
Vertovec, S. (2004). Cheap calls: The social glue of migrant transnationalism. *Global Networks, 4*(2), 219–224.
Vorderer, P. (2015). Der mediatisierte Lebenswandel. "Permanently online, permanently connected". *Publizistik, 60*(3), 259–276.
Voulgaridou, M. G., Papadopoulos, R. K., & Tomaras, V. (2006). Working with refugee families in Greece: Systemic considerations. *Journal of Family Therapy, 28*(2), 200–220.
Weine, S., Muzurovic, N., Kulauzovic, Y., Besic, S., Lezic, A., Mujagic, A., et al. (2004). Family consequences of refugee trauma. *Family Process, 43*(2), 147–160.
Watts-Jones, D. (1997). Toward an African American genogram. *Family Process, 36*(4), 375–383.
Wilding, R. (2006). "Virtual" intimacies? Families communicating across transnational contexts. *Global Networks, 6*(2), 125–142.
Yznaga, S. D. (2008). Using the genogram to facilitate the intercultural competence of Mexican immigrants. *The Family Journal: Counseling and Therapy for Couples and Families, 16*(2), 159–165.

Chapter 14
Innovations in Family Therapy and Systemic Practice

Peter Stratton and Maria Borcsa

Synopsis In this final chapter we use the inspiration from the 12 chapters to suggest five areas in which we see family therapy and systemic practice developing. We juxtapose a selection of material from the reports of original developments in our chapters under these headings to draw out the connections between them. The headings are: The political context of our work; Developments in family therapy theories; Novel practices in therapy and training; Developments within systemic theory and practice; and Wider resources and contexts of application. While the material drawn from this book illustrates the current liveliness of systemic couple and family therapy thinking and practice, the sections progressively point to wider resources that could be a foundation for future originality.

Introduction

This book consists of 12 descriptions by senior family therapists of trajectories from their origins in the field to their current originality, for each of whom to a greater or lesser extent, EFTA may have provided a secure base that allowed their creativity to flourish. Carefully reading the chapters generated for us a sense of how such trajectories could provoke many ideas about how systemic couples and family therapy (SCFT) could develop. We hope that bringing together and into conjunction, examples of material from all of the chapters will create a sense of the ways our field has progressed from its origins to its current originality. We have also been inspired by the emerging patterns to suggest some other potential developments that may launch us beyond the chapter content into further possibilities.

Every systemic family therapist continually encounters demands on them for creative originality. We need all our ingenuity as our clients bring ever new

P. Stratton (✉)
University of Leeds, Leeds, United Kingdom
e-mail: p.m.stratton@ntlworld.com

M. Borcsa
University of Applied Sciences Nordhausen, Nordhausen, Germany

M. Borcsa, P. Stratton (eds.), *Origins and Originality in Family Therapy and Systemic Practice*, European Family Therapy Association Series,
DOI 10.1007/978-3-319-39061-1_14

challenges; but also to make use of the political and financial contexts of our work; and the need to enthuse and challenge each new generation of trainees. Our field is having to recognise that achieving a sound level of habitual practice is no longer enough. As Ericsson (2006) says, after training and years of experience, practitioners "… are able to work as independent professionals. At that time most professionals reach a stable, average level of performance, and then they maintain this pedestrian level for the rest of their careers. In contrast, some continue to improve and eventually reach the highest levels of professional mastery." (p. 685).

This volume is a set of examples of how our founders and presidents have developed from their origins to be able to offer richly varied examples of originality. Our hope is that our readers will take this demonstration of many different ways "to achieve a step change from acceptable competence to a higher level of mastery" (Stratton and Hanks 2016, p. 8) as inspiration and encouragement to seek out their own forms of applicable originality. And that this continuing enhancement of our field will also find a home in EFTA in future years.

The Political Context of Our Work

Both the needs and the contributions of families are consistently undervalued by our governments and health, especially mental health, services. Despite rhetoric about the importance of families, wellbeing and stable relationships, work-life balance, importance of early years, etc., the actions of governments most often either ignore or undermine families while the provision of family therapy and other forms of family support is continually under attack. From within the mental health professions we face the increasing pressure to only treat, and obtain data about, people with a clear diagnosis which in terms of DSM increasingly requires a biological basis. With the financial resources for lobbying being held by the drug companies we see an increasing move back to having psychological distress treated with drugs or at best, by cognitive and behavioural treatments that can be packaged and researched in parallel ways.

As Juan Luis Linares says, "there is a place here for the diagnosis of psychopathology, not, however, as a way of labelling deviant behaviour, but rather as a system of guiding metaphors that facilitate our understanding of complex and dysfunctional relational phenomena." The most effective way of deconstructing conventional psychopathology is to achieve a deeper understanding of its relational bases.

Arlene Vetere adds that the task of explanation becomes one of integration, formulation and critical reflection and it needs to be useful. A plea that progress demands a more theoretically integrated approach, across all social and health care disciplines. We might add that it also requires a close engagement with our research base so that we are able to capitalise on it to demonstrate at every opportunity the unique and powerful contribution that SCFT can make to addressing mental health issues, to the welfare of families, and to progress towards well-functioning societies.

The reports in several chapters from the exciting early days of EFTA draw our attention to current needs for political involvement to support our field. EFTA has in many contexts led the way, especially Mony Elkaïm, Jacques Pluymaekers, and our successive presidents. See especially Jacques Pluymaekers' descriptions of the early days of radical SFT in Europe and Quebec, and Mony Elkaïm's account of the early movements to replace psychiatry, and the application of systemic approaches to societal and international conflicts. The need for such systemic radicalism has not diminished but reading about the heady early days does raise the thought that maybe as our profession has become established we newer generations might have lost some of the fire and courage of the originators. But the content of this book suggests that it might just be that we are agitating on many more different fronts so that there is less sense of a focussed campaign.

A major area of current concern is explored by Maria Borcsa and Julia Hille as they consider the changes brought about by the twin forces of increased migration and developing information and communication technologies (ICTs). Each of these has significance for altering family structures and while geographical changes may most often result in dispersion and reduced communication of families, the technological changes are often a means of ameliorating such effects. They also have consequences such as "deterritorialised identities" that will come to have political impact.

While EFTA members are politically active in many ways in different European countries we see in our first EFTA volume great diversity in the work with a variety of clienteles, contexts etc. and the achievements of this kind of wider application provide a base for the political action that is increasingly needed. We hope this book will provide authoritative material that readers can use to support the argument that family therapy and wider forms of systemic practice have a much greater potential contribution than is currently recognised.

A newer impetus that is less direct than the examples of political involvement of our founders and presidents, could come from elsewhere in the fields of systemics. Some opportunities for political involvement are suggested in the later section "Developments Within Systemic Theory and Practice".

Developments in Family Therapy Theories

A case can be made that the early forms of systemic family therapy were strongly influenced by a wish to differentiate from the dominant psychoanalytic models of the time. And that we have continued to promote each new advance by claiming it supersedes, and renders irrelevant, previous achievements. It does not take a very sophisticated use of systemics to recognise that the attempt to define yourself by your difference from a previous model inevitably leads to giving the previous structures a powerful influence in shaping your innovation. The pattern has applied more recently in attempts to create forms of family therapy that are claimed to reject the systemic model. One of the most obvious ways this has worked has been the ways that recent innovations such as narrative therapy and brief solution focussed therapy have often had more to say about treatments of individuals than of families. At the same time while practice involving individuals has less to say about working with wider systems, others are operating as if the best intervention for a family is to focus all efforts on changing the wider systems within which it operates.

A clear analysis of some of the unproductive moves of the last 25 years is presented by Juan Luis Linares' development of an ultramodern position to overcome the limitations he describes that have resulted from inappropriate importations of other theoretical positions see his critique of social constructionism and post-modernism, the rise of improvisation and a neo-Marxist tendency and his recommendation of returning the focus from just the individual or just society, to the family as intermediary between those two. His analysis leads to a proposal to ensure we recognise the privileged position held by the family system as an essential intermediary between the individual and society. As he says "we should put an end to postmodern dogmatism and throw open the windows of the systemic world to fresh and demythifying air that brings with it all that is good in the psychotherapeutic tradition".

Others among our authors offer significant developments in aspects of their theories without the need to reject our systemic origins or claim they are superseding all the wisdom we have painfully acquired. For Luigi Onnis the operation of time means that changes are irreversible: once a system is changed it cannot return to the previous system. Time is taken up in a very sophisticated analysis by Hugh Jenkins reviewing concepts of time both in different forms of therapy and other traditions of thought from the ancient Greeks through early Christians to a variety of more recent European perspectives. Leading to the concept of therapy as a "liminal" space, inhabited by patient and therapist, located at the margins.

For Juan Luis Linares the liberation from the reductionist cause–effect thinking eliminates the resulting paralysing issues of guilt and blame. From a systems point of view, nobody is to blame, but everybody is responsible for the necessary change in the pattern of interactions. In this way we can accept that the way in which some parents treat their children psychologically must cease to be a taboo for family therapy.

Theo Compernolle also argues in some detail that we should not expect to see linear cause–effect sequences but unique stochastic processes (transactions) so we must always look at wider (higher) systemic levels. We return to this theme later in this chapter.

Mony Elkaïm describes the influences and contexts of his moving on from early rather mechanical systems and cybernetics with the application to family systems of I. Prigogine's theory on systems far from equilibrium (Prigogine and Nicolis 1977). For Mony Elkaïm this led to the introduction of a new model for couple therapy as well as the development of his influential concepts of "resonances" and "assemblages". A similar progression is described by Luigi Onnis as a move from homeostatic to evolutionary models.

Juan Luis Linares takes the development to an even more advanced level with his account of an ultramodern position. He claims that this systems point of view "jettisons most turf fights and power struggles between professionals from different schools and disciplines and improves collaboration. Ideas about why people and families behave as they do, are resolved when these ideas are no longer formulated as truths, but as simplified representations of a part of reality at a particular systems-level and as hypotheses to be tested all the time in the therapeutic process. This does not mean that all methods and techniques are of equal value. We need research to find out how efficient and reliable they are."

Mony Elkaïm progresses to thinking less in terms of systems composed of individuals in interaction and more in terms of interrelationships of "assemblages", which supports his creation of the reciprocal double-bind concept (love me, don't love me) to his powerful analysis of resonance. Human systems can be analysed as relations between world view systems rather than between individuals. The use of resonance analysis thus becomes a crucial tool.

For Arlene Vetere, systemics provides us with a reflexive framework to map pattern and process and communication and meaning-making in our relationships, but not a theory of content. The integration of large and well-researched systems of thought—attachment theory, narrative theory, trauma theory—with systemic theory and practice provides a powerful explanatory model. She proposes the implications of attachment theory research to be:

(a) naming and regulating emotions, (b) standing in the emotional shoes of the other, (c) comforting and self-soothing, (d) information processing, (e) transformations in representational systems.

Attending to content and systemic context Kyriaki Polychroni describes concepts of "multi-level, multi-focal models of intervention", "subjective culture" and "cultural chronos and the multiplicity of inner voices "developed during the history of the Athenian Institute of Anthropos (AIA). Meanwhile Theo Compernolle suggests an eco-psycho-somatic approach to therapy to better integrate relevant knowledge from different scientific domains and to pay special attention to what goes on at the interface between them.

Novel Practices in Therapy and Training

As is to be expected from a book by highly experienced practitioners, we are offered many practical ideas about therapy and training that could be exported to our own contexts. Many are very relevant to our earlier suggestion of the centrality of creative originality in therapy and training.

Jorma Piha and Florence Schmitt give us an intriguing account of sculpting while verbal explanations are excluded so that the participants do not even know which family member they represent. While some readers may well be tempted to take up this technique, it raises a more general consideration which could be extended to other ways of preventing use of the dominant communication channel, e.g. planning therapy with a deaf or blind client. This deliberate removal of the sometimes over-dominant channel of verbal communication has a counterpart in Edith Goldbeter's process of turning an apparent obstruction, the unavailable but highly significant missing person, into a major resource for the therapy. These are two examples of how, through overcoming a clear limitation, we can transcend the limits of habitual practice. As Jorma Piha and Florence Schmitt say: "He/she has to combine rigour with creativity, meticulousness with flexibility and seriousness with imagination".

A model of these virtues comes from Jacques Pluymaekers' account of creating practice for under-resourced neighbourhoods in la Gerbe clinic. In Mony Elkaïm's chapter we also find the creativity that we see in his live presentations, conveyed by his description of moving from origins in network practices, through to his example of pictorial resonances. The goal of the supervision is not just to "understand" but to "feel differently" about the rapport with the patients: to change the affect.

In further suggestions of resources for therapists in action Hugh Jenkins describes ritual as a way of creating change, and of therapy as a rite of passage. Juan Luis Linares proposes that the ultramodern therapist is happy to submit his or her expertise to the family's judgment. The kind of intelligent therapeutic intervention that is sought by ultramodern systemic therapists incorporates collaborative conversation but does so in conjunction with scripts or road maps that give some direction when conversing. Family members are aware that the therapist "knows", and also that he or she will not use this knowledge to tyrannise them or impose upon them realities that they are not ready to accept. Mony Elkaïm provides an extension of this way of thinking in that through resonance the therapist's experience is amplified by the human system in which he/she is participating to reinforce the world views of the other members of the system.

In a chapter of very practical suggestions Edith Goldbeter explicates her concept of a "nodal" third—the missing person. How the absence of a person can lead to disorganisation which the therapy must help to be recognised and if necessary, mourned. As this is achieved we can start talking of "light thirds" instead of nodal thirds. As a practical technique she describes the use of the missing person's chair as a metaphor. As Maurizio Andolfi says, constructing metaphors is one of the best ways to strengthen a therapeutic alliance with the family.

For Luigi Onnis, practice involves a shift from an *epistemology of description to an epistemology of construction*, from an epistemology of observed systems to an epistemology of self-observant systems, which provides at least two important results: The first relates to the cognitive sphere: once the myth of neutrality and separation has been abandoned … the therapist withdraws the pretence of an objective knowledge of the therapeutic reality interpreted as an "absolute truth"; The second consequence relates more directly to the therapeutic process: the therapist losing their distant and "external" position, must also give up the claim to control the therapeutic process and predict outcomes.

Jorma Piha and Florence Schmitt's non-verbal sculpting which is used in the training of family therapists to increase their self-awareness of their family of origin issues, can additionally be used as a means of clinical supervision when trainees work with families. In this way the meaning and importance of non-verbal interaction within the family therapeutic system is highlighted. But they point out that monitoring the family sculpting process is demanding. The monitor has to be sensitive and mature as a person as well as professionally.

A different approach is how Maurizio Andolfi builds a solid therapeutic alliance with the family through the active collaboration of the problem child, who is invited to become a sort of co-therapist. In this way children are engaged in therapy as significant relational bridges in the dialogue/clash between generations. He analyses the cognitive and affective qualities required by therapists to enter with passion and empathy into the most difficult and painful issues of the family without a judgmental or culturally stereotyped attitude. For this, playing and playfulness represent the most articulate and personal means of engaging the family and the therapist in the therapeutic encounter. But he points out that it is, nonetheless, still little used by family therapists, who prefer by far an adult and serious model of communication.

Kyriaki Polychroni describes methods of application that include "systemic group therapy", and experiential training in family dynamics/therapy is described showing how the integration of other modalities into our family therapy models can optimise our systemic practice. "synallactic collective image technique" is essentially a cognitive-emotional tool that uses images in activating analogical processes, which facilitate the expression of personal stories. She describes later developments in which the incorporation of attachment and the Emotionally Focussed Therapy (EFT) have also affected the manner in which AIA conduct couple therapy groups. She draws attention to how including specific experiential inner dialogue exercises can help to foster partners' accessing primary emotions and attachment yearnings and other experiential tasks that guide couples in restructuring their relational patterns.

Maria Borcsa and Julia Hille conceptualise their interview process consisting of four parts, (1) the structural genogram; (2) uniqueness variables; (3) relational spaces of belonging; and (4) use of information and communication technologies. From this conceptual approach and by a careful consideration of the literature, they construct the "Genogram 4.0". They provide a table which shows sample items for each of these headings. The interview also builds up to a focus on the impact of ICT has on the life of the therapist; moreover, the authors suggest ways how the interview can be extended during training.

Developments Within Systemic Theory and Practice

Another theme that cuts across the three sections into which we grouped the chapters, is progression, liberation even, from early concepts of systemics. From here we feel it particularly appropriate to start using the insights of our authors as a springboard for more general considerations. Our field has progressed through increasing sophistication in the ways the systemic metaphor has been used as a basis for both theory and practice. As described above, in several chapters an account of such progression is reported by the author and taken together, these give a map of current systemic thinking. As we pull together the strands of innovation from the whole book, we are by now beginning to see areas which could be particularly fruitful in the future. The accounts of changing use of systemics could lead us to recent developments in other areas of systemic sciences which we introduce after reviewing some of the experiences of our authors.

Mony Elkaïm describes becoming liberated from von Bertalanffy and systems theory with its emphasis on homeostasis and keeping families stable, to Prigogine with the therapist's task becoming an agent of change rather than stability. Petros Polychronis had planned to present at the EFTA-TIC conference in 2015 an account of dissipative systems where being further from equilibrium creates more complexity and less linearity; chaotic dynamics are extremely sensitive to initial conditions where unpredictability allows for the emergence of novelty; downwards causality, etc. Luigi Onnis, also building on Prigogine advocates taking complexity theory as an important newer area of systemics. Though as Melo and Alarcão say "Family therapy has advanced, since its inception, in close connection with systems' sciences and cybernetics. But it hasn't kept up with the new developments in complexity sciences" (2015, p. 86).

So we might extend these considerations by opening our field up to current complexity theory. A first thought is that although the families we see are complicated, complexity has a more specific and carefully worked set of meanings. The difference is discussed by Poli (2013) writing on "the difference between complicated and complex social systems". Complexity science is not a single theory but is attempting to establish the general principles of complex adaptive systems. And it is highly interdisciplinary, seeking the answers to some fundamental questions about living, adaptable, changeable systems. The literature covers many different areas but with rather few references to families as objects of study from this perspective. If we start to engage rather more with other systems sciences we might hope not just to be consumers of their advances, but to recruit them to apply their insights to the systemics of families and their contexts.

For Theo Compernolle, "systemic" must include the system of the individual and the system of professional interventions, not just the family system. He maps out levels of systems saying the crucial task is to choose at which level to intervene. He echoes Juan Luis Linares in his call to consider unique stochastic processes which implies always looking at wider (higher) systemic levels.

Theo Compernolle's conclusion is that "systems theory, or developing a "systems zoom-lens" will help a therapist or coach to integrate learning from very different disciplines and schools. Medicine, neurology, biology, psychiatry, psychotherapy management, and family therapy for example are not in conflict with each other but they deal with different system-levels. On these levels one can make different observations, different hypotheses leading to different interventions. One can never totally understand what happens on one level only based on knowledge about other levels. One cannot, for example, fully understand what happens at an individual level with only knowledge about the family and vice versa. For the therapist this idea greatly widens her scope of observation and intervention".

As Luigi Onnis moves from pragmatics to complexity, we might think outside of our selective uses of systems theory to consider areas such as soft systems methodology and anticipatory systems theory (AST) (Stratton 2016). These approaches have already done some of the work that we will need in order to implement the proposals in this book of taking our systemic views further. Maria Borcsa and Julia Hille's Genogram 4.0 can be viewed as an extension of systemic levels perhaps best seen as an orthogonal dimension. Our old image of concentric circles of systems (individual, family, community, state etc.) is challenged by globalisation, transnational families, and the grafting on of systemic communicative capability through constantly evolving ICT.

The core principle of AST is that an anticipatory system is one that incorporates a model of itself which it can interrogate (Louie 2010). So whereas a basic (cybernetic) system is driven by feedback from the environment (judging the distance from a goal and taking action to move in that direction), an anticipatory system uses feedforward. In fact we routinely make use of this capability by inviting our clients to envisage themselves in a desired future so that we can work back to changes that would be needed now. In therapy AST suggests that instead of considering family interactions in terms of feedback which maintains stability, we become alert to the ways they are continually anticipating the thoughts, feelings and behaviours of themselves and each other. When an anticipatory system uses feedforward, rather than examining the environment it may be primarily examining its model. Of itself and its environment.

But we must leave the wider systemic possibilities here, and move on to other resources.

Wider Resources and Contexts of Application

Several of our authors point to areas beyond the strict boundaries of family therapy and systemic practice. Theo Compernolle suggests an eco-psycho-somatic approach to therapy to better integrate relevant knowledge from different scientific domains and to pay special attention to what goes on at the interface between them thereby integrating widely different approaches and contexts of application. And we have the extraordinary range of scholarship of Hugh Jenkins's discussion around concepts of time both in different forms of therapy and other traditions of thought. He particularly argues that we should tap resources from anthropology and neuropsychology.

It is not just sources of knowledge that we might access, but contexts of application. Kyriaki Polychroni attends to wider cultural contexts and how the rapid changes can leave families bewildered and unprepared, which suggests that we need to attend to current empirical work within the sociology of the family.

Luigi Onnis points to the existence of an isomorphism between different systems (in forms considered by Bertalanffy) and in another direction by stimulating a fruitful integration between the various fields of scientific knowledge.

There are so many areas of knowledge and research that we could draw on to spark our creativity and ground our practice: psychological development of the child; sociology and anthropology of families; major statistical data bases such as the UK household survey; cognitive psychology; and of course robotics, neurobiology and brain sciences are just a few.

Jorma Piha and Florence Schmitt point out: "At that time, we couldn't understand how research on infants, early interaction, pre-natal and post-natal communication would totally revolutionize our knowledge of the ontogenesis of narratives. The works by Stern (1985), Siegel (1999), Damasio (1999) and others in the late nineties and at the beginning of the new millennium opened new doors to understand how stories start from bodily movements and sensations."

Then we have Arlene Vetere's chapter showing how earlier work on attachment became integrated in her work with a narrative approach within a systemic framework. When describing transformations in representational systems she builds the analysis through psychological research on different forms of memory.

Maria Borcsa and Julia Hille review what is currently known about forms of communication and familial contact using ICTs. But both the hardware (like phones) and the contexts of use (like WhatsApp) are continually changing and we need to be aware of developments, even if not competent in them, if we are to understand their roles in families. We will progressively need to consider how can we use mass social media to give families systemic resources. As we write the *Financial Times* (2nd April, 2016) reports Satya Nadella, chief executive of Microsoft saying that a new force is sweeping through the computing world: the power of conversation. As an averagely insecure human I (PS) have found it entertaining that robots that have been set to learn how to converse by engaging with Internet conversations and the implicit assumptions of language have had to be taken off air because they rapidly develop extreme racist and misogynistic forms of speech. More practically, apps like MyChat (from China, with over a billion users since 2012) allow many different forms of individual and group conversations between people.

We hope that this first volume in the EFTA series will encourage therapists, supervisors and trainers to look more widely for inspiration both within our field and in other disciplines. For example we have already discussed the importance of creativity and Maurizio Andolfi calls creativity and playfulness "magic tools to produce change". So a final area we might draw on is that of studies of how creativity can be potentiated in the therapeutic and supervisory contexts (Stratton and Hanks 2016).

Conclusion

In this chapter we invite you, our reader, to use this book to consolidate your originality in thinking and practice. We hope that many of you will offer your achievements within the supportive context of EFTA so that our profession can continue to develop its contribution to the wellbeing of individuals, families and communities.

With people such as our authors and the current members of EFTA active in our field we can be optimistic about the outlook for family therapy and systemic practice and confident that we cannot predict which directions it will go in future.

References

Damasio, A. (1999). *The feeling of what happens: Body and emotion in the making of consciousness*. New York: Harcourt Brace.

Ericsson, K. A. (2006). The influence of experience and deliberate practice on the development of superior expert performance. In K. A. Ericsson, N. Charness, P. Feltovich, & R. R. Hoffman (Eds.), *The Cambridge handbook of expertise and expert performance* (pp. 685–706). Cambridge: Cambridge University Press.

Louie, A. H. (2010). Robert Rosen's anticipatory systems. *Foresight, 12*, 18–29.

de Melo, A. T., & Alarcão, M. (2015). Building grounded theories of family complexity in family therapy process research. *Human Systems, 26*, 86–102.

Poli, R. (2013). A note on the difference between complicated and complex social systems. *Cadmus, 2*, 142–147. Retrieved from www.cadmusjournal.org/.

Prigogine, I., & Nicolis, S. (1977). *Self-organization in non-equilibrium systems*. Chichester: Wiley.

Siegel, D. J. (1999). *The developing mind: Toward a neurobiology of interpersonal experience*. New York: Guilford.

Stern, D. N. (1985). *The interpersonal world of the infant*. New York: Basic Books.

Stratton, P., & Hanks, H. (2016). Personal and professional development as processes of learning that enable the practitioner to create a self that is equipped for higher levels of professional mastery. In A. Vetere & P. Stratton (Eds.), *Interacting selves: Systemic solutions for personal and professional development in counselling and psychotherapy.* (pp. 7–32). Abingdon, New York: Brunner-Routledge.

Stratton, P. (2016, in press). Integrating current systemic sciences into systemic therapy and training: soft and anticipatory systems theories. *Human Systems,* 27. In press.

Index

M. Borcsa, P. Stratton (eds.), *Origins and Originality in Family Therapy and Systemic Practice*, European Family Therapy Association Series,
DOI 10.1007/978-3-319-39061-1

MIX
Papier aus verantwortungsvollen Quellen
Paper from responsible sources
FSC® C105338

If you have any concerns about our products,
you can contact us on
ProductSafety@springernature.com

In case Publisher is established outside the EU,
the EU authorized representative is:
Springer Nature Customer Service Center GmbH
Europaplatz 3, 69115 Heidelberg, Germany

Printed by Libri Plureos GmbH
in Hamburg, Germany